TRANQU
DECODING

Aarthi Ramachandran is a political journalist who has worked with leading Indian newspapers such as *The Economic Times* and *Business Standard*. She has written about the Congress for the past seven years and tracked Rahul Gandhi's political career closely. She is now a freelancer, attempting the transition from being a full-time journalist to a full-time mother. She lives in Delhi with her husband and daughter.

DECODING RAHUL GANDHI

Aarthi Ramachandran

Foreword by
N. Ram

TRANQUEBAR

TRANQUEBAR PRESS
An imprint of westland ltd
Venkat Towers, 165, P.H. Road, Maduravoyal, Chennai 600 095
No. 38/10 (New No.5), Raghava Nagar, New Timber Yard Layout, Bangalore 560 026
Survey No. A-9, II Floor, Moula Ali Industrial Area, Moula Ali, Hyderabad 500 040
23/181, Anand Nagar, Nehru Road, Santacruz East, Mumbai 400 055
4322/3, Ansari Road, Daryaganj, New Delhi 110 002

First published in India in TRANQUEBAR PRESS by westland ltd 2012

Copyright © Aarthi Ramachandran 2012

10 9 8 7 6 5 4 3 2 1

ISBN: 978-93-81626-69-6

Typeset in 11/13 pts. Garamond Regular by SÜRYA, New Delhi
Printed at Thomson Press (India) Ltd.

For
Nandini, who mostly let her mother write, and Rima.

CONTENTS

ACKNOWLEDGEMENTS

When I began this book about two years ago, it was a blind leap from a precipice without knowing what lay in store for me. All I knew was two pairs of hands – those of my husband, Vivek, and Alam Srinivas who is all that one can ask of in a friend – would ensure I had a safe landing. That this book is out is due to them more than anyone else. Alam also acted as my first editor and without him, quite simply, the book would not have happened. I have often joked with him during the writing that he has midwifed the book. Thanks are due to both Vivek and Alam in more measure than I can say.

Though my close family members have put up with my absence, it was my three year old daughter, Nandini, who had to inexplicably contend with a mother who was there but not quite there. The book is dedicated to her because she allowed me time away from her – helped no doubt by 'Chhota Bheem' on Pogo TV.

I need to thank Hartosh Singh Bal who had enough confidence in me to introduce me to people who matter in the publishing world, and put in a good word. It was Hartosh who suggested I should work on this book when I was contemplating a break from the grind of daily newspaper reporting in mid-2010. My former bosses at *Business Standard* and *The Economic Times*, Aditi Phadnis and P R Ramesh have been two of the biggest influences in my career as a political journalist. Most of what I've learnt about the trade, I owe to them. Aditi was most generous with her time and shared with me her understanding of the 2012 Uttar Pradesh Assembly election verdict in great detail.

A host of 'beat colleagues' and friends gave freely of their time and information each time I called. I thank each of them, especially Sanjay Mishra, Dheeraj Kanojia, Kay Benedict, and Prabhanjan Verma. I also need to thank my former colleague at *The Economic Times*, Devesh Kumar, without whom I would not have negotiated the 2010 Bihar Assembly election coverage. I am grateful to Satish Kumar Singh, director of Cachet Pharmaceuticals (Alkem Laboratories Group) and Sudheer Kumar who ensured I was comfortable and well taken care of during the trip.

I also need to thank Mukul Kesavan and Ninad Sheth who helped with access to libraries and books; and Kanupriya Vashisht and Sree Srinivasan for help with information pertaining to Rahul's US education. Mukul used his enormous clout to let me use the India International Centre (IIC) library as my workplace for nearly six months. I wish to thank the IIC library staff for their help and support. Thanks are also due to the library staff at the Indian Institute of Public Administration, the Centre for the Study of Developing Societies and the Nehru Memorial Museum & Library.

I cannot but mention here the many Youth Congress and National Students' Union of India leaders, most of whom did not want to be named, as well as Congress leaders who chose not to be identified. They made it possible for me to understand Rahul Gandhi's thinking and way of functioning. I want to specially thank Ashleigh Lamming and Merrow Golden, who interviewed Rahul Gandhi for Cambridge University's campus paper, *Varsity*, in 2010. I am most grateful to them for having shared their unpublished interview notes with me.

A special thank you to my editor at Westland, Renuka Chatterjee, who patiently but firmly guided the entire project. Her support has been constant. I also need to thank Sudha Sadanand who helped in improving the book with her insightful comments on politics.

I wish to thank my family, especially my parents-in-law who travelled from Chennai to Delhi at short notice to facilitate my writing at a crucial time when I was stranded without childcare support. My parents, sister and other close family members have put up with my complete preoccupation with the book over the past two years. My brother Ashwin's weekly visits contributed immeasurably to keeping my spirits up as the book took shape. Sunita who looked after Nandini when I was shut up in my room, writing, will also always have my gratitude.

FOREWORD
by N. Ram

Contemporary India has its fair share of political journalists, political scientists, political pundits, and historians. But there is one significant deficit when we come to politics of the present. Serious biography writing has not made its presence felt in a theatre that offers abundant material for the biographer – a diverse and colourful cast of netas, national, regional, and local, framed against circumstances, issues, challenges, and opportunities that often seem way too much for them. There may be legitimate complaints about the stature and quality of contemporary political leadership, especially compared with what seemed to be in robust supply in the not-distant past. But it is a fact that we have been unfairly denied the benefits – in terms of information, insights, literary quality, and sheer pleasure – that the biographer's slog and art have conferred on readers in several western countries.

N. Ram is one of the country's leading journalists. He is the former Editor-in-Chief of *The Hindu* and other group publications, including *Frontline* and *Business Line*. He stepped down from his editorial role in January 2012 but remains a director of Kasturi & Sons Limited, publishers of The Hindu group of newspapers. In 1990, he was awarded the Padma Bhushan by the Government of India.

I cannot think of any Indian political biography of note that brings us closer to the present than Paul R Brass's *An Indian Political Life: Charan Singh and Congress Politics, 1937 to 1961*, which is the first in a multi-volume series on *The Politics of Northern India: 1937 to 1987*.

Rahul Gandhi, a late-arriving and apparently reluctant heir presumptive to (what is sometimes caricatured by right-wing opponents as) India's republican throne by virtue of being born in its most prominent political dynasty, is an inviting enough subject. He is an inviting subject for the curious, nose-to-the-ground political journalist, although not yet perhaps for a scholarly biographer like Brass, who would surely need critical distance, more time, and much more primary material than is accessible. The claim made by a recently published book (by two industrious and not uncritical journalists) to be 'the first authoritative biography' of Rahul Gandhi is nothing more than publishers' hype.

As the economy has run into trouble, as inflation and the crisis of livelihood have become key concerns for hundreds of millions of ordinary Indians, and as corruption has emerged as an overarching national issue, politics in India seems to be trapped in a state of dispirited uncertainty, systemic pessimism, and low expectations. *Stasis*, the old Greek term of art, best describes the present.

As political parties and key actors begin to eye 2014, everything points to a steep decline in the political stock of the party and coalition ruling at the Centre – the Congress and the United Progressive Alliance respectively. But the so-called national alternative, the Bharatiya Janata Party, is in no better shape, presenting the spectacle of a house divided at every level, and going through a time of troubles; and the National Democratic Alliance does not look like a confident challenger. The widespread impression in the polity and news media is that this is once more the time of regional parties and that a combination of them will come to power at the Centre, for however long and whatever that will be worth, in 2014.

Rahul Gandhi's star, which was so visibly in the ascendant three years ago and was given huge and exaggerated credit, especially in the news media, for the impressive overall Congress performance in the 2009 Lok Sabha election, no longer shines bright. But just as the rise of the heir presumptive was seen through a distorting lens three years ago by sycophants and enemies alike, the nature of his decline too is being hyped up. Politics is a complex game played on many tracks, involving numerous, contradictory and unpredictable components in its transforming processes. Simple-minded assertions made on the assumption that the rise or decline of the stock of a party or formation, or the mode of political articulation of a section or sections of society, will be linear and uninterrupted can be rejected out of hand. Thus viewed, 2009 was no more the zenith for Rahul Gandhi than 2012 (with the Uttar Pradesh Assembly election fiasco capping a series of demoralising electoral defeats for the Congress) is the nadir.

Aarthi Ramachandran's attempt to 'decode' – or rather, deconstruct – Rahul Gandhi does not set out to be a biography, let alone an 'authoritative' one. Anyone can see that would not be possible. What she offers instead is a hard-nosed, nuanced, and critical exploration of her subject's evolution as a politician. For one thing, she does not believe he was 'a reluctant heir'. The book title derives from the fact that Rahul Gandhi is widely regarded in his party and in the polity as some kind of enigma and therefore needs decoding. What is clear is that he has arrived; what is not is what political propositions and values he represents and where he is headed.

Although much about his life remains unknown, the basic facts about his education at St. Stephen's (discontinued for security reasons), Harvard (discontinued, probably for the same reasons, although he also does not seem to have relished his time at this university), Rollins College, Florida (where he graduated with a bachelor's degree in international relations), and Trinity College, Cambridge (where he took an MPhil. in development studies) and pre-political working career (nothing special) have now been confirmed. The price paid for inaccessibility of an extreme kind has been a lot of nonsense written about his education and personal life in sections of the press, leading Rahul Gandhi on one occasion to put this memorable correction on record: 'My girlfriend's name is Veronique, not Juanita. She is Spanish and not Venezuelan or Colombian. She is an architect, not a waitress, though I wouldn't have a problem with that. She is also my best friend.'

Journalism, if it is worth anything intellectually, is a discipline of verification combined with a sceptical temperament. Ramachandran demonstrates this with a meticulousness and resourcefulness that taps every accessible source and opportunity – and yields a surprising body of insights into 'brand Rahul', what makes him tick, what explains the 2009 surge and the subsequent ebb.

This exercise in deconstruction is based on the author's field observations as a reporter of Rahul Gandhi's campaigning and political style, mining a variety of newspaper and other sources (including the unpublished interview notes of two student reporters who interviewed him in 2010 for *Varsity*, Cambridge University's campus publication), and talking to an assortment of Youth Congress and National Students' Union of India leaders as well as Congress leaders. Unsurprisingly, given Congress political culture, most of these leaders did not want to be named.

We learn that Rahul Gandhi is an obsessive organization man, who believes in applying business management strategy and methods, including the 'Toyota Way', to grassroots political organization. He espouses meritocratic notions of seeking and nurturing talent, and opening up opportunity for career advancement in Congress politics. While he has not been above playing the dynastic card, he has been candid about how he got to where he is today, declaring himself to be 'a symptom of this problem', which he wished to change. He does not seem to be good at building coalitions or dealing with existing or potential allies. He favours going it alone but, unlike, say, Bahujan Samaj Party leader Mayawati, he has no core social constituency. In the heat of campaigning, he has made his share of political gaffes and over-the-top allegations against opponents. He has been an indifferent parliamentarian whose sporadic interventions on issues, including corruption, have impressed no one except the party faithful. His secular credentials are not in question; in fact, he holds no known religious faith and has gone so far as to declare the national flag to be his religion.

The two great personal tragedies that hit his family – the brutal assassination of his grandmother in October 1984 and of his father in May 1991 – toughened his inner fibre and demonstrated to the nation his resilience as well as his dignity in the face of calamity. Paradoxically, while he found it difficult to understand why his father had entered the rough and tumble of politics after the death of Sanjay Gandhi in 1981 and still entertained doubts about this in late 1989, the assassination of his father gradually freed him from doubts about taking on a political role – because he felt that after his grandmother's and father's ultimate sacrifice, it was his duty to 'serve the people of India'. But he insisted that he would do this only after he had prepared himself and had something to offer.

And what about his ideological make-up and world-view?

His mother, Congress President Sonia Gandhi, is a declared social democrat who has been known to advocate and push for ambitious welfare measures such as the National Rural Employment Guarantee Act (NREGA) championed by the Left, presumably to soften the impact of the Manmohan Singh regime's determined pursuit of neo-liberal economic policies. Rahul Gandhi too has lobbied for welfare and relief packages following his field visits but his interventions on the side of the poor, the dispossessed, and the marginalized are seen as opportunist or at best instrumentalist and his ideas on socio-economic issues are criticized as inchoate. He told his interviewers for *Varsity* in 2010 that his time in Cambridge, and especially the economic theory he studied, was 'immensely influential in shaping the person I am today.' He added the revealing caveat (not reported, surprisingly, in the published interview but made available to Ramachandran from the interview notes) that he had 'changed a lot' since then and that 'I am a lot less left wing than I was, for one thing.'

Rahul Gandhi's larger frame of political reference, in lieu of a coherent ideological frame, is the idea of 'two Indias' – one empowered and confident, the other disempowered and languishing. His ideological and political predicament, it seems, is what to do about this. In any case, the disconnect between the hard organizational work that he has insisted on and led within the student and youth wings of his party and the larger livelihood and other issues that shape class and mass politics has opened up a credibility gap. Much was made, in the wake of the 2009 triumph, of the generation divide and of Rahul signalling the arrival of an unstoppable new force, India's youth, as though they formed a mostly coherent mass with a political mind who would gravitate towards one leader and one pole. No one cares to offer that kind of analysis now.

What about Rahul Gandhi's vision of emerging and future

India? Within the country, visions of its future in relation to the world have ranged from the bullish and upbeat to the sceptical and the positively downbeat. The supporting analyses and arguments are rooted, at one end, in overly optimistic projections of Indian economic performance and development and in uninhibited *realpolitik* – leading to the grand goal of India becoming a developed country by '2020'. At the other end, they are rooted in a preoccupation with the basic livelihood and human development issues and with moral concerns over recent and current foreign policy directions.

To his credit, Rahul Gandhi has not bought into '2020', which was always a pipedream and is now, in the midst of a global and national economic downturn, recognized to be such. To be a true believer, you needed to persuade yourself that the world's largest mass of basic deprivations and other features of a less-developed society (such as a preponderance of the population living in the countryside, subsisting on agriculture and handicrafts, and lacking modern amenities) could somehow be overcome in the intermediate term. And this without doing the hard, foundational work of social development that, for example, Amartya Sen and Jean Dreze advocate in their book *India: Economic Development and Social Opportunity*, an analysis of endemic mass deprivation and the role of `public action' in meeting the challenge.

After all, in mid-2004, 'India Shining', a ruling party's presumed killer slogan, bombed in a general election in which close to 400 million people voted, offering salutary lessons to all political players. And Uttar Pradesh 2012 offers a salutary lesson to the politics of superficiality and a narrow-laned organizational obsessiveness that promises radical change but refuses to engage with issues that matter to ordinary people.

I do not wish to reveal more about the deconstruction of Rahul Gandhi essayed in this book. You will find that by confining herself strictly to the factual and the verifiable, deploying her journalistic skills and *nous* to tap every accessible source, and not being shy of putting forward her critical insights and value judgments, the author lives up to the promise of the book title in surprising measure.

Chennai
July 2012

LIST OF ACRONYMS

ABVP	Akhil Bharatiya Vidyarthi Parishad
AIADMK	All India Anna Dravida Munnetra Kazhagam
AICC	All India Congress Committee
AIIMS	All India Institute of Medical Sciences
BJP	Bharatiya Janata Party
BoP	Bottom of the Pyramid
BPL	below poverty line
BPO	Business Process Outsourcing
BRIC	Brazil Russia India China
BSP	Bahujan Samaj Party
CAG	Comptroller and Auditor General
CBI	Central Bureau of Investigation
CCS	Centre for Civil Society
Congress-I	Congress-Indira
CPI	Communist Party of India
CrPC	Criminal Procedure Code
CWC	Congress Working Committee
DMK	Dravida Munnetra Kazhagam
DTC	Delhi Transport Corporation
DUSU	Delhi University Students' Union
EC	Election Commission
EOB	elected office-bearer
FAME	Foundation for Advanced Management of Elections

FERPA	Family Educational Rights and Privacy Act
FMCG	Fast-Moving Consumer Goods
GD	group discussion
GM	General Motors
ha	hectares
HDW	Howaldtswerke-Deutsche Werft (submarine)
HUL	Hindustan Unilever Limited
ILID	Institute of Leadership and Institutional Development
IYC	Indian Youth Congress
JD	Janata Dal
JMM	Jharkhand Mukti Morcha
JNLI	Jawaharlal Nehru Leadership Institute
JP	Jayaprakash Narayan
KPCC	Kerala Pradesh Congress Committee
LARR	Land Acquisition Rehabilitation and Resettlement
LDF	Left Democratic Front
LJSP	Lok Jan Shakti Party
LTTE	Liberation Tigers of Tamil Elam
MAP	Multidisciplinary Action Project
MBA	Masters in Business Administration
MBC	most backward class
MDMK	Marumalarchi Dravida Munnettra Kazhagam
MISA	Maintenance of Internal Security Act
MIT	Massachusetts Institute of Technology
MKSS	Mazdoor Kisan Shakti Sanghatan
MoEF	Ministry of Environment and Forests
MP	Member of Parliament
NAC	National Advisory Council
NCP	Nationalist Congress Party
NDA	National Democratic Alliance
NGO	Non-Governmental Organization
NREGA	National Rural Employment Guarantee Act

NRHM	National Rural Health Mission
NSUI	National Students' Union of India
OBCs	Other Backward Classes
PCC	Pradesh Congress Committee
PDP	People's Democratic Party
PDS	public distribution system
PIO	person of Indian origin
PMK	Pattali Makkal Katchi
PMO	Prime Minister's Office
PPP	public-private-partnership
R&D	Research and Development
RGCT	Rajiv Gandhi Charitable Trust
RGF	Rajiv Gandhi Foundation
RGICS	Rajiv Gandhi Institute of Contemporary Studies
RJD	Rashtriya Janata Dal
RLD	Rashtriya Lok Dal
RoC	Registrar of Companies
RTI	right to information
S&P	Standard and Poor's
SC	Scheduled Caste
SC	Supreme Court
SOP	standard operating procedures
SP	Samajwadi Party
SPG	Special Protection Group
ST	Scheduled Tribe
SVD	Samyukt Vidhayak Dal
TPS	Toyota Production System
TRS	Telangana Rashtra Samithi
UDF	United Democratic Front
UIDAI	Unique Identification Authority of India
UNI	United News of India
UP	Uttar Pradesh
UPCC	Uttar Pradesh Congress Committee
US	United States

PART ONE

THE FORMATIVE
YEARS

1

YESTERDAY ONCE MORE

In April 2009, Rahul Gandhi went to Purulia, one of West Bengal's poorest districts and a traditional Maoist base, on an election tour. He was probably not aware of the more adventurous trip to the place his grandmother, former prime minister of India, Indira Gandhi, had made four decades ago – thereby missing out on not just an oratory trick but also a sense of personal history. When Indira Gandhi visited this very place in 1970, she had an eventful time. The one piece of heartening news for her at the end of her Purulia trip was of Rahul Gandhi's birth. Even if Rahul failed to make the connection, some in the crowd belonging to an earlier generation, didn't.

Bespectacled and wearing his all-white, khadi kurta-pyjama with the same devotion an investment banker reserves for the pinstripe suit, Rahul wasted no time in connecting with the eager audience, wrapped up his speech quickly, shook hands with the people as security personnel struggled to keep the crowds in check, and took off for another election rally in his chopper, all in a matter of half an hour[1].

The contrast with Indira Gandhi, who was a master at

scripting dramatic moments in politics, was stark. While touring Purulia and Bankura which were in the grip of drought in June 1970, Indira encountered angry protestors at Purulia. They resorted to stone-pelting as she addressed the crowds who had gathered to meet her at the government circuit house.

She had stood up to the stone-pelters. 'Undaunted, Mrs Gandhi continued her speech for a short while, standing on the bonnet of a police jeep, with a police helmet on her head.'[2] Some reports[3] said 'a moment later she threw away the helmet, pushed aside those around her and resumed her speech still standing on the bonnet' in complete disregard of security measures.

Before her speech, there had been a scuffle between people who wanted to meet the prime minister and the police who were restraining them from entering the circuit house. The police resorted to a lathi-charge when some sections of the crowd hurled stones at them. Indira saved the situation by coming out herself to meet the crowds. Even as people complained to her about the police violence, 'several hundred people with Marxist Communist and Jan Sangh flags were heard shouting anti-police slogans'[4]. When she began her speech, some in the gathering threw stones that fell near her.

The next day, all the top headlines were about how the prime minister had braved the unruly mob with utter disregard to her security. The *Tribune*[5] had a big front-page story on the PM's stand against the stone-pelting agitators. Towards the end of the story was a small box item. 'PM becomes grandma', said the headline of the single-column story, which had used a UNI (United News of India) wire report from Patna, dated 19 June.

'Prime Minister Indira Gandhi became a grandmother today. Mrs Gandhi, now on a tour of Bihar and West Bengal, was about to board an aircraft for Patna at Panagarh airport when she received a telephone message about the birth of a son to Mrs Sonia Gandhi, her Italian-born daughter-in-law, in a Delhi hospital this afternoon. The prime minister arranged for sweets for the officials and newsmen accompanying her,' the report read.

She would not know it then, but the same grandson would follow her into politics years later. He too would undertake a journey that would bring him to Purulia, and require him to make similar promises about improving the condition of people's lives, albeit in much calmer circumstances, and with far less impact.

Before Rahul, it was the turn of his father, Rajiv Gandhi, and his mother, Sonia, to join politics. Both made the decision under different circumstances, despite not being keen about politics initially. Rajiv was not the political type despite growing up in the household of prime ministers and die-hard politicians during politically charged times. The elder of Feroze and Indira Gandhi's two sons, he was born on 20 August 1944, three years before Independence. Feroze was born in a Parsi family and grew up in Allahabad where the Nehru family home was located. Feroze and Indira had a tumultuous marriage. They were separated after Indira came to stay with her father, India's first prime minister, Jawaharlal Nehru, in New Delhi, but never got divorced.

As a result Rajiv's early years were spent in Teen Murti House, the imposing and verdant official residence of the prime minister in New Delhi. Indira acted as the official hostess at the many lunches and dinners that Nehru had to give. In time, she would also become a political assistant to her father.

When Rajiv and his younger brother, Sanjay, were old enough, Nehru, who had been educated at Harrow and later, Cambridge, sent his grandsons to The Doon School. Doon was an elite boarding school situated in the northern hill-town of Dehra Dun, that had been modelled after the best British public schools. From there Rajiv went to Cambridge University in England for higher studies. However, he left without a degree, not having sat for his exams[6]. He moved to the Imperial College of Science and Technology in London for a course in mechanical engineering but did not complete it either. He would admit later that he was not interested in 'mugging for his exams'[7].

On his return to India, he chose a career outside politics. After training as an airline pilot he joined India's national carrier, Indian Airlines, in 1968. He got married to Sonia Maino, an Italian student he met while he was at Cambridge. She was learning English at a private language institute in the university town.

Sonia was born on 9 December 1946, the second of three daughters born to Stephano and Paola Maino. She was raised in Orbassano, a town in Northern Italy near Turin. Sonia's biographer Rashid Kidwai in his, *Sonia: A Biography*[8], says Stephano was a 'self-made man' who had been through 'some very tough times'. Stephano had then 'made good' in a small construction business in Orbassano which had developed in the post-war boom in Northern Italy in the early 1950s. Kidwai characterizes the town that Sonia grew up in as being lower middle class. He also says that Stephano brought up his daughters in a 'traditional Catholic way'.

Rajiv and Sonia came from distinctly different backgrounds. But Sonia made the big decision to settle down in a foreign land and live in an Indian joint family with her mother-in-law, Indira Gandhi, after their marriage in 1968. Indira had become prime minister in 1967 after Nehru's successor, Lal Bahadur Shastri's death. Sonia appeared to have adapted to her new surroundings relatively well for somebody who knew very little of India before their marriage. Rahul was born on 19 June 1970 and his sister, Priyanka, on 12 January 1972.

Rajiv and Sonia Gandhi had their 'small but own close circle of friends'[9]. Rajiv never appeared inclined to dabble in politics. His biographer Minhaz Merchant says in *Rajiv –End of a Dream* that the couple's life was 'comfortable, settled and a trifle ordinary'[10]. According to him, they valued their privacy and avoided the politicians who were constant visitors at 1 Safdarjung Road, the prime minister's house, and 'scrupulously kept out of all political activity'[11].

Rajiv as a father was 'loving and approachable but strict' says Sonia in *Rajiv*, a book she put together as a tribute to her husband after his assassination in 1991. 'He could not tolerate any symptoms of what he considered "spoilt brat" behaviour such as fussing over food or wasting it. The children had to finish whatever had been prepared for them, whether they liked it or not and however long it took. He would not allow even his mother to intervene. He had a strong aversion to rudeness or bad manners, and would revert to the old school of punishment – for instance, make the children write 100 times, "I will not bang the door"[12].'

Merchant says[13] Rajiv had many interests, among them music, photography, ham radio, target shooting and flying. He was a good photographer and encouraged his children to take up photography, Sonia says in *Rajiv*. He taught them about sensitivity to colour, instructed them about keeping small notes about how they were faring and how they could improve. Rahul and Priyanka continue to be enthusiastic about photography to this day. In Priyanka Gandhi Vadra's 2011 book of photographs, *Ranthambore: The Tiger's Realm*, which she co-authored with friends Anjali and Jaisal Singh, she says she takes photographs because her father taught her to and for no other reason[14].

It wasn't just photography though. Rajiv passed many of his interests to his children. Sonia Gandhi[15] writes that on Rahul's first birthday, when he was presented with a set of things to choose from that could indicate his future preference, such as a pen for learning, Rajiv was overjoyed when Rahul chose a mechanical car. One of the first presents that Rahul was given by his father was a mechanical tool kit, she writes.

Feroze Gandhi had taught his sons to work with their hands as children, inculcating in both Rajiv and his younger brother, Sanjay, a love for all things mechanical. Indira Gandhi's friend and biographer, the late Pupul Jayakar recounts in *Indira Gandhi: An Intimate Biography*[16] that after Feroze was elected to the Lok Sabha from Rae Bareli in 1952, he came to stay in the prime minister's house in New Delhi. She says he found the atmosphere 'stifling' and soon shifted to a house of his own in the MPs quarters. On the weekends the boys would go over to their father. 'When they visited their father, Feroze gave them total attention. He showed them how to pull apart and put together toy trains and cars. He taught them how to plant and care for roses.'

Like his father and his uncle, Rahul went on to become interested in mechanics. He is known to have an interest in motorsport, and like both of them he too has a flying licence. Rajiv was also a technology buff. He was a ham radio operator and persuaded his entire family to get into it. His personal computer was his constant companion much like the BlackBerry is for Rahul today. He would pass on an interest in technology to his son and is known to have asked Sam Pitroda, the tech-entrepreneur from the United States (US) who became an important part of his team as prime minister, and is now adviser to Manmohan Singh, to send computer-related appliances for Rahul[17].

Rahul has managed to sustain the interest in technology and gadgets. He manages practically all his work on his BlackBerry, thumbing the phone relentlessly whether on a padayatra or campaign trail, and does at least some of his reading on the iPad.

Rajiv continued to be a pilot for well over ten years after Rahul was born. He quit his job only at the end of 1980 after Sanjay Gandhi's death in a plane accident on 23 June the same year put enormous pressure on him to help out his mother. Indira Gandhi had become increasingly dependent on Sanjay after he joined politics towards the mid-1970s, while Rajiv Gandhi and his family went about their lives. During the internal Emergency and later when Indira Gandhi was out of power, there was talk of Rajiv and Sonia contemplating leaving India for good to settle down abroad, possibly in Italy. Merchant notes that Rajiv while refusing to be 'unequivocal on this matter . . . denied the suggestion'[18]. Another biographer, Nicholas Nugent, while making the same point about Rajiv and Sonia wanting to move to Italy, talks of their desire to 'avoid the additional attention and resentment the Emergency brought to Indira and Sanjay, who were daily being accused in the press of destroying Indian democracy'[19]. Indeed, it is possible politics and its impact on their growing children during the post-Emergency years might have been one of the reasons why Rajiv and Sonia contemplated leaving India.

Politics however caught up with Rajiv's family with Sanjay's death. Rajiv decided to take the plunge but had to face stiff resistance from Sonia, who says she 'fought like a tigress'[20] to stop him from entering politics. She says in *Rajiv* that she understood 'Rajiv's duty'[21] to his mother but at the same time was 'angry and resentful towards a system which . . . demanded him as a sacrificial lamb'[22]. She says, 'It would crush him and destroy him – of that I was absolutely certain'[23].

Though she eventually accepted that politics would be part of her life, her discomfort with it always remained. Meanwhile, Rahul had been sent as a boarder to Doon School in 1982 and Priyanka was to follow him to Welham Girls' School, also in Dehra Dun, a year later in 1983. They had been educated at Delhi's Modern School until then. 'Rajiv was firm in his views that the experience would help them grow up to be strong and independent, but he was constantly concerned about . . . the intensified personal onslaught on the family. The children had faced similar problems earlier at a school in Delhi when schoolmates sometimes taunted them, but we had been close by to support them,'[24] Sonia writes.

Both Rajiv and Sonia had built an invisible wall around themselves to keep politics out of their lives. Yet there was nothing they could do beyond a point since politics was in their home, at the centre of their lives in the figure of Indira Gandhi.

Indira Gandhi was an important early influence on Rahul and Priyanka. She contributed to the shaping of their personalities and sense of values. She was generous in affection and demonstrative in love in the manner that her own grandfather Motilal Nehru (1861-1930) had been towards her[25].

Motilal was a self-made man who worked his way to the top of the legal practice in Allahabad, an important centre of power at the beginning of the twentieth century with the high court of the province situated there and a university having been set up. His talent and hard work soon brought him a booming law practice and he shifted his family into a palacelike house with forty-two rooms, a swimming pool and tennis court in 1900. Anand Bhavan (abode of joy), as the house came to be called, became the Nehru family home. Indira was born and raised in that large house which was ruled over by Motilal with an 'abundance of love'[26] but without any 'challenge to his authority'[27]. Indira's biographer Inder Malhotra believes that Indira modelled herself on her grandfather in her later years, turning into a 'possessive and protective matriarch of the Gandhi family'[28] as Motilal had been a 'patriarch of the larger Nehru clan'[29].

Motilal's presence filled up Anand Bhavan in the same way that Indira's did in the much more modest but incredibly powerful 1 Safdarjung Road, where Rahul and Priyanka grew up.

Indira had become a national heroine after the 1971 war with Pakistan which had led to the creation of Bangladesh. Over the next few years she was to become the centre of all political power in her own party, the Congress. During the years of the Emergency between 1975-77, she became even more powerful by suspending people's fundamental rights and curbing press freedoms. If she was Durga, the Hindu goddess who had vanquished a thousand demons in battle, at the end of the Bangladesh war, then in a few years' time she was the Indira of D K Barooah's iconic sycophantic tribute – 'Indira is India and India is Indira'.

Priyanka says her 'own identity was confused'[30] up until her adolescence because she 'idealize(d)'[31] her grandmother. 'I grew up in a household where she was the head and she was an extremely powerful woman. Not only politically powerful, but she was also a powerful human being to be around. So being this little girl and seeing this woman who was so strong and stood for so much, it did have an effect on me'[32].

Rahul has not spoken in such direct terms about his grandmother's influence on him, but it is clear he also looked up to her. In fact, his reverence for her was underlined by a closeness that may have eluded his sister. Indira Gandhi's personal assistant, Usha Bhagat writes in her memoirs, *Indiraji Through My Eyes* that Priyanka, who 'knew her mind and was very poised from the beginning'[33] would not get into trouble, while Rahul, whom she decribes as 'naïve and carefree'[34], was often in a spot of trouble. Then 'the grandmother was then very protective towards him'[35], she says.

There are several hundred photographs, scattered over books, in Rajiv Gandhi's photo collection, and in photo essays on the then prime minister, of her playing with Rahul, Priyanka, and Feroze Varun, Sanjay and Maneka Gandhi's son, born on 31 March 1980. When they were small children, Indira would participate in their simple games, play catch with them, take them for a walk in the garden, or just watch over them. She would bring back presents from her foreign visits. A 'really big stuffed monkey'[36], a 'mechanical car'[37] and other such objects made their way back to the prime minister's home after her trip to Zurich in 1981.

She also took them along with her on some foreign visits. P C Alexander, who was principal secretary to Indira Gandhi from 2 May 1981 to 3 November 1984, recalls that Indira's grandchildren, along with other family members, accompanied her to Kenya, the United States of America, and Yugoslavia in 1981 and 1982.

'I could see a lot of Mrs Gandhi as a caring and affectionate grandmother . . . She would personally attend to the smallest detail concerning the children . . . At the game park for wild animals which we visited (in Kenya), the grandmother in her took great delight in telling the children about the different animals and their habits and proved to be more knowledgeable on those subjects than the professional guides who were escorting us'.[38]

In photographer Raghu Rai's book-length photo essay, *A Day in the Life of Indira Gandhi*, there is a whole section on Indira and a bib-wearing, possibly two-and-a-half-year-old, Rahul. The child would see off his grandmother each day as she set out for her office. The pictures show an indulgent grandmother waving goodbye to a grandson who delightfully plays out what was a daily ritual for the two of them. 'Getting in (her car), she (Indira) waves to Rahul. He waves back, leaning forward to get a better look as the car glides away . . . "Gaee!" (She's gone!) he shouts, waving his arms above his head . . .'[39]

Another photo shows Indira taking Rahul by the hand across the lawn to another part of her house where people awaited her daily darshan. This was where Indira would meet common folk, party workers, journalists and others who might want to pass on a petition to her. The tradition dated back to Nehru, who as prime minister would meet common people between eight and nine in the morning. On entering political life, Rahul himself gave darshan to people though it was less ostentatiously described as a 'jan sabha'. I attended one of these meeting in October 2009 and had a chance to interact with him on a one-to-one basis at 10 Janpath where the sabha was held. The account of that meeting follows in a later section of the book.

As he grew up, Rahul became especially close to his grandmother who doted on all her grandchildren but developed a special attachment towards her first grandchild. Rahul seems to have become a pole for Indira's affections in the aftermath of her favourite son, Sanjay's death. Indira Gandhi, according to Pupul Jayakar, was left with a 'vacuum surrounding her'[40] after Sanjay's death. She needed 'someone whom she could trust totally, who would act strongly and swiftly, and keep the windows to the outer world open for her'[41]. That role was taken over by Rajiv, whose decision to enter politics was primarily influenced by the need to 'help out'[42] his mother. Jayakar says Indira also needed 'physical closeness and support'[43], which was provided by Sonia whose relationship with Indira 'changed dramatically from that of a daughter-in-law to the role of a daughter'[44]. She adds, 'And for comfort, she gathered her three grandchildren close to her'[45]. After Sanjay Gandhi's death, all the grandchildren, including the baby, Varun, slept in Indira's room[46].

However, little Varun, in whose every gesture she saw Sanjay[47], was to leave Indira's household by the end of March 1982. His 23-year-old mother, Maneka, had a bitter falling out with her mother-in-law over Sanjay's succession. The battle for supremacy between Rajiv, who was his mother's choice for succeeding Sanjay, and Maneka, who thought herself the rightful claimant to her husband's political legacy, ended in a potboiler of a climax, played out in full view of the national media. Maneka left Indira Gandhi's household with her son, the underlying insinuation being that she had been thrown out. Indira's supporters claimed that Maneka had plotted to be thrown out in order to gain public sympathy and political mileage. The episode brought their relationship to an irreconcilable pass.

The result of this ugly row was that Rajiv Gandhi and his family became the centre of Indira's life in her last years, and her 'bond'[48] with Rahul possibly a vent for her unexpressed affection for Varun.

Priyanka was to admit years later in self-deprecating banter, that Rahul was Indira's 'favourite'[49] and that 'the idealizing granddaughter would be kind of marginalized for the favourite grandson'[50]. Priyanka says Indira 'taught'[51] Rahul and 'spent a lot of time with him, talking to him'[52]. Indira had wanted to build up his character and make him ready to face his fears. In one anecdote Rahul describes a common enough childhood fear and how his grandmother helped him overcome it. Speaking to young children at the opening of a science fair at a Delhi school in November 2010, he told them how he was scared of darkness when he was young as he felt it held 'ghosts'[53] and 'bad things'[54]. Then, he said, one day his grandmother had asked him why he didn't go and see for himself what was inside darkness. So, he had walked into the garden in the dark and he had kept walking and then realized suddenly that 'there was nothing there in the darkness to be scared of'[55].

The instruction from his grandmother may have come in handy – there was a lot that Rahul and his family would go through in the next few years from Indira's own assassination to Rajiv Gandhi's murder at the hands of the Liberation Tigers of Tamil Elam (LTTE), the Sri Lankan Tamil separatist outfit.

Indira Gandhi was shot dead by her Sikh security guards with automatic guns inside her own house-cum-office on 31 October 1984, as retribution for the Indian army's attack on the Golden Temple, the holiest of the Sikh shrines. Rahul and Priyanka had already witnessed one unexpected death in the family with Sanjay's death.

Speaking to students at Kashmir University in September 2011, Rahul, who described himself as a Kashmiri to the 1,200 students gathered in the hall, spoke[56] about the day his grandmother died. 'I was only fourteen years old, I was sitting inside the classroom looking out of a window and suddenly someone came in the classroom and the teacher stopped teaching. He shared something with the teacher and asked me to come to (the) principal's room. A woman, on phone, told me to reach home immediately. My grandmother had been killed,' Rahul Gandhi said.

Maybe, Indira Gandhi had wanted to prepare her 'favourite grandson' for another death, this time her own. She had spoken to him about her intuition that her life was at an end. 'She told him to be brave when the time came: she had lived her life and done all she had to do and could do; he was not to cry for her.'[57] She had also discussed her own funeral arrangements with Rajiv and Sonia and written down instructions[58].

But all she may have been able to do was avert a fourteen-year-old Rahul from going into deep shock. Cry he certainly did as the photographs of a grief-stricken Rahul being consoled by his father at Indira's funeral show.

After Indira Gandhi's assassination, Sonia Gandhi's discomfort with politics became a deep-rooted fear. P C Alexander describes the scene between Sonia and Rajiv at the All India Institute of Medical Sciences (AIIMS) on the day when Indira Gandhi was assassinated. With Indira's body still in the hospital, the Congress decided to appoint Rajiv Gandhi as the caretaker prime minister.

'The scene which I witnessed as I moved close to Rajiv was an extremely poignant one. Rajiv was clasping Sonia by both hands in a corner of that room and talking to her very animatedly. Sonia was holding him very tightly and with tears rolling down her cheeks was ardently pleading with him not to agree to be prime minister. Rajiv was kissing her forehead and trying to convince her that he had to accept the office as it was his duty to do so in that hour of grave crisis.'[59]

But, Sonia's pleas were in vain. Here is Sonia's description of the same scene in *Rajiv*.

'As he spoke to me it sank in that they had asked him to

become the party leader. He was going to be sworn in as prime minister. I begged him not to let them do this. I pleaded with him, with others around him, too. He would be killed as well. He held my hands, hugged me, tried to soothe my desperation. He had no choice, he said; he would be killed anyway.'[60]

The entire family took a long time to overcome the shock[61] of Indira's violent death[62] but Rahul, Priyanka, and Sonia came to 'constantly fear for'[63] Rajiv's life. But the most crushing consequence of Indira's death for Rahul and Priyanka was that there would be severe restrictions on their movement from that day. 'The day of my mother-in-law's assassination was the last day Rahul and Priyanka ever attended school . . . For the next five years the children remained at home, studying with tutors, virtually imprisoned. The only space outside our four walls where they could step without a cordon of security was our garden,'[64] Sonia wrote.

They grew up in a severely protected environment which restricted their interaction with a wide crosssection of people. Rajiv Gandhi had tried his best to compartmentalize his political and his family life. A former bureaucrat who worked in the Prime Minister's Office (PMO) recounted that there was a strict demarcation between his work and home life and those on one side did not usually cross over to the other side.

Earlier, their schooling had been disturbed when Rahul and Priyanka were brought back from their boarding schools in the spring of 1984. That was the time when the security risk to Indira Gandhi's family was considered grave in the backdrop of growing militancy in Punjab.

Rajiv Gandhi makes the poignant point in one of the letters he wrote to his children when they were about to enter college, that they had been denied the freedom to go out and explore the world like other young people their age. 'Both of you have been living under very difficult conditions for some years now. This is the period in your life when you should have been getting about, meeting others your age, finding out about the world as it really is. Unfortunately, circumstances have been such that we have not been able to give you both a normal life . . .'[65]

Like his mother, Rahul too developed a wariness for politics and politicians during his growing up years. In a story which Rahul narrates[66], he once asked Rajiv at the end of the tiring campaign for the 1989 Lok Sabha elections, 'Papa, . . . why do you do this? Have you ever thought that you should just leave this?' He felt politics was 'non-stop work' and also that it was 'dangerous' for his father. The son had felt that the father had never wanted to do this to begin with and wanted to be a pilot. But, Rahul says, his father had been 'surprised' by his question and replied 'that he had never thought about it (leaving politics)'. When Rahul asked why, Rajiv had replied that was because 'he believed in the people of India'.

The anecdote is interesting because it shows that a nineteen-year-old Rahul was not terribly enamoured of a life in politics. However, it also shows that Rajiv Gandhi had come a long way from being the son who had entered politics in 1981 to 'help out'[67] his mother.

Rahul related that exchange with his father at the launch of Congress MP Mani Shankar Aiyar's book, *Rajiv Gandhi Ki Smritiyan* (Remembering Rajiv) in August 2008. Aiyar, while recalling the same anecdote[68], pointed out that once Rajiv Gandhi had learnt 'to have great faith in the people of India' during his five years as prime minister, it was as if there was 'no alternative to being in politics'. Rahul has travelled a similar path himself from reluctance to full acceptance of a role in politics.

At that time, though, he thought differently. Speaking at a workshop conducted for members of the National Students' Union of India (NSUI), the Congress' student wing, many years later he would recall[69]: 'From the time I saw him in politics, each moment of his life was lived for India . . . he used to talk of computers . . . I was small but even then I used to feel he was right. I saw there were so many people who made fun of him. Today's big leaders who are in the Opposition today used to say why does India need computers. India is a country of poor people . . . Rajiv Gandhi does not know anything . . . I saw that his entire effort was being negated. I could see what he was saying was the truth . . . I thought here was a man who was giving his life and people were trying to stop him. First the effort to stop him was through ordinary means and in the end the effort to stop him was that he was killed. That's the reality. This had a big effect on me. I felt I should develop myself in such a way that I could help my father. This was my thinking.'

Though Rahul has not spoken of it explicitly it is possible he felt it was not just his father but their entire family which was being targeted. When Rahul entered Delhi's prestigious St. Stephen's College in 1989 after finishing his schooling, the Bharatiya Janata Party (BJP) claimed his admission, under the sports quota for his skills in rifle shooting, was invalid[70]. The allegation appeared to be that with 61 per cent marks in his school-leaving examinations, Rahul was not academically bright enough to enter the college. The BJP's Delhi chief at that time, Madan Lal Khurana, claimed that Rahul's certificates in shooting were fake[71]. The BJP also asked its student and youth wings to launch a campaign on the issue[72].

The Congress and the prime minister's house took the

position[73] that Rahul was entitled to a seat in the college under the sports quota and claimed that by the standards of other sportsmen, 61 per cent marks were decent. They also rejected the claim that Rahul's skill in rifle shooting had been invented to help him into the college. They said Rahul had won two shooting gold medals at the state level and was ranked fourth at the national level. The National Rifle Association and the Olympic association also issued statements about Rahul's ability as a rifle shooter. Rahul's shooting skills attracted much media scrutiny and the incident is likely to have affected Rahul.

The fear of losing Rajiv to a terrorist attack never left Rahul and his family. It is possible he accompanied his father during the 1989 election campaign and later to Meham in Haryana in 1990, which was the site of unparalleled poll violence, out of a protective instinct. Sonia writes in *Rajiv*[74] that Rahul would telephone from America 'consumed with anxiety' about his father's security arrangements. She says Rajiv's specialized security cover was withdrawn after he became leader of the Opposition and it was replaced with a force not trained for this specific task. Rahul, who had gone to the US in June 1990 to start his undergraduate studies at Harvard University, insisted on coming back to India at the end of March 1991 for his Easter break. He accompanied his father on a tour of Bihar and was 'appalled to witness the lack of elementary security around his father'. Sonia says that before going back to the US Rahul had told her that if something was not done about it, he knew he would soon come home for his father's funeral.

~

Rajiv Gandhi was assassinated on the night of 21 May 1991 in Sriperumbudur by a suicide squad of the LTTE. LTTE operative Dhanu, chosen for the suicide blast, that would kill Rajiv and thirteen others next to him, set off the bombs strung around a waist belt even as she bowed to touch Rajiv's feet in a gesture of respect after garlanding him. 'Sonia went into deep shock. It was Priyanka, devastated by the news and yet remarkably composed, who took charge,'[75] writes Minhaz Merchant . He says Rahul returned from America on Thursday 23 May, joining Amitabh Bachchan, film superstar and a family friend of Rajiv's, who was flying back from London. 'The two arrived in Delhi together, having linked up in Paris, and quickly took charge of the arrangements, easing some of the burden on Priyanka.'[76]

Merchant adds: 'Rahul, who had shared a special bond with his father, stayed the longest by the side of the body (which was lying in state in Teen Murti House), often alone, long after his mother and sister had returned home to 10 Janpath'[77]. He lit the funeral pyre on the evening of 24 May 1991, after a Hindu ceremony during which he went around the pyre seven times. 'Throughout the heat-soaked ordeal, Rahul remained composed. Priyanka stood close to her mother, arm around her shoulders'[78]. He adds, commenting on one of the main reasons for the enduring allure of the Nehru-Gandhi family in Indian politics: 'To the millions who watched the poignant ceremony on Doordarshan that Friday evening it seemed truly remarkable that a family which had suffered so much could conduct itself with such enormous dignity.'[79]

Rajiv Gandhi's ashes were then taken in a special train to the Nehrus' ancestral home, Anand Bhavan, in Allahabad. When his father died, Rahul showed the same composure that his father did when Indira had died. He was in charge during the train journey from New Delhi to Allahabad. He was greeting mourners at each station with folded hands and even attending to the relatives and guests who were travelling with them in the all-white railway compartment. He broke down only after his father's ashes had been immersed in the Ganges[80].

This is also the journey that Rahul has described as a turning point in his own life. On one of his first visits to his constituency, Amethi, after he was elected in 2004, he spoke about how 'something clicked inside' during that journey[81]. 'When we entered UP, there was a huge crowd running with the train, very emotional and upset . . . I felt then that I had a certain responsibility towards these people.'[82]

Many years ago, his father Rajiv Gandhi speaking to TV cameras for a documentary[83], had described his son as a 'sensitive' boy. That is likely to have been at the end of the 1980s, and Rahul must have been in his late teens. He was very attached to his father and, in fact, feared for his life. He has said that it took him 'years' to get out of the 'shock' of his father's death and that he had decided to work for the people his father served when he saw his body.

Priyanka says she was 'furious with the whole world'[84] after her father died even though she did not realize it herself. It is possible that her father's death made her introspective and forced her to ask what she wanted of herself and from life. Both Rahul and Priyanka however believed that their father and their grandmother had died 'for the country'.

Merchant says Sonia's decision to turn down the Congress Working Committee's (CWC) offer of becoming the Congress president after Rajiv's death was due to Rahul's and Amitabh Bachchan's point of view on the matter. 'The two were vehemently opposed to Sonia even considering a political career,'[85] he says.

Rahul Gandhi's college education, like his schooling, was disturbed after his father's death, ostensibly due to security concerns. Rahul had to shift from Harvard University to a lesser-known and smaller college in Florida called Rollins

College. He got his BA in international relations from Rollins in 1994 and then went on to Cambridge University, his father and great-grandfather's alma matter, to get an MPhil in development studies in 1995. This is dealt with in more detail in the next chapter.

∼

Rahul and Priyanka had a strange contrast operating right through their childhood. Their parents themselves were not eager participants in matters political. Their dinner table conversations would revolve around politics and political events because it was inescapable in the Indira household. Rajiv and Sonia tried their best to protect their children from the influence of politics. Rajiv Gandhi has spoken about how he wanted to keep his children away from politics when he was the prime minister.

Rajiv and Sonia, like other upper class Indians, initially had an attitude of discomfort, bordering on disdain, for politics and politicians.

Then when their father entered politics, Rahul and Priyanka were deprived of a normal childhood. After Indira Gandhi's assassination in 1984, they were pulled out of school for security reasons and home tutored. They were totally barred from leaving their home whenever the police announced a red alert[86].

They 'justified'[87] their father's and their grandmother's assassinations with the idea that it was 'for the country'. It is possible these tragedies fostered in them a desire to work for the people they believed their father and grandmother had laid down their lives for.

Rahul has spoken of his father's assassination as the event that made him realize he felt 'a certain responsibility' for the grieving crowds who came in large numbers to meet the special train carrying Rajiv's ashes to be immersed in the Ganga at Allahabad. He has also spoken of wanting to carry on the work his father was doing when he was killed.

Sonia too said she joined politics because she felt the party that her husband, her mother-in-law and other members of Rajiv's family had given their life to was becoming weak[88]. Her politics was centred on the Congress, whose upkeep, she believed, was her moral responsibility and duty as a member of the Nehru-Gandhi family.

Rahul entered politics in 2004 when his mother needed the support of her children as the campaign against her foreign origins refused to die down. By bringing her son into politics, Sonia was furthering the Nehru-Gandhi dynasty. The tradition began with Indira who brought both her sons into politics. To Rahul a sense of duty to his immediate family is connected to a larger sense of duty to the nation and the Congress which is the vehicle through which this work is to be done.

Sonia and Rahul Gandhi both developed a fear and antagonism to politics after Indira Gandhi's assassination. This was probably strengthened after Rajiv Gandhi's death. When they made their way into politics, it led to a deep reluctance in them for posts and positions of power.

Sonia and Rahul have framed their politics in terms of 'working for the people', 'helping the poor' and 'serving the nation' as opposed to 'going after power'. It is important to remember that this position was expressed in opposition to an image of corruption which had attached itself to Rajiv Gandhi after the Bofors scam. Though he was not legally indicted for it, the scam was one of the principal reasons for his losing the 1989 general elections. The Congress would work hard to obliterate Italian businessman Ottavio Quattarocchi's connection to the Bofors deal after being elected to power.

Sonia turned down the prime minister's post after the Congress win in the 2004 general election, a decision that would become an important part of her identity as a politician. Rahul also refused any posts or positions on entering the Congress in 2004. However, while they may have given up posts they did not really give up power. Sonia continues to be the most powerful politician in India. Rahul enjoys the status and clout of being the next Nehru-Gandhi heir. Sonia and Rahul have often been criticized for practising a brand of politics that involves wielding their considerable clout in politics and policymaking with very little accountability.

2

EDUCATION AND WORK

In October 2008, Rahul Gandhi attended a question-and-answer session with college students in Uttarakhand as part of his efforts to promote the National Students' Union of India in the state. In the course of the session, a participant railed against reservations for students from socially and economically backward classes – OBCs or Other Backward Classes – in higher educational institutions as the biggest problem with Indian higher education. Rahul responded with what he thought were the real issues in Indian education.

'The biggest problem in Indian education is that there is not enough of it . . . There should be a massive increase in the number of educational institutions and a massive increase in the quality of these educational systems. I have been educated in the United States. I have been educated in England. And I will tell you . . . what I learnt here and compared to what I learnt, and the way I learnt, in the States and England, there was a difference. We in our system, we don't ask people to ask questions . . . You're told basically to remember things. I remember I was at St. Stephen's. Asking a question was not a good thing in class. You were looked down upon if you asked too many questions,'[1] he said.

His comments would have struck his contemporaries at St. Stephen's as a tad ironical. Rahul had been the quintessential 'quiet boy' in class for most of the one year he spent at the college. Yet, here he was all these years later, holding up St. Stephen's as an example to highlight India's education problems.

It is important to understand Rahul Gandhi's years abroad as a student and as a professional, because it left a deep imprint on his thinking. This experience would guide him in his initial years in politics to a great extent.

Rahul did his undergraduate studies at Harvard University and Rollins College in the US. He graduated with a BA in international relations in 1994 from the latter. He then went to Cambridge University in England from where he received an MPhil in development studies in 1995. After completing his education, he went to work as management strategy consultant with Michael Porter's management consultancy firm, Monitor, in London. Before he entered politics in 2004, he also dabbled in business for a while, setting up his own engineering design outsourcing firm, Backops Services, at the peak of the Business Process Outsourcing (BPO) boom in India in the early 2000s.

His chosen field of education and his stint as a management consultant in an organization in whose Bible competitive strategy (both for nation states and enterprises) figured prominently, moulded his outlook on issues connected with economic development in poor countries and the importance of long-term strategic planning for organizations. His years spent at these elite international campuses made Rahul more aware of the gulf between the quality of education in India, even at the best of institutions, and the West.

These influences would later become evident in his work with Non-Governmental Organizations (NGOs) in his constituency, Amethi, with education and women's self-help groups; his backing for a contentious legislation to bring foreign universities to India; his support for large social sector schemes such as the Congress-led coalition government's flagship rural job guarantee scheme; his long-term vision for the revival of the Congress party and the revamp of the Youth Congress and its student wing, the NSUI.

Despite the importance of this period in determining the characteristics and idioms that would make up the personality of Rahul Gandhi, the politician, strangely little was known about this passage of time when he took the plunge into politics. Unfortunately, this lack of clarity about Rahul's education, his brief professional career, and the even more short-lived foray into entrepreneurship, still persists to a great extent. Rahul's opaque way of functioning, a tactic his mother has developed into an art form, contributes enormously in festering the rather pointless confusion around his educational qualifications and professional capabilities. And this confusion provides fertile ground for many uncharitable conspiracy theories about Rahul and his immediate family.

~

Rahul Gandhi spent just over a year at St. Stephen's College. He enrolled there in mid-1989 to read history. Life in college was anything but enjoyable and fun-filled for Rahul the teenager. Even in a college where there was no dearth of students from some of the most powerful political and bureaucrat families, Rahul could not evade the spotlight. Being constantly surrounded by safari suit-clad security personnel hardly helped his chances of interacting with friends and doing the kind of things nineteen-year-olds do.

Sunil Manoharan, a St. Stephen's classmate, says that the heavy security cover is a defining memory of the days he spent alongside Rahul. 'About twenty or twenty-five Special Protection Group (SPG) guards would be all over the college. They would be carrying sling bags in which we all assumed were guns. Everyone knew who Rahul was,' he said in a telephonic interview from Singapore where he now works with the satellite broadcaster ESPN Star Sports as a syndication manager. Manoharan was also a year senior to Rahul at Delhi's St. Columba's school which counts several celebrities including Bollywood superstar Shah Rukh Khan as its alumni. Rahul was enrolled at the school for a brief period on his return from The Doon School where he studied for two years from 1982 to 1984. The security threat to Indira Gandhi's family in the backdrop of militancy in Punjab had led to both Rahul and Priyanka being withdrawn from their boarding schools. Rahul was admitted to St. Columba's and Priyanka to the Convent of Jesus and Mary in the spring of 1984[2]. Rahul was at the school until Indira Gandhi's assassination in October 1984. After this, his sister and he were home-tutored by teachers from the same schools[3]. 'Rahul was a quiet and shy boy in school and he continued to be a quiet and shy boy in college,' Manoharan said.

As a student Rahul was always marked out as different because he was the son and grandson of prime ministers. At school, the nastier of his classmates taunted him, the nicer ones thought to themselves that he too would grow up to be prime minister someday. It is not the kind of attention that would have helped a self-conscious youngster. Not surprisingly, Rahul did nothing to attract more attention to himself. 'He would come in quietly and sit at the back of the class (at St Stephen's),' Manoharan recalled.

He also remembers Rahul as not being regular at college.

Whenever he did attend, he came across as a 'regular kind of a guy' Manoharan said. He said there were other students at college who could be described as 'brash', but Rahul was not like that at all despite his family background of power. Manoharan recalls Rahul accompanying some students in their class to the residential blocks nearby after lectures ended for the day. 'He was such a simple guy that he would accompany us on occasion (to the hostel blocks). We would fool around and I remember him engaging in a bout of arm-wrestling once,' he said. It is possible if he were not weighed down by the restraints of belonging to a powerful family and restrictions of the SPG, Rahul might have been an easy-going and 'sporting'[4] kind of boy with a large circle of friends. The peculiar circumstances in which he grew up meant that there was no way he could lead a life like that even if he wanted to.

Security concerns were always a step behind him and would catch up with him now and then. 'It was the first year of college and people were getting to know each other. One of our friends, who lived on campus, invited Rahul to his birthday bash. Rahul said that he really wanted to come but it was the SPG which decided his itinerary. He didn't turn up for that party,' Manoharan said. Rahul had told his classmates how he would get ready for college but on some days, he would not be able to leave home since security men would not deem it safe enough for the Gandhi family members to venture out. 'He hardly turned up for classes mainly because of the security problem,' Manoharan said.

The security imperative interfered with his making new friends as well. Earlier at St. Columba's too he faced the same situation. 'His life was tightly controlled. He would come and then he would be taken back. He would not hang back in school like the rest of us,' Manoharan recounted.

Even this minimal interface with others his age stopped

after his grandmother's assassination. 'The security personnel came to take him away from school. That's how we got to know that something was wrong,' Manoharan said recalling the morning when Indira Gandhi was killed by her own security guards. Rahul's education was disrupted due to that incident and he dropped a year of school, possibly the same year that Indira died. Rajiv was asked how both Rahul and Priyanka were in the same class during an interview in 1988. 'Only one year separates them. And with all the shifting, they came to be in the same class. But that has one advantage: they can be taught each subject by the same tutor. Now, we can't possibly keep separate tutors for each of them, that would be too expensive,'[5] he quipped – both children were by then being home tutored.

This possibly explains the bond between Rahul and Priyanka. They were not only siblings but also classmates and playmates. Their childhood traumas had drawn the two of them close and made them protective of each other and their mother. There is an image of Priyanka and Rahul walking arm-in-arm, the camera capturing them from the back, as they walked into their mother's house, 10 Janpath, on the day the 2012 UP election results came out. After the Congress' drubbing in the UP elections, Rahul Gandhi had come out to meet the press teams outside Sonia's house. This had been his campaign from the word go and he was now going to own responsibility for the party's crushing defeat. As he fielded questions from a large gathering of journalists, some TV cameras zoomed into a jeans-and-kurta clad figure inside 10 Janpath, trying to stay away from the public gaze and yet not quite willing to let her brother face a grilling session from the press all alone. As he walked back after his brief statement to the media, Priyanka came forward to meet him. He put his arm around her and she reciprocated as the two of them walked back. That was the moment the cameras had captured, so evocative of their close relationship.

The brother and sister who were home-tutored together all those years back might have learnt to depend on each other in the uncertain and isolated years they grew up, but once their school years ended both had to step out. Once they began attending colleges, it is but natural they might have wanted to experience life as regular students and leave behind the security concerns to the extent that they could. It is possible that this was one of the primary reasons why Rahul decided to go to the US for higher studies.

On his twentieth birthday, Rahul Gandhi travelled to the US to enroll for an undergraduate course at Harvard University. It is possible Rahul did not take immediately to Harvard in Cambridge, Massachusetts. Part of this may have just been the New England weather. It was too cold and wet for someone raised in India, according to a source in the know about Rahul's years abroad. Rahul has also spoken about how he was able to settle in quickly in Britain as compared to the US in an interview he gave in early 2010 to Merrow Golden and Ashleigh Lamming, politics students from Cambridge University, for their campus paper, *Varsity*. When he was asked whether he had any particularly fond memories of his time in Cambridge University he replied: 'I remember walking down Trinity Street, looking at the college buildings thinking, this feels so much more like home (than America)! There's a strong connection between the UK and India, and that definitely helped me to settle in quickly'[6].

It has been widely reported in the Indian media and some foreign publications that Rahul took courses in economics at

Harvard. Neither Rahul nor Harvard officials have confirmed this. Rahul did not respond to questions about his course of study and the time period for which he was at Harvard in a questionnaire sent to him for this book. His office resolutely refused to clarify on this seemingly innocuous matter about Rahul's higher education.

Harvard too said it could not disclose details about Rahul Gandhi's time at the university. This was in response to an email seeking confirmation of media reports which said he was at the institution between 1990 and 1993 for an undergraduate degree course in economics and lived off-campus. The university's Director of News and Media Relations, Kevin Galvin, said: 'I can confirm that our records show Mr Gandhi was a student here during that period, but federal laws governing student privacy (in the US) are fairly restrictive. I will not be able to address the specifics of your other questions.'

US laws robustly defend the confidentiality of students' academic records. Students can even disallow parents from checking their records even if they happen to be paying the fees. The law states: Third Party Disclosures are prohibited by FERPA (Family Educational Rights and Privacy Act, 1974) without the written consent of the student. Any person other than the student is defined as Third Party, including parents, spouses, and employers. All educational officials are required to secure written permission prior to the release of any academic information.

This closes the possibility of the universities in the US sharing information about Rahul's educational background. This information can come to light only if Rahul himself decides to put it out for public scrutiny.

What is known about Rahul's course of study at the university is that it was interrupted on account of his father's assassination in May 1991. Rahul was in India for a few months after his father's death. Priyanka Gandhi, who was enrolled for an undergraduate degree in Psychology (Honours) at Delhi's Jesus and Mary College, had gone back to her studies by October 1991[7], but it is not clear when Rahul returned to Harvard.

For a long time after he joined politics there was no clarity about Rahul's college education or his work experience. He had not mentioned his graduation degree at all in his affidavit[8] to the Election Commission of India while filing his nomination papers as a candidate from Amethi in 2004. In the section on educational qualifications he talked of his senior secondary exams (Central Board of Secondary Education) in 1989 and an MPhil in development economics from Trinity College, Cambridge in 1995. There was no information on where he got his graduation degree despite citing a post-graduate MPhil qualification. Later, it would turn out that he had also got the name of his course at Cambridge wrong. He had been awarded an MPhil in development studies and not development economics though the latter is a core component of the course he had completed.

To return to the confusion about his education and work, *Newsweek* magazine reported in a story published in December 2006 that Rahul had taken economics courses at Harvard and Cambridge but 'failed to earn a degree'[9]. It also said that Rahul had worked for Monitor in London in 1994 but 'didn't stick with the job for very long'[10].

Rahul, through his lawyer, Congress spokesperson Abhishek Manu Singhvi, sent a notice to the publication. The magazine was forced to print a retraction. It apologized to Rahul Gandhi for 'several inaccuracies'[11] in the earlier article and offered a clarification to its readers. The magazine's clarification was based on an apology drafted by Singhvi. *Newsweek* said: 'While

Gandhi was at Harvard in 1991, his father, Indian Prime Minister Rajiv Gandhi, was assassinated. Serious, immediate and life-threatening security concerns compelled Gandhi to transfer to Rollins College in Florida, from which he graduated with a BA in 1994.' It said he had then received an MPhil in development economics from Trinity College, Cambridge University. That mistake would come to light only in the 2009 general election campaign when another publication, *The New Indian Express*, verified Rahul's MPhil degree from Cambridge and found that he had been a student of development studies and not development economics. In any case, at that time the information that *Newsweek* had published in its clarification was all that was known with any degree of certainty about Rahul's education and work experience. The magazine also said in its clarification that Rahul had joined the Monitor Group, a leading global strategy consulting group in London, where he worked for three years. 'Hence the references in *Newsweek's* article to Gandhi having "failed to earn a degree" or that he did not "stick with the job for very long" are wrong,' it said.

In the run-up to the 2009 general elections, Rahul's MPhil degree became controversial. *The New Indian Express*[12] alleged that Rahul had not only got the name of his course wrong but also the year. The paper said he had attended the course only in 2004-05. It produced a certificate from the university as evidence of its claim. Rahul once again sent a notice to the newspaper through Singhvi. With the notice was a letter[13] issued by Cambridge University in which its vice-chancellor said she 'regretted the recent controversy in India' over his qualifications. She clarified that Rahul was a student at Trinity College from October 1994 to July 1995. She also said that he was awarded the MPhil in development studies in 1995.

Rahul's unwillingness to be open about his educational

background is similar to the Gandhi family's secrecy over Sonia Gandhi's illness. Sonia and her family have been resolute in their silence on her medical condition despite speculation in the Indian and foreign media that she is suffering from some kind of cancer. All the family has been willing to reveal is that she has undergone surgery abroad for her medical condition. It can be argued that her health is a matter of public interest given that she is the de facto head of the Congress-led coalition government in Delhi. In the same way, Rahul Gandhi's educational qualifications are of importance to the public at large since he is perceived to be a future prime ministerial candidate of the Congress and is a Member of Parliament (MP).

∼

To complete his undergraduate studies, Rahul shifted from Harvard to Rollins College in southern US. Rollins College is located in Winter Park, an affluent suburb of Orlando in Florida. The city was developed as a resort town for wealthy Northern Americans to escape the harsh winters in that part of the country[14]. If Rahul had indeed found New England in the north difficult weather-wise, then this would have been an ideal place to shift to complete his education.

Rollins itself is a small, private, liberal arts institution known for its undergraduate teaching. It is not as high-profile or well-known as the Ivy League Universities on the north-east coast of the US, but is well respected in Florida. In fact, the US News & World Report, a well-known authority on college rankings in the US, puts Rollins College at the number one spot among the regional universities in the southern United States in its 2012 'Best Colleges' edition [15]. Rollins is known for its low student-to-teacher ratios, which means students get more individual attention from instructors, and for attracting top-notch teaching staff.

The college is now working on attracting more students, including Indians, to its undergraduate International Business major. This has led to a turf war amidst the teaching faculty. Some of the faculty in the liberal arts does not want the college to go the commercially-oriented way and believes this does not bode well for the future of the college. In Rahul's time, these pressures were possibly not there and Rollins is likely to have been a low-profile but academically sound liberal arts institution, if not quite a member of the Ivy League like Harvard.

Rollins' public relations and community affairs official Ann Marie Varga confirmed that Rahul Gandhi had graduated from Rollins College in 1994 but said all other information was 'confidential at the individual's express request'. However, the college website lists Rahul as having graduated in International Relations.

Tom Lairson, a professor of political science and international business at the college, who had taught Rahul said he would not discuss his academic performance citing his own policy, that of Rollins, and the US law on student confidentiality. However, he said: 'Rahul was a student in several of my classes and I was also his academic adviser. I enjoyed having him in class, our conversations outside class and his return visits to Rollins after graduation.' The comment is significant because it reveals two important details about Rahul from this phase in his life. Firstly, that he appears to have enjoyed his time at Rollins College on the whole. He became part of the college community and continues to have links with his former professors and classmates. Some of the friends Rahul made at Rollins still continue to be close to him, one professor at the college revealed. Secondly, it shows a completely different side to Rahul's personality than the one which would emerge in his early years in politics and the one that had dominated his student years in India at school and college.

He has also spoken about how allowing foreign universities in India would lead to education not being viewed through silos, a throwback to his background in liberal arts education that focuses on inter-disciplinary learning.

He refused to engage in discussions at any political forum whether public or closed-door immediately after he became an MP. One well-known Delhi-based academic recalls that the Rajiv Gandhi Institute of Contemporary Studies (RGICS) would arrange private sessions with MPs to discuss important forthcoming legislations at the time Rahul had stepped into politics. These sessions were meant to be educative and provide an opportunity for the fifteen or so young first-time MPs and the subject experts called by the RGICS to exchange views. The institute would have closed-door sessions on policy matters that were likely to be discussed and debated in the Parliament. However, Rahul hardly ever spoke at these gatherings though other young MPs were known to have expressed their points of view. His trademark in those early years was to listen rather than speak. Rahul is not someone who is, by nature, given to reticence as Professor Lairson's interactions with him indicate. However, he appears to get bogged down in situations where he is under intense scrutiny for being the Nehru-Gandhi heir.

In situations where he is required to speak, whether it is the Parliament or his election speeches, he is uncomfortable. He is only now beginning to find his public speaking voice. For the most part, however, he has tended to avoid speaking in public or to the press on issues. He comes across as a politician who is reluctant to share his views on issues of national importance or worse as someone who does not have views at all.

~

Looking back on his years at Trinity College in Cambridge, Rahul Gandhi would tell *Varsity* magazine, 'My time at Cambridge was immensely influential in shaping the person I am today'[16]. When his interviewers had asked him why, he said[17] it was mainly so in terms of what he learned on the course, in particular the economic theory he covered. He didn't, however, mention any specific theories.

Development economics is one of the 'core papers' that students of MPhil in development studies at Cambridge have to take. Debraj Ray, a development economist at New York University, in the *New Palgrave Dictionary of Economics*[18] describes development economics as a subject that studies the economics of the developing world. *The Economist* in its glossary of economic terms describes development economics in this manner: 'Spawned by the end of the colonial era in the 1950s and 1960s, a whole branch of economic theory grew up around the question of how to promote economic development in poor countries'[19].

Though Rahul spoke of how he had been influenced by the economic theory he studied at Cambridge, he qualified this by talking of how he had 'changed a lot'[20] since then. He said he now disagreed with a lot of what he was taught at Cambridge. 'I'm a lot less left-wing now than I was, for one thing,'[21] he said.

Rahul Gandhi's brush with development economics at Cambridge is likely to have given him a broad framework to think about India's development challenges. To that extent, it may have led him to back his mother's and her kitchen cabinet, the National Advisory Council's (NAC), proposals for the National Rural Employment Guarantee Act (NREGA) scheme and other large social sector measures such as the proposed food security legislation .

Rahul also described his Cambridge year as a 'very strange time'[22] from the point of view of a student living away from home. 'My father had just died, and I went from being at the centre of all that to being completely on my own and being in a place where no one knew who I was,'[23] he said. He didn't do much at Cambridge outside of his course, he said. 'I did boxing, and played squash, but I spent most of my time studying, and I only really got to know people in my course'[24].

When he was asked what was the most important thing he learned at Cambridge, Rahul said it was 'the importance of compromise'[25]. Ashleigh Lamming said he elaborated on this comment, saying the Cambridge teaching system had helped him learn how not just to argue his own opinion, but to find a solution that takes all points of view into account[26].

The interviewers had also asked him where he would like to see Indian education going in the future. He replied with a candour that is usually missing in his public utterances: 'The Indian education system is about 800 years behind the British one. We still teach as if we were living in medieval times, as if universities had a monopoly on knowledge and books were the only source of information. Back then a teacher could have told their student this [a wooden object] was made of metal and they'd have believed them. Nowadays students have access to information from so many sources – from the internet, TV, mobile phones, books – and the teacher is just one competing source of information. If you told a student today that something wooden was made out of metal they'd say you were an idiot. Teaching, and the whole education system has to move on. Education can't be about telling students what to think anymore because kids just won't believe them. The role of the teacher should be about helping children to manage all the different sources of information, and make decisions for themselves about what they believe based on critical evaluation of the competing sources of information'[27].

Ashleigh Lamming described her impressions of Rahul during her interview with him in an email. She said she remembered thinking that he expressed himself like an 'economist'. She said: 'He tended to talk about things using economic language – he talked about affirmative action (for Dalits and women which he supported) as being a problem of "supply and demand", and . . . talked about teachers no longer having a "monopoly" over information, but being one of many "competing" sources of it. At this point in the interview, he reached for a pen and paper and drew an elaborate economic diagram to illustrate a teacher as being one competing source of information.' She said he appeared 'very fond of Cambridge as a town, and of Trinity College in particular.'

A few years after Rahul had passed out of Cambridge, he met the Nobel prize-winning economist Amartya Sen. The meeting possibly took place towards the end of the 1990s or in the first couple of years of the new millennium when Rahul was working in London. Sen recounted that meeting to *Outlook* magazine in 2009. He said in the interview he had been impressed by Rahul Gandhi. When he was asked what impressed him, he replied: 'I think he is very talented . . . We had a meal together when I was Master of Trinity and we chatted about what he was planning to do. At that time, politics was not part of his plan at all, and he told me that. I believe those were his genuine views and he changed his mind later. It was very clear to me that he was very committed to Indian development. I pointed out to him there were ways for him to dazzle the world with the money he could make. But he wasn't in the least interested. I would say, since I have known Manmohan at the same age, that there was a very similar commitment in both of them, in terms of being deeply concerned about deprivation in India and wanting to make a change in that. And to devote one's lifetime to that'[28].

Rahul's college years were a time of wider exposure to the world of ideas for him. It played its part in setting him on a trajectory, economically speaking, that would bring his stated economic position close to what economists Amartya Sen and Jean Dreze, the author of the NREGA, describe as 'growth mediated' development[29] or using the rapid economic growth to fund social services, especially in healthcare and education, aimed at the poor.

It is at Cambridge that he also met his girlfriend, Veronique[30]. The gossip circuit in Delhi had known of Rahul's Columbian love interest back in London when he came down to help his mother with her maiden campaign tour in 1998. Then he was spotted and photographed watching an India England World Cup cricket match in Edgbaston, Birmingham in 1999, with a leggy young woman, rumoured to be his girlfriend. This was about the same time that the political campaign against Sonia Gandhi's foreign origins was gaining steam in India. The photograph of Rahul and his friend fuelled speculation about the status of their relationship. It raised the politically-laden prospect of another foreigner coming into the Nehru-Gandhi family. At that time it was believed that Sonia did not particularly approve of the relationship given its politically uncomfortable connotations. The rumours were given a fresh lease of life when Rahul was spotted holidaying with her in the Andamans at the end of 1999. By then her identity in the press had crystallized as Rahul's mysterious Columbian girlfriend.

It might have been ignored after a point, were it not for a

year-end family vacation in Kerala and Lakshadweep in 2003. Rahul and his friend were accompanied by his sister Priyanka and her family during that trip. By this time, the press had presumed her name to be Juanita. Finally during the 2004 Amethi election campaign Rahul shed some light on his relationship with this mystery woman while speaking to journalist Vrinda Gopinath of *The Indian Express*. 'My girlfriend's name is Veronique not Juanita . . . she is Spanish and not Venezuelan or Columbian. She is an architect not a waitress, though I wouldn't have had a problem with that. She is also my best friend,' he told her[31]. After he won from Amethi, he held a rare informal interaction with journalists in his constituency. They asked about his girlfriend's nationality to which he replied she had been living in Venezuela for a long time although her parents were Spanish[32]. He also said that he was not planning on getting married anytime soon. That was the last time he openly spoke about his romantic relationship to the press. He continues to be a bachelor and not much has been heard of Veronique since Rahul's revelations in 2004.

Rahul had attained the legal age for contesting elections to the lower house of Parliament in India, twenty-five years, by the time he passed out of Cambridge in July 1995. This triggered speculation that Rahul might contest elections and embark on his political career. *The Times of India* reported on 21 August 1995, that 'speculation was rife in the Amethi parliamentary constituency that Rahul Gandhi will enter active politics by filing his papers from there in the next Lok Sabha elections'[33] which was less than a year away.

Rajiv Gandhi had won the election from Amethi in the

1991 elections, half-way through which he had been assassinated. In the by-poll held in Amethi after Rajiv's death, the seat had been retained by Captain Satish Sharma, a flying buddy of Rajiv's who had also become an important member of his political core team. Sharma was made the minister of state for petroleum in the P V Narasimha Rao government which had come to power in the 1991 polls. He offered to resign his seat to make way for Rahul once he was old enough to contest polls. He said he had contested the election only at Sonia Gandhi's behest. He also made it clear that he had been nurturing the constituency all these years for a member of the Nehru-Gandhi family. This was also the time when Sonia Gandhi began to show signs of her willingness to step outside 10 Janpath, where she had practically secluded herself after her husband's death. She addressed a public meeting in Amethi on 24 August 1995 where she publicly took on the P V Narasimha Rao government for what she saw as the slow pace of investigations into Rajiv Gandhi's assassination[34]. This was the meeting from where Rahul's career was set to be launched. He had returned to India by that time. However, he did not travel to Amethi with his mother and sister for the meeting.

Less than a year later he was back in London working for Michael Porter's management consultancy firm, Monitor. Many years ago, Rahul was asked during a ragging session by senior students at St. Stephen's College, what he would do after completing his graduation[35]. He had replied that in most probability he would get a Masters in Business Administration (MBA). Though he did not get an MBA degree, the career he chose for himself in management consultancy was what an MBA-holder would have aspired to.

Monitor describes itself as a 'strategy consulting firm that focuses on top management issues most critical to long-term competitiveness'. It works with large multinational corporations, governments and non-profit organizations and is known to be notoriously guarded about its clients. Michael Porter, a management guru from Harvard Business School, was one of the co-founders of Monitor. He wrote the seminal *Competitive Strategy: Techniques for Analyzing Industries and Competitors*, published in 1980, that in many ways defined the field of strategic planning.

Talking about the importance of strategic planning, Porter says: 'The emphasis being placed on strategic planning today in firms in the United States and abroad reflects the proposition that there are significant benefits to gain through an *explicit* process of formulating strategy ... Increased attention to formal strategic planning has highlighted questions that have long been of concern to managers: What is driving competition in my industry or in the industries I am thinking of entering? What actions are competitors likely to take, and what is the best way to respond? How will my industry evolve? How can the firm be best positioned to compete in the long run?'[36]

The last question is particularly pertinent in understanding the impact of strategy consulting on Rahul. Till date his efforts in politics have focused on reviving the condition of the Congress by looking at long-term solutions such as organization and leadership building. He has also worked on the reform of the election system within the Congress – what he has dubbed the adoption of 'internal democracy' in the Indian Youth Congress (IYC) and the NSUI. This exercise has seen a heavy emphasis on ideas borrowed from management theory to structure and build those two organizations. It shows a coming together of his understanding of political systems in the US and Britain and his own professional experience as a management strategy consultant.

Monitor refused a request for an interview with Rahul's colleagues at the firm. It also declined information on Rahul's role within the organization, his key result areas or the industry sectors that Rahul had specialized in during his stint at the company. Monitor's Michael Goldberg, however, confirmed in an email that Rahul Gandhi had worked for the company 'starting late June 1996 through early March 1999'.

According to sources, who have known Rahul from his time at Monitor, there were no problems with his performance at the firm. He worked there under an assumed name and his colleagues did not know of his real identity, said a Monitor employee who was at the firm around the same time as Rahul. 'His looks gave it away to those of us who knew who he could be,' the source said.

Rahul has spoken of the long hours he used to put in while at the firm during his first election campaign from Amethi. An interviewer had asked him how he would adapt to a life in politics, which is not as easy compared to the 'relaxed life' he had led. Rahul responded: 'I never had any relaxed lifestyle. When I worked in London, I used to work long hours daily. If anyone did not deliver at Monitor, he would be told to go. So I worked hard, and the culture of working hard is in my blood. That is what I need in politics too, I believe.'[37]

After three years at Monitor, Rahul came back to India to help his mother with the 1999 general election campaign. Sonia had taken the plunge into politics before the 1998 general elections. Rahul had come down from London to be by his mother's side during that campaign as well. In the 1999 mid-term polls, Sonia was contesting elections to the Lok Sabha for the first time. He was his mother's constant companion even as his sister, Priyanka, restricted herself to managing her mother's campaign in Amethi, which she did almost single-handedly. Unlike his sister, who all but outshone Sonia during the 1998 election campaign, Rahul was a presence in the background. He would wave to crowds now and then, but that was it. He was physically present by his mother's side as a protective figure, in the way that he had wanted to do for his father many years back. The Congress lost the 1999 election decisively. The party touched its all-time low in Parliament with just 114 seats.

Rahul disappeared from the political firmament once again after the elections. There is no exact information about any other job Rahul might have taken up in the intervening years after he left Monitor in March 1999 and returned to India for good in late 2002.

Rahul's performance on the job at Monitor was to a large extent determined by his own talent and skills. This was an important formative experience for him. His entire politics has been marked by an engagement with issues that are long-term in character, whether it pertains to his working on reviving the Congress' organizational structure in states where it has weakened or developing new leadership by bringing young people into the organization. These concerns have dominated his politics rather than an emphasis on issues of immediate political concern. While this may make sense from a professional management or strategy consultant's point of view, Rahul's role was never meant to be that of an organizational consultant to the Congress party. This has become a problem area with his politics and went against him in the way he was perceived in the Congress and outside.

It is telling that on his resume on the Parliament website, Rahul Gandhi still continues to call himself a 'strategy consultant' in the column under 'profession'.

～

At the turn of the century, the idea of outsourcing manufacturing and services functions to low-cost destinations such as India and China was keeping strategy consultants awake at night. Rahul Gandhi too was hooked on to the idea of doing things cheap in India for well-heeled Western clients. Rahul made the transition from consultancy to entrepreneurship in 2002 by setting up a firm called Backops. The new firm's name left no one in doubt about its nature of work. Rahul himself described the company as an engineering design outsourcing firm. In the articles of association filed with the Registrar of Companies (RoC), Backops was in the business of providing back-office and advisory support to domestic and international clients across industry segments; to act as a consultant, adviser and representative in the field of information technology, legal, commercial and business management, Research and Development (R&D) and computer analysis; and to provide and market products and services, web solutions and set up websites for e-commerce. In 2002 when he forayed into this business, India was emerging as one of the hottest destinations for BPOs. The domestic economy was booming. The ecosystem for entrepreneurs in sunrise industry sectors had developed in India. For a globally networked 32-year-old, it was a time as good as any to jump on to the outsourcing bandwagon and put to test the business ideas he dispensed as a consultant.

The secrecy that surrounds almost every affair of the Gandhi family accompanied Backops as well. Although Rahul did declare his 83 per cent ownership of Backops in his mandatory affidavit filed with the Election Commission while contesting from Amethi, the country first heard of the details of the venture when the Mumbai daily *Midday* carried a story soon after Congress' surprise victory in the 2004 elections. The paper made some sensational claims about this little-known Rahul-owned firm. The story said that Backops, a company not many had heard of, had secured plum projects like the city's (Mumbai's) international airport terminal building, the commercial complex at Phoenix Mills, Belapur railway station, the Wockhardt Hospital in Mulund, and buildings at the Osho Commune, Pune. *Midday* said: 'The impressive line-up may have a lot to do with the fact that Rahul Gandhi, now MP from Amethi, owns 83 per cent of the company's shares'[38].

It was improbable that a start-up would bag parts of such key projects whose value ran into crores of rupees. Backops' office was a non-descript rabbit warren in South Mumbai's Colaba. Did he use his family's new-found political clout to grab these projects? Why and how did he get into this business in the first place? Was Backops a front for some other larger political design?

These were some troubling questions that began to surround Backops. Matters weren't helped by the usual stonewalling and silence from Rahul and his associates. It was somewhat surprising that Rahul chose to provide engineering design services. His educational background suggests he had no expertise whatsoever in the subject. Did he pick up some skills during his stint at Monitor? It is unlikely. *A Times of India*[39] report in March 2004 said that he had done a course in computer-aided engineering design. Is that enough to start a specialized firm?

A *Business Standard*[40] story a month later provided some answers. According to the incorporation documents filed with the RoC, Rahul was the company's majority owner while three other friends – Anil Thakur, Ranvir Sinha and Manoj Muttu – owned the rest of the company. Backops had an authorized share capital of Rs 25 lakh divided into 25,000 equity shares of Rs 100 each. Rahul was the largest shareholder with 2,500 shares, while Muttu held 250.

Anil Thakur and Ranvir Sinha, both residents of Delhi, held 150 and 100 shares, respectively. Of the 25,000 authorized shares, 3,000 were subscribed to. There was no other financial information about the company. No income statement was filed since its incorporation two years ago. The company's registered office was in central Delhi's Deen Dayal Upadhyay Road. When a *Business Standard* correspondent visited the address, he found not Backops but a chartered accountancy firm called Thakur Vaidyanath Aiyer and Company. Employees there hadn't heard of Backops, and some became a little nervous when queried further.

When the paper contacted Rahul directly for information on his company, he was livid. Not in India when the correspondent called, he accused him of breaching his privacy and claimed he wasn't obliged to speak to the media about his private affairs before hanging up. Surprisingly he called back a few minutes later, and in a perceptibly calmer state of mind offered to answer some queries, provided the questions were short. Rubbishing the claims *Midday* had made about Backops bagging a dozen big-ticket infrastructure projects, Rahul explained that Backops was a fairly 'small' company whose revenue was less than $100,000 or Rs 45 lakh back then. 'It is a start-up that employs just eight people. I can't talk about Backops' exact revenue at this point of time, but it is in the sub-$100,000 region,' Rahul said.

At that time he said, Backops currently had three overseas clients that outsourced detailing and technical analysis related work to the company. 'There is nothing mysterious about the firm and I am open to talking about it through proper channels,' Rahul added. He seemed fairly keen to grow the business despite his full-time involvement with politics. He was looking for a CEO who would look after Backops' day-to-day affairs.

But politics had taken a toll. He quit as a director of the company in 2009 with Priyanka replacing him. Backops isn't a going concern today. There is no income to speak of; and no business expenditures made in 2011. In all likelihood, Backops would cease to exist even on paper very soon.

Rahul's stint abroad allowed him a freedom that had eluded him in India. According to a source who knows the Gandhi siblings, a majority of the people he encounters in India come to him with their heads bowed. Not surprisingly, many of Rahul's friends are foreigners, the source said.

There was a quest for normalcy, of getting away from the trappings of being a Nehru-Gandhi scion that was part of Rahul's growing-up years as much as an identification with the family he came from. The security cover, that was necessary but also restrictive, was responsible for making it hard for him to enjoy the freedom that that other people his age could have. While he was in London, for a few years he attempted to live a regular life, putting his life at risk and doing away with his security guards[41]. While he was in the US, he would take trains and during his commute strike up conversations with his fellow passengers. He has remarked[42] about how they were not interested in knowing anything about his background except what work he was doing. He said they never asked about caste, community, or religion and that's the vision he had for India when he joined politics.

He became a professional working and living in one of the world's foremost financial and commercial hubs, London, as a management consultant with a leading global firm in the sector. This is the holy grail for most young Indian B-school graduates. Yet while this might have been something he aspired to and worked towards, there also seems to have been a desire in Rahul to do more with his life than make money abroad as he told Amartya Sen. There was no overt inclination towards politics at this stage in his life, but there was not a ruling out of it either because he was part of his mother's election campaigns.

It is possible he wanted to succeed on his own steam before he joined politics. That was perhaps one of the reasons why he did not jump into politics right away after finishing his education. He has spoken about how he could have joined politics right after his father's death but 'he had nothing to offer'. This idea followed him when he entered political life. He would talk of wanting to 'learn and understand'[43] rather than take up posts in the Congress-led Central government and in the party.

PART TWO

ENTER RAHUL

3

FAMILY AS POLITICS

A 33-year-old Rahul Gandhi was one of the most sought-after candidates in the run-up to the 2004 Lok Sabha polls.

Rahul was young, good-looking, modern, English-speaking and, on the whole, very un-politician-like. He was the face of the next generation of the Nehru-Gandhi family; he brought back memories of the heyday of his father, Rajiv. In 1984, Rajiv won his party a historic near-three-fourth majority in the national elections following Indira Gandhi's assassination. The media was in love with the forty-year-old Rajiv for a while. Twenty years later, when Rahul decided to contest the election from his father's constituency, Amethi, the media was no less besotted with him.

Amethi is part of the Avadh region in Central Uttar Pradesh (UP), India's most populous state, which holds the distinction of sending the most number of MPs to Parliament (80 out of 543) despite its dire socio-economic backwardness. The Nehru-Gandhis can trace their relationship with this part of UP to Rahul's great-grandfather, Jawaharlal Nehru. He lent his backing to the peasant unrest in the United Provinces (now

UP) against the payment of burdensome taxes over and above the rent that had been imposed by the landlords. This unrest was especially severe in several districts of Avadh in 1920-21. Jawaharlal Nehru's biographer M J Akbar[1] holds the 'links forged . . . in this agitation' as being responsible in 'some part at least' for the Nehrus and Gandhis being elected from Rae Bareli and Amethi.

Over the next nine decades, Amethi sent four Nehru-Gandhis to Parliament – Rahul's uncle and Indira's second son, Sanjay; Rajiv; Sonia; and Rahul himself, who was elected in the 2004 and the 2009 general elections.

Rahul's decision to contest from Amethi signalled he would take charge of the family inheritance. This put an end to the speculation about his sister, Priyanka, whom Congressmen favoured more than Rahul. She was compared with Indira because of her resemblance to her grandmother, her ability to charm crowds, and her aggressive campaign demeanour during Sonia's campaign in 1999. Rahul was seen as politically less gifted, and viewed as reluctant as far as politics went. Sonia's biographer and journalist, Rasheed Kidwai explained that this perceived reluctance was largely due to the 'visibility factor' since Rahul had lived abroad for more than a decade after Rajiv's death in 1991. 'Rahul was simply not around. And the Brahmins of UP (Congress leaders) would see Indira in Priyanka,' he said.

The impression that Rahul was a reluctant heir was a mistaken one. He knew all along that the job was his for the taking. But he waited until the right time, or what he thought was right. 'I could have joined politics soon after my father died . . . but I was just nineteen and had nothing to offer. I made a commitment to myself, I will do it one day,'[2] he said in an interview during his first election campaign.

However, the road to that decision was not straightforward.

Rahul faced a dilemma similar to Priyanka, and even Sonia, when he thought about politics and the official posts and positions that were inevitably part of the package. At one level, they were hurt by the assassinations of Indira and Rajiv, who had been murdered for decisions they had taken while they were in office. Indira was killed by her Sikh bodyguards for the attack on the Golden Temple; Rajiv was killed by the LTTE. Politics, and the burden of official decisions, had been traumatic for them. For Rahul and Priyanka, the rhythm of growing up had been broken. But all the three believed that Indira and Rajiv had died 'for the country'. So, they wished to follow those footsteps, and there was a push factor to enter politics.

Sonia's answer to these contradictory pulls was the urge to save the Congress as she owed it to her deceased family members to protect their legacy. Her decision to enter political life in 1998 was aimed at stopping the country from being overrun by 'communal and divisive forces'[3], her shorthand for the Bharatiya Janata Party or BJP. The pro-Hindu, majoritarian party was on an upswing in the same period in which the Congress declined. It won its highest tally of 182 seats in the 1998 general elections. It was back with the same number of seats in the 1999 mid-term polls when the Congress put in its worst performance in the Lok Sabha elections till then with 114 seats.

But Sonia had an instinctive reluctance for positions of power which had claimed two lives in her family. In her eyes – and her children's – she resolved this conflict by turning down the prime minister's post in 2004. Viewed another way, she practised a brand of politics that demanded little accountability for the decision-making power she wielded.

Priyanka felt her mother went 'against her grain'[4] to embrace politics, and she wouldn't make the same mistake. She would not do it out of 'a sense of duty' to 'some ideal', 'the party', or her 'family'[5]. Her solution was her rationalization that she wanted to work for the people. 'I am very clear in my mind. Politics is not a strong pull, the people are. And I can do things for them without being in politics.'[6] She displayed the same reluctance for posts and positions.

Yet, she couldn't disassociate completely from politics. She campaigned for her mother and brother. Just as in the 2007 UP Assembly elections, in 2012 she was Congress' chief campaigner in Amethi and Rae Bareli. She ventured into the adjacent Sultanpur Lok Sabha constituency in the 2012 elections. She brought her children to election podiums and watched on as they waved to the audience.

Still, from Priyanka's viewpoint, she was not in politics. She described her work as her duty to Sonia and Rahul. She would not contest elections or expand her role beyond Amethi and Rae Bareli. Seen from a different viewpoint, even more than Sonia, Priyanka is twice removed from political accountability despite her immense clout. She holds neither a post in the party nor in a legislative position.

Rahul grappled with the same idea to work 'for the people' without contesting elections. Amartya Sen believes[7] politics was not part of Rahul's plans at all when the two met towards the end of the 1990s or in the early 2000s. He felt those were his 'genuine views' at that time and that he 'changed his mind later'. He spoke about Rahul's 'concern about deprivation in India and wanting to make a change in that'. At that time Rahul was working in London.

It is possible Rahul was unsure about the form and shape of his political associations. The backdrop of reluctance to positions of power in the family cannot be ignored. Over the years he has maintained this. Asked after his Amethi win in 2004 how he felt when his supporters described him as the 'next best prime minister', he said: 'Please do not take it as any kind of arrogance, but having seen enough prime ministers in the family . . . it is not such a big deal. In fact, I often wonder why should you need a post to serve the nation'[8]. At a press conference during the 2012 UP campaign, he said he was not 'obsessed' with becoming prime minister but with the development of the state.

In fact, when he came back to India in late 2002, he set up his own business in a field far removed from politics – engineering and structural design outsourcing services. But, at the same time, he kept indirectly in touch with politics. He was involved with the Rajiv Gandhi Foundation (RGF) and the Rajiv Gandhi Charitable Trust (RGCT)[9]. The RGF was set up by Sonia in June 1991 after her husband's death. Its declared aim is to 'work in areas which were of deepest concern to Rajiv Gandhi'. It counts literacy, health, disability, empowerment of the underprivileged, and livelihoods as the areas that it has been involved with over long years. RGF and RGCT were involved with developmental work in Amethi.

On his first trip to Amethi after his return to India, he was asked[10] what he felt about the immense pressure on him to join politics. 'You have to feel it, if you want to do it at the right time, you do it . . . You can't be pressurized,' he said. When a reporter persisted that he was clearly not the type who was averse to politics, Rahul thought about it for a few seconds. 'I am not averse to politics, but that does not mean I am going to join politics . . . Both my sister and me do think about it, and we discuss it as well. But we haven't made any decision on it.'

Two months later, he decided to contest from Amethi. Sonia told *Hindustan Times* in April 2004. 'We all knew that at some stage we would have to decide one way or the other (about Rahul contesting elections). That was a given. We sat down and discussed it like all families do and then Rahul decided to file his nomination'[11]. When asked whether the decision was made years ago, she denied it: 'No, not years ago. It was as the campaign drew nearer that we finally sat down and discussed it'[12].

Although it is unclear, Rahul's decision was influenced by the desire to help out his mother, whose foreign origin was still a controversial issue. Earlier, he felt the desire to 'help' his father, when Rajiv went through a political rough patch in the late 1980s. He told[13] National Students' Union of India (NSUI) leaders at a workshop conducted after he took charge of the organization post September 2007 that Rajiv's 'entire effort was being negated' and he felt he should 'develop' himself in such a way that he could be of assistance to his father. When Sonia stepped into political life, Rahul accompanied her on election tours. In those days, his role was more of a personal aide rather than a political one, which was assigned to Priyanka.

But, in 2004, Sonia needed a regular political aide. The feeling within the Congress in the run-up to the 2004 polls was that a more 'authentic' Nehru-Gandhi face would help the party. Everyone, including Congress leaders, expected the BJP to win in the general elections. After his sister decided to stay out of politics, Rahul might have felt he owed it to his mother to help her. Rajiv had joined politics when his mother, Indira, needed a political aide after Sanjay's death. Rajiv had overruled his wife's objections then. His decision was made under far more trying circumstances.

Unlike his father, Rahul did not make that choice out of familial compulsion alone. He identified with the legacy his father had stood for – the Nehru-Gandhi legacy – and the one his mother safeguarded. It is possible he believed that his duty to the country was intertwined with his duty to the Congress; like his mother he felt the Congress was the only party that represents all Indians.

After he won Amethi, his reasons to take the political plunge were reflected in his two primary areas of interest. The first was to continue his father's work in Amethi and to 'bridge the gap between modern India and traditional India'[14] that he believed his father had been doing when he was killed. This idea would later become part of Rahul's political lexicon. He would speak of 'two Indias' – the rich and poor, and the urban and rural – and talk of the need to focus on economic redistribution. The second area that obsessed him was the imperative to revive the Congress party and make it organizationally stronger. Since he was averse to electoral offices, it would give his politics a skewed NGO-like emphasis.

As part of the organization-building exercise in the Indian Youth Congress and NSUI, Rahul would aim to bring changes to a system that traditionally favoured family connections and money power. This was never an ideological position as much as it was a management issue. He looked at politics through technocratic prisms. In his head, he had compartmentalized his decision to continue the Gandhi dynasty and parallely hold free and fair internal elections within the youth and student wings to do away with the influence of family and money. He could, therefore, call himself a 'symptom'[15] of the problem that affected the Indian political system and yet continue to function as the heir apparent in the Congress. This contradiction would riddle his project to 'democratize' the IYC and the NSUI with a serious inconsistency.

But before we get into Rahul's work with rebuilding the Congress organization, we need to analyse the state of the Congress party that Rahul inherited in 2004, when he decided to become the next Nehru-Gandhi heir.

4

THE CONGRESS THAT
RAHUL INHERITED

In 1977, when Indira Gandhi rode Moti, an elephant, to reach Belchi, a remote village in Bihar to commiserate with Dalits whose kin had been burnt alive in a violent caste clash, it marked her first steps on a comeback trail after she was routed in the 1977 elections post the internal Emergency. It was the beginning of a process to mend her broken relationship with the people. The event and the image of a heroic Indira who braved the floods and an unhelpful local government to be with the Dalits in their hour of grief was enough to turn the tide. The Emergency memories began to fade from that moment.

More than thirty years later, Rahul Gandhi gave policemen a slip and rode pillion on a motorbike to reach Bhatta Parsaul in the wee hours of 11 May 2011. The twin villages in UP's Greater Noida district were the site of violent skirmishes between the police and agitating farmers who felt the Mayawati government took away their fertile farmlands cheap, only to sell it to fat-cat industrialists. The state government enforced prohibitory orders in the area, and the step reinforced fears of police excesses. Rahul's dharna in Bhatta Parsaul was a challenge to the state authorities. The media flocked in large numbers to Greater Noida (it was conveniently located only a couple of hours from the headquarters of several TV channels) to enthusiastically chronicle Rahul's heroics. The whole event was tailormade for TV.

Unlike in the case of Indira, Rahul did not become an overnight hero, or set the Congress on the road to political recovery in UP. Unlike his grandmother's impromptu and emotional trip, Rahul's adventure appeared choreographed. The Congress' opponents called it a tamasha, and so it seemed.

It was not merely the lack of spontaneity on part of Rahul that led to the assessment. The fact was that something had fundamentally changed in the thirty-four years since his grandmother's elephant-ride. The Congress' position in Indian politics and the Nehru-Gandhi aura had drastically diminished during the period.

≈

The Congress grew out of a mass movement for complete independence from British colonialism. Founded in 1895 by A O Hume, a retired civil servant, it was dominated by the educated elite and professionals – mainly lawyers and doctors. In its early years, it asked for better opportunities for work and education and greater political participation for Indians under the colonial rulers. Later, when it stood for Independence, and was symbolized by Mahatma Gandhi, it took the form of a national movement that attracted the masses. But it was led by the elite and the professionals.

Post-Independence, the Congress was a loose formation of several interest groups, which transformed into India's 'party of power'. In the first three general elections held in 1952,

1957, and 1961, it won an over two-thirds majority of seats in the Lok Sabha[1]. It became the ruling party in most states with the exception of Jammu and Kashmir, Kerala and Nagaland[2].

Once several powerful leaders, including Mahatma Gandhi and Sardar Vallabhbhai Patel died soon after Independence, Jawaharlal Nehru, the first prime minister of India, centralized power in his hands within the Congress during his uninterrupted reign as prime minister for seventeen years from 1947 to 1964. That's when the seeds of the dynastic succession norm were sown, though there is still considerable debate over whether Nehru himself intended his daughter, Indira, to be his successor.

After Nehru's death, power passed into the hands of the Congress organization. Some of its most influential regional satraps banded together and were nicknamed the 'Syndicate'; its members[3] were Atulya Ghosh from West Bengal, Biju Patnaik from Orissa, S K Patil from Mumbai, Neelam Sanjiva Reddy from Andhra Pradesh, and S Nijalingappa from Karnataka.

After the Lal Bahadur Shastri interlude, which lasted less than two years, Indira Gandhi took over as prime minister in early 1966, only because the Syndicate thought it could treat her as a political puppet. However, they gravely underestimated her. She took on the Syndicate and 'appealed to the people directly over the heads of the party bosses'[4] in the March 1967 elections 'pitt(ing) her mass appeal against their (Syndicate) skill in manipulating the party machine'[5]. Indira emerged as the Congress' most popular leader after Nehru.

But the party suffered damage. In the watershed election, the Congress lost grip over large parts of India. Its strength in the Lok Sabha came down to 283 out of 520 seats, from 361 out of 494 seats in 1962. Its vote share was down from 44.7 per cent to 40.8 per cent. It lost power in eight out of sixteen states including Tamil Nadu. The Syndicate burnt its fingers too; K Kamaraj, one of its leading members, lost his state, Tamil Nadu, to the Dravida Munnetra Kazhagam (DMK), as also his seat.

The post-1967 period 'represent(ed) a secular decline in Congress strength nationally and in state after state'[6]. As far as Indira was concerned though, the 1967 verdict meant that although she had unshackled herself from the Syndicate, the battle with it was far from won. She continued the tug-of-war until the first Congress split of 1969. She marginalized her rivals and centred the Congress completely on herself after that. The process ended with the second split of 1978 after which the party simply came to be known as Congress (Indira) or Congress (I).

From 1972, Indira stopped holding organizational elections in the Congress. She made sure there would be no leader to equal her stature. She surrounded herself with 'small men', who would be loyal to her and appointed her own people as chief ministers in an attempt to make sure nobody rose too high. She continuously played one faction within the party against another, and controlled access to herself to make sure that she did not give anything away.

The coteries around her changed during her reign – from January 1966 to March 1977, and later from January 1980 to October 1984. However, they came to be dominated by alleged wheeler-dealers. The most prominent among them were L N Mishra of Bihar, the party fundraiser and minister for defence production who was pilloried as 'nagad narayan' (money-spinner) in Parliament[7], yoga guru Dhirendra Brahmachari, who came to known as the 'flying Swami' after his penchant for helicopters, and Bansi Lal of Haryana, who wasn't known for a squeaky clean image and later facilitated the construction of Sanjay Gandhi's Maruti factory in Gurgaon, on the outskirts of Delhi. As Haryana chief minister he arranged for over 300 acres of land, much of it agricultural, to be handed over to Sanjay Gandhi's project at prices lower than the market rate[8]. Indira's office assistants, Yashpal Kapoor and later R K Dhawan, worked behind the scenes and facilitated the alleged deal-making that politics demanded. They were among the most sought-after people in the party because they controlled access to Indira.

Indira became all-powerful during the internal Emergency (1975-77). The immediate provocation for the declaration of the Emergency was a Supreme Court (SC) judgement delivered by Justice V R Krishna Iyer on 24 June 1975. It granted only a conditional stay to an earlier judgement by the Allahabad High Court which had struck down Indira Gandhi's election from Rae Bareli in 1971 and debarred her from contesting elections for six years. After the SC judgement, Indira's continuance in office had become questionable as she could attend Parliament but not vote. The Opposition parties, backed by the socialist Jayaprakash Narayan (JP), had been building up a campaign to remove her from power. They used the judgement to immediately press for her resignation. On 25 June, in consultation with West Bengal Chief Minister Siddhartha Shankar Ray, Indira decided to impose Internal Emergency under Article 352 of the Constitution. V Krishna Ananth in *India Since Independence* writes that she told President Fakhruddin Ali Ahmed on 25 June that the JP movement could be defined as an 'armed rebellion' (JP had been appealing to the armed forces not to take orders from an 'illegitimate' government) and hence warranted a Presidential proclamation of the Internal Emergency provision. The President signed the proclamation late at night and it came to be known as the midnight proclamation after that. Indira had not consulted her Cabinet members or sought their approval for the proclamation. The Cabinet was intimated about the development only in the wee hours of 26 June. It met at 6 a.m. and cleared the proclamation without any resistance from the ministers. Sanjay Gandhi played an important role in the developments leading up to the declaration of the Emergency as well as in the large-scale midnight arrests of Opposition leaders and a few Congressmen under the Maintenance of Internal Security Act (MISA). He was also instrumental in making sure the power supply to Bahadur Shah Zafar Marg, where most newspapers offices in Delhi are located, was cut so that the news of the Emergency and the midnight arrests did not reach the people. Indira now had powers that were dictatorial in scope. She put in place press censorship, suspended people's fundamental rights and had the powers to arrest and jail anyone without citing reasons.

The Emergency period benefitted Sanjay who used his influence with his mother and those within her establishment to set himself up as a parallel centre of power in the Congress. His eventual plan was 'to capture the Congress through the Youth Congress'[9] which Rahul attempted years later. The regional leaders realized his importance and tried to outdo one another to pre-empt and fulfil Sanjay's wishes.

Under Sanjay, the Youth Congress became a feared organization and its activists came to be known as Sanjay's 'goondas'. Part of this had to do with the absolute power that Sanjay himself wielded during the Emergency years. Senior journalist Vinod Mehta in his *The Sanjay Story* (1978) says by June 1976 Sanjay was 'running a parallel government from inside his mother's house'[10].

Sanjay presided over forcible slum clearance programmes which were undertaken in several places including Delhi to 'beautify' the city. Slum clearance was part of his five-point programme[11] that also included the dreaded family planning drive which Mehta describes as the 'lynchpin of Sanjay's

Emergency activities'[12]. Protests against the demolition of slums at Delhi's Turkman Gate resulted in the deaths of 150 people in police firing[13]. Of Sanjay Gandhi's 'achievements' as far as the family planning or sterilization programme went, Krishna Ananth says it was one of 'large-scale coercion, abuse of authority and scores of men sterilized under duress'[14]. The Youth Congress became involved with these ventures, especially the mayhem that passed in the name of family planning. Journalists John Dayal and Ajoy Bose write in *For Reasons of State: Delhi Under Emergency*: 'The Youth Congress was directly coordinating with Sanjay Gandhi, and through him got the local official machinery (in Delhi) to act as their back-up organizations to implement their blackmail and threats which were to become the main tool of getting ever-increasing numbers of vasectomies'[15]. But it wasn't just because of the Emergency activities that the Youth Congress came to be associated with hooliganism. Mehta says[16] after Sanjay became a member of the Youth Congress executive council in December 1975, he launched a recruitment drive to 'swell the membership as fast as possible', giving all 'procedural formalities' a go-by. The Youth Congress quickly became 'an umbrella organization which sheltered a variety of goondas, thugs, pick-pockets, criminals' – all the 'bad characters' and 'anti-social' elements police usually kept a record of'[17]. He says Youth Congress is remembered in Delhi in the years immediately after the Emergency for 'hounding and subverting the entire commercial life in the city'[18].

The Emergency excesses related to the forcible imposition of family planning strictures finally swept Indira out of power after she declared elections in 1977.

Indira had reduced the Congress to a family cult. By the time she was through, the Congress was dependent on the Nehru-Gandhi family. It became weak organizationally in a relative sense. This coincided with the period when the party's political fortunes witnessed a gradual decline in the states. Amidst this, the Rajiv Gandhi era began.

≈

With Sanjay's unexpected death on 23 June 1980, Indira needed somebody to fill the void. She looked to her elder son, Rajiv, who gave up his life as an airline pilot and entered Parliament from Amethi in 1981. But he did not see himself as someone who would step into Sanjay's shoes. He wanted to pursue his own brand of politics. Rajiv distanced himself from 'the gaggle of lumpen rich that Sanjay had brought into the party and from the Sanjay hordes'[19], though, eventually, some of the prominent figures of his younger brother's faction such as Kamal Nath became part of the Rajiv establishment.

Rajiv tried to bring reforms in the Congress organization. He wanted professional and educated people to join the party. He talent-spotted and pushed the cases of younger people from the Youth Congress, whom he liked. He created a new team which would work directly under him. His key men, Arun Singh and Arun Nehru, were corporate managers who gave up plum jobs to join him. Rajiv's biographer, Minhaz Merchant, says Arun Nehru was 'the wunderkind President of Jenson and Nicholson, a Calcutta-based paint multinational'[20] and Singh, who hails from the Kapurthala royal family, was marketing controller at Reckitt and Coleman also in Calcutta. It led to an enthralling quote by the maverick Ram Jethmalani, who, in his trademark style, said that India was being run by 'a planewallah (Rajiv), a paintwallah (Arun Nehru) and a boot-polishwallah (Arun Singh)[21]'.

Rajiv positioned himself as one who wanted a complete break from the corruption and wheeling-dealing of his mother's era. In a famous speech delivered at the Congress centenary session in Mumbai in 1985, Rajiv denounced the 'brokers of power and influence who dispense patronage and convert a mass movement (Congress) into a feudal oligarchy'[22]. In the same breath he identified these power brokers as those who belonged to 'self-perpetuating cliques' who were given to 'self-aggrandizement', 'corrupt ways', 'linkages with vested interests in society', and 'sanctimonious posturing'.

He dispensed with his mother's intermediaries such as Dhawan. Rajiv wanted to 'recreate the party in his self-image'[23]. He announced in his press conference on 7 July 1985, the first after he took over as prime minister, that Congress would have organizational elections the next year[24].

However, the promises never materialized. Rajiv proved inadequate to the task. His own aides, Arun Singh and Arun Nehru, fell out with him within a few years. The Rajiv Gandhi government was bogged down by allegations of kickbacks to the tune of Rs 64 core[25] paid to middlemen in the purchase of the Swedish Bofors guns. The government's 'stonewalling' of demands to bring the guilty to book in the Bofors case and other corruption scandals destroyed Rajiv's image as 'Mr Clean'. Ramchandra Guha in *India After Gandhi* says the 'stonewalling prompted speculation that the middlemen were somehow linked to the prime minister himself'.

The Bofors scandal came out in the backdrop of the friction between Rajiv and V P Singh, who was Rajiv's finance minister and was later shifted to defence. Singh had resigned in the wake of allegations of kickbacks in another defence purchase – the HDW (Howaldtswerke-Deutsche Werft) submarine deal with West Germany, into which he had ordered an enquiry as defence minister. Singh was expelled from the party and became the face of the Opposition campaign against Rajiv by the time the 1989 elections arrived.

Even as his government battled corruption charges, Rajiv's mishandling of the Shah Bano and Ram Janmabhoomi-Babri Masjid issues showed a complete deficit of political management. The opening of the locks in the Babri Masjid to allow worship of the Ram idols in February 1986 and allowing the shilanyas (foundation stone laying ceremony) for the proposed Ram temple at the disputed site in November 1989 began the process of Muslims leaving the Congress. It culminated after the demolition of the Babri Masjid on 6 December 1992. Under Rajiv, there were also a series of Assembly election losses in the states that nibbled away at the strength of the Congress. In early 1989, with the next Lok Sabha election on its way, Rajiv had re-inducted R K Dhawan as a special assistant in his official set-up.

He lost the 1989 elections. The reason for his ouster from power had to do with his political failings. He was not rooted in grassroot politics the way his mother and grandfather had been. His entry into politics had to do with Indira's need to have someone from her family on whom she could depend politically.

The shift of support away from the Congress after 1989 was unlike what the party experienced in the 1977 elections when it was trounced by the Janata Party. It was a change 'rooted in the shifts in party organizational strength and support base at the state level . . . in India's political economy and changing patterns of social mobilization'[26]. After the 1989 polls, the Congress' downward slide across India was rapid and seemingly irreversible.

It declined in the Hindi belt; the rise of OBC politics in the early 1990s along with the BJP's emergence on the scene in the era of Mandir-Masjid politics in India would make the Congress a shrinking force in the Hindi heartland. In the Assembly elections in 1989-90 the Janata Dal (JD) or the

Janata Dal-BJP alliance displaced the Congress in UP, Bihar, Gujarat, and Orissa among others[27], where it had been a dominant power.

Before he died in 1991, Rajiv Gandhi made another attempt to introduce internal elections in the Congress organization to reverse the decline. The idea was on the verge of being accepted by the party's apex decision-making body, the Congress Working Committee (CWC), according to Rajiv's aide, Mani Shankar Aiyar. It had to be put on the back burner when the 1991 elections were announced. Rajiv was killed during the poll campaign.

∼

After Rajiv's death, the party which was completely dependent on the Nehru-Gandhis, turned to his widow, the Italian-born Sonia. She refused the offer to become the Congress president. This allowed the Congress factions to compete for dominance. Senior Congress leader from Andhra Pradesh, P V Narasimha Rao, became prime minister after the 1991 general elections, but Sonia's role was crucial in the subsequent intra-party politics. Rajiv's group and Rao's opponents in the Congress continued to press for Sonia's entry into politics. She stayed away but did not demur when her name was used to take pot-shots at Rao. Much later, on 28 December 1997, she decided to campaign in the next year's general elections. She became the Congress president in March 1998, replacing Sitaram Kesri in a coup.

Her bigger challenge came from Maharashtra stalwart Sharad Pawar. Aided by P A Sangma and Tariq Anwar they staged a revolt against Sonia's leadership in May 1999. They raked up her foreign origin issue, a sore point for Sonia who had been fighting the BJP on the same issue. Pawar, Sangma and Anwar were expelled from the party during a dramatic phase when Sonia resigned and then took back her decision. The trio later formed the Nationalist Congress Party (NCP).

Sonia used Indira's methods – she controlled access to herself and played factions one against another, albeit less as a means of marginalizing rivals and more as a means of keeping the primacy of the 'high command' intact. The Congress became dependent on Sonia or the Nehru-Gandhi family. This was what Indira had done; so, it was easier for Sonia to replicate it.

There were differences between Indira and Sonia as well. The latter shared her late husband's view of politics and wanted to change the way the party was run. She appointed Ahmed Patel as her 'political secretary' and formalized the role. She brought in non-political professionals into prominence, whom she tended to trust more. Manmohan Singh's eventual ascension to the prime minister's post is an outcome of this mindset. The National Advisory Council can be seen as an extension of the same idea.

Sonia's mandate on taking charge of the Congress in April 1998 was to pull it out of the dire straits in which it found itself after being voted out of power at the Centre in 1996. However, her presence did not benefit the party at the national level immediately. In fact, the party posted its lowest ever tally in Parliament in the 1999 general elections. The BJP steadily gained strength through the 1990s. It would win more seats in the Lok Sabha than the Congress in 1996, 1998 and 1999, though the Congress remained ahead in terms of vote share[28].

~

Sonia's and the Congress' ability to defeat the BJP, which had been in power since 1999, in 2004 was in serious question after Congress was badly defeated in Madhya Pradesh, Chhattisgarh and Rajasthan in December 2003. Many in the party felt the BJP's attack on her 'foreign origin' would be effective.

The Nehru-Gandhi charisma was no longer an article of faith in Indian politics. By the time Sonia entered politics, India had had a Congress prime minister who was not a member of the dynasty and had completed a full term in office. The economic reforms during the Narasimha Rao government's regime, with Manmohan Singh as the finance minister, had raised the standards of living of many middle- and upper middle-class Indians. For this constituency, the break from the Nehru-Gandhi dynasty was something that worked. The changes in demographic trends meant that there was a generation of new Indians who had few memories of Indira and none directly of Jawaharlal Nehru. Therefore, Sonia's relevance as a Nehru-Gandhi legatee was not to the larger Indian electorate. This impression was strengthened with the coming to power of the BJP-led National Democratic Alliance or NDA government under Atal Bihari Vajpayee in 1999 after three years of instability.

However, the Nehru-Gandhi family remained relevant within the Congress. In fact, it became more powerful as it was the only centre around which the entire Congress edifice could hold together. It was now an amalgam of pressure groups which were interested in power, and their one-way ticket to it was through proximity to the Nehru-Gandhi family.

Surprisingly, the Congress made an unexpected return to power at the Centre in 2004. Its victory was possible due to pre-poll coalitions with regional players in at least seven states[29]. The party, under Sonia, decided to actively build an anti-BJP coalition putting aside a decision taken at a conclave in Pachmarhi in Madhya Pradesh in September 1998. The mood at Pachmarhi had been against giving up Congress' 'primacy'[30] in the affairs of the country even as it described the coalition era in Indian politics as a 'transient phase'; at a subsequent conclave at Shimla in 2003, the party signalled a change in this position.

In 2004, the Congress' allies included the DMK, Marumalarchi Dravida Munnetra Kazhagam (MDMK), and Pattali Makkal Katchi (PMK) in Tamil Nadu, the NCP in Maharashtra, K Chandrasekhara Rao's Telangana Rashtra Samithi (TRS) in Andhra Pradesh, Lalu Prasad's Rashtriya Janata Dal (RJD) and Ram Vilas Paswan's Lok Jan Shakti Party (LJSP) in Bihar, Shibu Soren's Jharkhand Mukti Morcha (JMM) in Jharkhand and the People's Democratic Party (PDP) in Jammu and Kashmir. In Himachal Pradesh it negotiated a merger with its breakaway Himachal Vikas Congress of Sukh Ram.

The victory did not mark the ascendance of Congress; it became a national-level player with a dependence on regional parties and a shrinking role in most states. This continued despite the Congress coming back to power in the 2009 general elections with 206 seats and a vote share of 28.55 per cent in the Lok Sabha, its best performance since the 1991 elections when it had 232 seats and 36.26 per cent of the votes.

It was now one of the two main political parties contesting for power in states such as Madhya Pradesh, Rajasthan, Kerala, Andhra Pradesh, Maharashtra, Karnataka, Punjab, and others. But it was a distant third – or even fourth in some cases such as UP – in states where regional parties had established themselves, such as Tamil Nadu, Bihar and West Bengal. In states such as Gujarat, it was seen as a non-existent Opposition party to the BJP.

5

THE 'PROFESSIONAL' POLITICIAN

Rahul Gandhi's entry into politics coincided with the Nehru-Gandhi family becoming the key decision-makers at the Centre again. Rahul's clout was second only to Sonia Gandhi's, in the ruling establishment. But neither did he accept a government post nor did he choose to play a key role in the party affairs.

In a controversial interview to *Tehelka*[1] in September 2005, he said: 'I believe in educating oneself. I believe in going out, and finding out for yourself what it's like and then learning to do something to improve things. I am still learning. I am very clear about what I want to do. I will do politics my own way and in my time. Nobody can force me to do anything. My idea of politics is very different from what is being done now.' Two ideas emerged from these statements. The first was about personal education and the learning curve; the second was to pursue a 'different' kind of politics.

In both respects, Rahul was like his father Rajiv Gandhi who, in 1982, more than a year after he joined politics, said: 'They (the Congress) are pushing me into an important position . . . I would rather start at the base and rise little by little'[2]. Rajiv also desired to build a different Congress as he nudged it in the direction of professionalism.

There were other similarities between them. Both grew up in the same upper class, Westernized environment. Both went abroad for higher studies. Rajiv was a commercial pilot for thirteen years before he became a full-time politician; Rahul had at least a three-year stint with the private sector in London. Therefore, both saw themselves as 'professionals' rather than as politicians.

One can safely assume that Rajiv's experiences in politics influenced Rahul, who possibly did not want to be caught unawares like his father. While Rajiv wanted to wait for his time, he had to suddenly take over the Congress' reins in 1984. However, his son, who wished he had something to 'take . . . to the table'[3], hoped to gain exposure and knowledge till he felt he was ready.

Sonia's role in shaping Rahul's ideas still aren't clear as the mother-son relationship is a complex one. Although he was protective towards her during Sonia's initiation into politics, and possibly joined politics to support her, he had an independent streak. But he wouldn't dismiss her ideas entirely too.

A senior Congress functionary who has worked with both of them gave some insight into the kind of relationship Sonia and Rahul have in the context of a trip Rahul made to Aligarh in August 2010 to make common cause with the farmers protesting against inadequate land compensation. 'It was raining when he left. He called her (Sonia) up from halfway (to his destination) to inform her that he had left. She asked whether he had taken his clothes and other things. Rahul replied that he would take care of himself.' He added that unlike Sanjay Gandhi, who was known to have violent disagreements with Indira, Rahul did not fight with Sonia.

~

After he became an MP in 2004, Rahul focused on development work in Amethi. He aimed to improve educational and health facilities. His pet project was an education plan to ensure that every youth in Amethi attained fundamental literacy[4]. With help from Pratham, an NGO which specializes in providing education to underprivileged children and ran a programme in Amethi then, Rahul set up his own team to work with children and young adults who had dropped out of school. NGOs were important to Rahul as they were 'professionals' in the development sector. As experts, they could be counted on to monitor and deliver results.

In the *Tehelka* interview, he said: 'If you come to Amethi after a month, you will find every Congress worker teaching children in his or her house. Each one will teach one or two children. That is the way I work. That is meaningful work'[5].

Rahul's development approach was different from that of his father. Rajiv had helped set up industrial units in Amethi, many of which turned sick later. After Sonia became MP, and the constituency came under Priyanka's charge, she worked with women's self-help groups and NGOs such as Pratham. Rahul continued Priyanka's work.

He visited schools in Amethi and in more developed states such as in Karnataka to assess the quality of education in rural schools. As he told *Tehelka,* he wanted to find out for himself what the problems were and then learn 'to do something to improve things'.

In his first full-length Parliament speech, he spoke on education during the Budget discussions of 2006-07. 'About a year ago I visited a village school. I walked up to one of the children and asked him, '*Beta bade hokar kya banoge?*' (What will you become when you grow up?).The silent stare I got in reply disturbed me. In school after school, I have asked this question and got no answer. Many students, teachers and parents believe that our school system is a dead-end. In village after village, there are children who don't have the opportunity to go to school . . . But I have also visited schools where every child aspires to greatness . . . There are village schools where the same system which destroys aspirations elsewhere makes the child of a landless labourer dream of becoming a software engineer.'

He went on. 'I am new to politics and still have a lot to learn. But if there is one thing I have learnt it is that people who are closer to a problem understand it best. Empower them. Make them accountable and you will get results. Community institutions can play a powerful role in improving the quality of local schools. Teacher absenteeism and poor performance are major problems. Handing decision-making to parents and communities directly affected by the problem, is our best bet at solving it'[6]. To improve the efficiency of delivery mechanisms and ensure accountability have been favourite themes with Rahul.

He emphasized that higher education and vocational training 'cannot function in a vacuum'[7] in an India that was emerging as a 'global power'[8]. He said that '. . . education needs to be connected to the job market . . . deepen its links with industry, with research and development, with technology and with finance. It is only by building these links that we will move from creating job seekers to entrepreneurs'[9]. He made a pitch to develop India 'as a global education hub'[10].

However, Rahul's overall parliamentary record in that era is poor. He participated in Parliamentary proceedings on just seven occasions during the 14th Lok Sabha (2004-09). Of these, three pertained to unstarred questions, or those that did not require oral answers; of the three, two related to higher education. On 13 December 2005 he asked whether the government planned to set up an 'institute on the lines of ISO certification to benchmark public and private technical education institutions?'[11] A week later he asked whether the government was aware of the 'very weak linkages between vocational training institutions . . . and evolving needs of the industrial and service sectors'[12] and sought details about it.

Even later, during the ongoing 15th Lok Sabha, he spoke on just one occasion – on the proposed anti-corruption legislation, the Lok Pal Bill – and hasn't asked any questions in the past three years.

Rahul defended this non-participatory streak to *Tehelka*. 'I don't ask questions in Parliament because I like to think things through. Just look around at the questions that are asked in Parliament, and you'll know why I don't ask questions'[13]. He added he would talk about issues only when he was 'properly educated'[14].

~

In the initial years as MP, Rahul, the professional politician, put himself through the classroom of politics and governance. He attended international seminars for young leaders. These provided him exposure and gave him a chance to meet high-profile, upcoming leaders in various fields from other countries.

For example, he went to the World Economic Forum's Young Global Leaders Summit held in Zermatt, Switzerland (24-27 June 2005). Among his Indian batchmates was DMK's Dayanidhi Maran, the then Union minister for telecom and information technology, and steel tycoon L N Mittal's son, Aditya Mittal.

He attended a two-week seminar at the Bucerius Summer School on Global governance in Hamburg (7-21 August 2005), an annual seminar organized by the ZEIT-Stiftung Ebelin und Gerd Bucerius, a German private foundation set up by Gerd Bucerius.

The Bucerius Summer School, according to its organizers, harks back to Henry Kissinger's International Summer Seminar at Harvard University which brought together emerging leaders from the world over for a summer course of debates and lectures in the 1960s. In 2005, the Bucerius School's theme was 'challenges faced by the world community in the 21st century'.

Later, Rahul fondly recalled the time he spent at the seminar. 'Like some of you in this room, I have attended the Bucerius Summer School. The knowledge I left with and the friends I made have stood me in good stead. Just before I came here, I leafed through the notes I took while attending the school. I can say with the benefit of hindsight and some humour that I only vehemently disagreed with one speaker. But what was important was that, like most of you, I had fun while I learned'[15].

In his *Tehelka* interview, he again spoke of Hamburg. 'I am not going to learn if I don't go to other countries ... (In Hamburg) there was this president of a small country, a young guy who I am not going to name. He sat in front of me, and was quiet for a long while. Then he looked at me and said it all depends on aid ... I wondered what's wrong with this guy. How can development rest on aid? Then he laid it out for me. He broke it up into little facts and showed me how important aid is. I go to Hamburg and this is what I get. How am I going to pick up something like this in India? How can I learn anything if I stay put in India and keep doing the same things as everybody else? I need to keep an open mind.'

In the early political days, Rahul visited Afghanistan (28-29 August 2005) with Prime Minister Manmohan Singh and went to Singapore (June 2006) on the invitation of Singapore's first prime minister, Lee Kuan Yew. He went to South Africa (March 2005) to receive that country's highest honour for foreigners, The Order of the Companions of O R Tambo, conferred on Jawaharlal Nehru posthumously. These visits were seen as part of the grooming routine for a future prime minister. His grandmother Indira Gandhi had accompanied her father on several foreign visits including the famous ones to the former USSR and USA. Indira too took along Rajiv on some of her foreign trips after he became an MP.

Before the week-long visit to Singapore, Rahul borrowed a biography of Lee Kuan Yew from the then foreign minister K Natwar Singh. 'I told Rahul there were probably just two people in Delhi who had read the book and that he was one of them,' Singh reminisced. When the book was returned to him, it was marked and underlined. Rahul, with his background in consultancy and interests in delivery mechanisms and accountability, must have been impressed by what he saw in the city-State.

Singapore's story of transition from a third world to first world country in less than four decades has evoked admiration across the world, including within certain sections of the Indian middle class. Many in this group feel India can make the same leap, but only if the 'right' people come to occupy the 'right' positions within the government.

Journalist Sunanda K Datta-Ray, author of *Looking East to Look West – Lee Kuan Yew's Mission India* spoke to Rahul about his visit: 'He saw the Singapore experience as an opportunity, and despite huge differences of scale – which he stresses – not altogether irrelevant to India'[16]. But Rahul recognized that a dictatorial control, even benign, would not be possible in India. 'There's a lot we can learn if we are flexible,'[17] he told Datta-Ray.

Datta-Ray says Rahul, who was accompanied by his team

member Kanishka Singh, went to see Singapore's port, airport, colleges, and public corporations. He attended a special dinner hosted by Lee Kuan Yew, and the octogenarian leader advised him not to take the leadership reins until he understood the country's complexities and had an able team in place[18].

Singapore's education minister, Tharman Shanmugaratnam, accompanied Rahul to the country's premier Institute of Technical Education and explained the country's system of technical and vocational education and training. There, Rahul saw a beauty therapy course, among other training facilities related to healthcare and information technology.

In India, Rahul had gone to the Planning Commission in September 2005. Deputy Chairman Montek Singh Ahluwalia refused to discuss what he described as a 'private visit'. But media reports[19] suggested that Rahul sat through a two-hour presentation by IT venture capitalist Vinod Khosla on the UPA government's Bharat Nirman project, which is aimed at building infrastructure in rural areas.

Rahul was keen to learn about Uttar Pradesh politics before he set about improving the Congress' position in the state. He approached it too in a professional manner, turning to academics and political scientists, rather than to the expertise of politicians. He approached it like an analyst would. He was faced with a new subject and was turning to the expert to help him get an overview of the issues.

Among the many academics he met to get a better grasp of political equations and social trends was Professor Sudha Pai of the Jawaharlal Nehru University or JNU. Pai, an expert on the Bahujan Samaj Party (BSP) and Uttar Pradesh politics, had written the book, *Dalit Assertion and the Unfinished Revolution:*

The BSP in Uttar Pradesh. When he met her, he asked questions based on the book. 'He had actually read the book,' Pai said describing Rahul as 'well-read and not arrogant'.

Rahul also attended a seminar on 'Uttar Pradesh in the 1990s: Critical perspectives on society, polity and economy' held at JNU in March 2005, where Pai and other scholars presented papers. Pai had earlier been an invitee at the Congress' brainstorming session-cum-youth training camp held at Chitrakoot in January 2005. The Chitrakoot session had seen other experts such as retired bureaucrat N C Saxena (author of the report that opposed Vedanta's proposal to mine bauxite in Orissa's Niyamgiri hills) and Magsaysay award winner Sanjay Pandey .

Pai feels that Rahul is a politician with positive qualities. His 'dislike of sycophancy' was evident from the fact that 'nobody (was present) on the dais at Chitrakoot (from the Congress)'. He did not believe in theatrics. 'Rahul came to Chitrakoot quietly (despite the fact that the Congress was launching its UP revival mission under Rahul). Indira Gandhi would have started from Lucknow, had chai along the way (at roadside stalls). The media was disappointed with Rahul. They missed the theatre,' she said.

≈

In the initial years, Rahul refused to reveal his mind on critical issues. He didn't present a blueprint for India's development. So, there was no clarity about what he stood for. He hardly spoke in Parliament or to the media. At one of his earliest press conferences[20] within a few months of becoming an MP, he displayed his political naïvete . When asked what he thought 'on the record of tainted ministers' in the Congress-led UPA coalition, he replied: 'The tainted ministers are not Congress ministers . . . And if there were Congress ministers who were tainted, I would have something to say about that. The ministers are part of the coalition government and obviously there are compromises that need to be made.'

His first interview with a mainstream publication, *Tehelka*, became controversial. He reportedly said he could have become the prime minister at twenty-five; he felt there was 'no trace of governance' in UP and the then Centrally-administered Bihar. The latter statement was seized on by the political opponents. Finally, the Congress clarified. 'Rahul Gandhi would like to state that he did not give any interview to *Tehelka*. The write-up projected as an interview contains several misrepresentations and . . . It arose from a casual conversation,' said the then Congress spokesperson, Abhishek Manu Singhvi[21]. He mentioned specifically that Rahul wanted to state that he had not said, 'I could have been prime minister at the age of twenty-five if I wanted to'[22].

Tehelka first refuted the Congress' claim but, within hours, put out a new statement. 'This seems to be a clear case of misunderstanding. Mr Gandhi thought he was having a casual chat whereas our reporter took it to be a proper interview'[23]. It also said 'any errors in the interview are inadvertent and regretted'[24]. *Tehelka's* website has an edited version of the interview. It continues to have references to the lack of governance in UP and Bihar but without Rahul saying he could have been prime minister at twenty-five. Since then, Rahul has not given exclusive interviews.

The problem is that Rahul's political reclusiveness, and his caution in public life run contrary to his personality trait of being curious, questioning, and willing to speak his mind, if not being outspoken, on issues he is interested in.

6

A TEAM TAKES SHAPE

For his team, Rahul Gandhi looked for like-minded, young professionals with work backgrounds similar to his. When his father was putting together his core team after joining political life, he too had recruited corporate professionals such as Arun Singh and Arun Nehru rather than relying on the Congress organization.

Team 'RG' took shape around the work he did in his constituency. One of his recruits was Kanishka Singh, who became his chief political aide. He looks after Rahul's appointments; he is the point man for most Congress leaders and journalists to access Rahul. He oversees the planning of his political meetings. He is in Rahul's shadow, travels with him and is always at hand when required.

When I contacted Rahul Gandhi for a meeting and interview for this book in July 2010, it was through Kanishka. The request was turned down. According to Kanishka, Rahul felt it was too early for a book on him. During the brief conversation, he explained that once Rahul decided something, he did not usually change his mind easily. Kanishka suggested that instead of a book on Rahul perhaps one on the Indian

Youth Congress and the National Students' Union of India transformation exercise might be a better bet. He was speaking of a detailed study of the organizational revamp of the Congress' youth and student wings that Rahul had begun after taking over as All India Congress Committee or AICC general secretary in 2007. Kanishka indicated that Rahul would be willing to cooperate for such a venture.

Over the next year-and-a-half I attempted to seek a meeting with Rahul or his close associates such as Kanishka and Sachin Rao a number of times for the book. On most occasions, it was through Kanishka; I also sought Rahul's cooperation to accompany him on his tours. There was no response from Rahul Gandhi's office in all instances. Finally, I wrote to Rahul directly and sent him a long list of questions I had about his politics. Since a meeting with him had not taken place, I needed to reach out to him one last time before the book went to press. Rahul did not respond to the last round of communication either. Till the time of publication, he did not respond to the questionnaire.

To return to Kanishka, when I spoke to him about the book over the telephone – in 2010, he came across as polite but unyielding. He appeared practised in dealing with a multitude of requests to meet Rahul in the five years or so that he had been manning the Nehru-Gandhi scion's office and screening visitors. His immense power in the Congress flowed from the single fact that he alone had the power to make that elusive meeting with Rahul Gandhi actually happen.

This is reflected in the way Youth Congress functionaries or others connected with the revamp of the two organizations talk of Kanishka Singh. Respect for his position, envy, and a tinge of fear are almost always evident.

Kanishka's clout is belied by his appearance. At thirty-four, he is bespectacled, slightly-built and on the shorter side. He is courteous and suave without being imposing.

His father, the late S K Singh, was an erudite and skilful diplomat; he was India's high commissioner to Pakistan, ambassador to Austria and Afghanistan, and the country's foreign secretary (1989-90, towards the end of Rajiv Gandhi's tenure as prime minister). After retirement, his father became the governor of Arunachal Pradesh in December 2004 and of Rajasthan in 2007.

Kanishka has a joint degree in international studies and business from the University of Pennsylvania. He passed out in 2000 with *cum laude* honours which indicates that he was a reasonably bright student. According to information[1] from the Registrar's Office at the University of Pennsylvania, he got a BA from the School of Arts and Sciences where he majored in International Studies (Rahul has a BA in International Relations) and minored in German. From Wharton, the university's business school, he has a BS in Economics where he majored in finance and legal studies. Before that he read Economics at Delhi's St. Stephen's College where he was several years junior to Rahul. He came to politics after a three-year stint in investment banking with the Wall Street firm Lazard in its New York office. Richard Creswell, senior vice president of global communications at Lazard, confirmed that Kanishka worked as an associate at the firm between 2000 and 2003. At Lazard, associates work as part of 'client teams'[2] which offer services such as general financial advice, help companies strategize mergers and acquisition deals, and raise money from the global markets. Its associates need a strong quantitative analysis background and good verbal and written communication skills. Not surprisingly, Kanishka is well-known within Congress circles as a number-cruncher, who has laptops full of caste and community specific data.

After moving back to India, Kanishka worked for Delhi

Chief Minister Sheila Dikshit's successful re-election campaign in December 2003 and on the Congress' 2004 Lok Sabha campaign.

In the run up to the 2004 general elections, a rout for the Congress in the polls and the return of a Vajpayee-led government was seen as a certainty among pollsters and in the media. In this environment, Kanishka wrote an article comparing Sonia Gandhi to John Kerry, the Democratic presidential candidate in the US, where elections were due in November 2004. The write-up appeared in the *Outlook* magazine just before elections kicked off in India. It argued that there were many similarities between the Congress campaign in India headed by Sonia, and Kerry's Democratic campaign. 'Kerry and Sonia Gandhi are fighting against right-wing incumbents who have the worst record on jobs of any leader in the history of their nations and are seeking to use foreign policy insecurities to bolster their domestic appeal'[3], he wrote. He ended his piece by hoping for an upset victory in the polls in both countries that would carry these similarities to their 'logical conclusion'. He proved to be half-correct. Kerry lost. But the Congress and Sonia won in India, and with that victory came his entry into Rahul's team.

Kanishka was put in charge of NGO-run development projects in Amethi not very long after Rahul won from the seat[4]. He was also involved with the setting up of the Indira Gandhi Eye Hospital and Research Centre in Amethi. The hospital, inaugurated in December 2005, was set up in association with the Madurai-based Aravind Eye Care System, an organization in the Bottom of the Pyramid (BoP) business space that believes there are profits to be made in products aimed at the world's poorest, that has won recognition for providing quality and affordable eye-care services to the poor. Kanishka, according to media reports[5], also developed an IT-based system to handle Amethi constituents' grievances and appeals to its MP in a time-bound manner.

As he became increasingly entrenched in Rahul Gandhi's team, his biggest asset was the trust his boss came to repose in him. He had a sharp mind when it came to facts and figures and ideas; he was discreet and unassuming – all qualities that Rahul prized a great deal.

During a brief informal interaction with Kanishka during Rahul's padayatra through Western Uttar Pradesh in July 2011, I found him using economic jargon in a conversation about the land acquisition row in that part of the state. The backdrop was a discussion on how some farmers, who had sold their land to the state, were building new houses with the compensation even though others found it inadequate and agitated for more. He had facts about the local Banjara community on his fingertips and recounted their struggle to be recognized as a Scheduled Tribe (ST).

He appeared to have a curious and attentive mind, the kind that would file away crucial bits of information for later reference. Rahul often turned to Kanishka during the tour to ask him to take down details and accept petitions. At one point Rahul looked for Kanishka and on not finding him, remonstrated with him for not being around when he needed him.

The young boys of the Youth Congress were distinctly aware of the strict hierarchy in 'Team RG' and regarded Kanishka as their de facto boss. Even the senior members of Rahul's IYC and NSUI team did not want to be seen as doing anything that he had not sanctioned. One such person, a well-known subject expert, whom this writer met during the trip spoke informally about his experiences of working with Rahul and the IYC and NSUI. The conversation happened on the road during the course of the padayatra. However, as soon as the procession stopped for lunch, the expert asked this writer to 'scoot' as he was going to meet Kanishka.

A Youth Congress leader explained how powerful Kanishka and another aide of Rahul's – Sachin Rao – were. According to him all information that reaches Rahul is filtered by either of these two people when it came to the work in the IYC and the NSUI.

But Kanishka's influence goes beyond the IYC and the NSUI. His command over caste break-up percentages and detailed information on each community, especially with regard to UP, have made him influential when it comes to distribution of election nominations. With Rahul relying on this kind of information a great deal when he makes decisions regarding candidate selection in elections, Kanishka's role became all the more important during the 2012 UP election campaign.

In a rare 2011 interview, Kanishka spoke about the reasons for quitting his Wall Street job. 'The whole thing was about how much money you will make in the end . . . You make money, then you are burnt out, you probably divorce your wife and your family has fallen apart. I thought, what a meaningless life'[6].

Sachin Rao, who joined Rahul in 2006-07, was also not enamoured of merely making money. A software engineer who grew up in Mumbai, he spent seven years developing software for global clients and got an MBA from the University of Michigan in the US. His focus at Michigan was on corporate strategy and international business. There he became associated with management guru C K Prahalad, a much celebrated proponent of the 'Bottom of the Pyramid' philosophy.

The Michigan MBA programme had a Multi-disciplinary Action Project (MAP) under Prahalad's guidance and Sachin was chosen for it. For his case study, he chose ITC's e-choupal initiative to demonstrate how the BoP venture benefitted both the company and the farmers, who directly sold their agricultural produce to the company. His study found that ITC's investment in technology – computer-based information kiosks at the village level – and manpower – an intermediary, who is always a farmer – boosted the company's revenues. But it brought about a range of positives for the farmers who, apart from money, felt a higher sense of self-worth as they were treated with 'dignity'.

Sachin's newly-acquired outlook on business which brought together profits and 'poverty eradication', was to prove pivotal to his own life story. He has described how his association with Prahalad and his work on the MAP left an imprint on his way of looking at his own 'aspirations'[7]. 'My personal lesson was that genuine impact begins with revolutionary aspirations that are undiluted by a fear of failure. When I am asked what I want to do with my life, my unabashed answer today is that I want to change the world.'

After a short stint at the consulting firm Booz Allen Hamilton in Chicago, he returned to India to work with an economic right-wing think-tank, run by another management guru and ex-corporate honcho, Gurcharan Das. He furthered his work on the BoP ideology at the Centre for Civil Society (CCS), and spoke at seminars and workshops.

'The idea that commercial engagement with the world's poorest presents corporations the opportunity to "do well while doing good" is rapidly becoming part of mainstream corporate strategy . . . Local entrepreneurs represent the vital "last leg" of distribution systems that get a range of products to BoP markets . . . Organizing local entrepreneurs and getting their outputs to the world markets presents some of the most compelling opportunities for social enrichment through corporate intervention,' said a January 2005 advertisement for a seminar on 'Poverty, Profits, and Entrepreneurship' on the CCS website with Sachin Rao mentioned as the contact person.

These ideas were bound to be part of Rahul's thinking when Sachin joined him. He became an important part of Rahul's experiments to reach out to the BoP space in electoral politics, that is to target the most marginalized communities such as Dalits and Adivasis. He also attempted to reach out to the BoP space within the Congress, represented by the local karyakarta or party worker who has been made completely powerless by a structure in which authority is vested with the high command.

A member of Rahul's team in the IYC described how Sachin reacted when a Youth Congress leader opposed affirmative action at a party meeting. He asked two people at the meeting to line up at one end of the room. He then asked one person to run and the other to limp. In that way, he conveyed his conviction about reservations forcefully and passionately.

In retrospect, it seems logical for Rahul to have found Sachin and Kanishka, or vice versa. Kanishka, before he became an integral part of Rahul's structure, had made a visible case for 'a younger leadership' to take charge in India through his articles in the print media. In an *Indian Express*[8] piece on the Congress' 'epochal' victory in the 2004 general elections, he noted that the Congress had 'firmly established itself as the party of and for young India'. He wrote about the 'solid and inimitable group of new, young leaders' in the party, citing the likes of (and in that order) 'Milind Deora, Sandeep Dikshit, Rahul Gandhi, Sachin Pilot, Jitin Prasad and Jyotiraditya Scindia'. He said 'the Congress is beginning to endorse and empower new and some very young leaders', which was a 'trend' that 'resonates' with the vast majority of India's voters. He believed that India was a 'polity' that had 'outgrown the grey-hair syndrome'. In a piece in *Seminar*[9] magazine, Kanishka wrote that India had evolved into a 'gerontocracy' in the 'post-Rajiv Gandhi era', and that 'a younger leadership in India will, by default, have the ability to think and act beyond a limited five-year time horizon'.

The outlook of the new leaders was visibly different. Kanishka said that [10] 'there is also a desire (in them) to apply, in governance, a skill set, which is imparted today in schools and at universities and in the rough and tumble world of private business corporations, something that was absent a decade or two heretofore.'

After Sheila Dikshit's win in 2003, he wrote[11] that 'the single most important lesson' for the Congress to learn from it and apply in the upcoming national election was that the voter, 'regardless of how literate or educated, behaves like a rational consumer and is aware of his or her best interest'. He said the voter must therefore be treated as a 'discerning consumer' and this would 'fundamentally change the focus away from electoral arithmetic based on religious, caste and regional lines that the Bharatiya Janata Party and other groups are seeking to exploit.'

Before Kanishka and Sachin, Rahul depended on Jairam Ramesh, one of the architects of the Congress' 2004 *'Congress ka haath, aam aadmi ke saath'* campaign. An engineer from IIT-Mumbai, who went on to study public management at Carnegie Mellon University, and then technology policy, economics, engineering and management at a new course developed at Massachusetts Institute of Technology or MIT, he has kept in close touch with Rahul without actually being in his team. Initially, he saw his role as something of a chaperone to Rahul, guiding him to things and people he might find useful in educating himself about politics. For example, he would tell Rahul about an interesting seminar on politics in Uttar Pradesh being held at the Jawaharlal Nehru University in Delhi and Rahul would drop in to listen.

Among the group of young Congress MPs, often described in the press as the 'babalog brigade' for being the sons and daughters of Congress leaders of the previous generation, Rahul is close to Milind Deora. The others in this group such as Sachin Pilot, Jitin Prasada, Jyotiraditya Scindia, Deepender Singh Hooda and Sandeep Dikshit became affiliated with the work Rahul was doing. But he did not go out of his way to be seen as part of this group of young inheritors. His core team was made of people he chose himself based on their talent and ability to deliver results. Along with Kanishka Singh and Sachin Rao, the team expanded to include the likes of Congress leaders like Meenakshi Natarajan and Jitendra Singh – they were both appointed AICC secretaries in the same exercise in which Rahul was made a general secretary in September 2007 and assigned to him. Singh, the present head of Alwar's royal family and a junior minister in the Union home ministry, reportedly underwent training in automobile engineering in Germany[12]. Natarajan, who made it to the headlines in May 2012 for drafting a controversial Private Members' Bill to regulate the media, is a post-graduate in bio-chemistry with a law degree. Meenakshi Natarajan rose in the Congress ranks through the NSUI, of which she was the national president between 1999 and 2003.

7

RAE BARELI BY-ELECTION, 2006

In January 2006, the Congress held its 82nd party conclave in Hyderabad's giant GMC Balayogi Athletic Stadium complex, constructed three years earlier for the 2003 Afro-Asian games. In theory, the party's plenary conclave is where some of its top office-bearers in the Congress Working Committee are elected and in-depth discussions about programme and agenda are held. In practice, however, the Congress plenaries have become occasions for the party to reiterate the primacy of the Nehru-Gandhi family in the party hierarchy. Typically at these jamborees, the Nehru-Gandhis are explicitly and implicitly serenaded by an unending string of Congress leaders big and small. The ceremony is given the stamp of popular approval through loud cheering and slogan-shouting in support of the family, which is left for the 'ordinary Congress worker' to supply. These ordinary Congress workers are usually delegates to the Session or turn up uninvited in large numbers.

The Hyderabad conclave of the Congress, the first plenary Session of the Congress after Rahul Gandhi formally stepped into politics, was going to be 'historic' for that reason alone.

There was also the small detail about the Session being held in Andhra Pradesh strongman and the then Chief Minister Y S Rajasekhara Reddy's home turf. It was an opportunity for YSR, as the chief minister was popularly known, to display his might to the party and he succeeded in overawing the Congress with the scale of the preparations[1] for the plenary.

Rahul Gandhi was without doubt the star attraction at the event[2] which an estimated ten to fifteen thousand[3] people attended. As soon as the second day's proceedings began, several groups of Congress workers began sloganeering for a bigger role for Rahul Gandhi in the party organization. They wanted him to be made a CWC member and take a place on the dais with the senior leaders of the party. The noisy demands threatened to hold up work at the Session. Rahul was forced to take the stage twice in order to pacify the crowds. They calmed down after he promised he would make a speech the next day.

When Rahul finally addressed them the following day, he spoke about the party's problems in states where it had become 'weak'. He chose UP as an example and pointed out that the Congress' 'failure' there had been organizational rather than political. 'We have failed because we lost that ability by which we could bring forward the true worker of the Congress,' he said, asking the party to give 'the anonymous mass of workers' a 'voice in the organization'. The difference between a 'true leader' and a 'neta' or powerful politician, he stressed was that – the former would have to be built 'brick by brick' as there was 'no fast path to success in creating leaders'. Then there was a call to the Congress leadership to 'embrace the young of our country', and an appeal to 'open the doors' of the Congress to others who wanted to join it.

Towards the end, he narrated a personal anecdote. Someone had once asked him what his religion was. He had thought about it for a while and replied: 'The Indian flag is my religion.' He concluded that after his father had died, he had promised himself that he would 'serve the people this flag represents'. It would be a 'disservice' to both his 'religion and his party' if he took up 'a job' before he knew what 'our workers and people feel and need'. His 'place right now was to learn and understand'. He thanked the party for its 'feelings and support' and promised he would 'not let them down'.

The speech should have cheered the hearts of the Congressmen and women present. However, for an organization such as the Congress, reared on the infallible sense of the Nehru-Gandhi dynasty's entitlement and belief in their charisma, it had an overarching message that would have sounded off-key. He was telling the Congress that he did not want to become a 'neta' – clearly, a derogatory word in his dictionary – by which he meant someone who was important in the party as a result of the 'posts and positions' he or she held, rather than the one who worked at the grassroots level and listened to the people.

Rahul Gandhi clearly thought organizationally rather than politically. That is, his was not the speech of a Nehru-Gandhi scion. His was a business strategy consultant's roadmap for organization building. He was seen as the party's charismatic face who would infuse a sense of purpose in the rank and file and enthuse voters to support the Congress. Instead, Rahul saw himself as the man who would look for ways to make the organization more effective. He was not thinking like a politician at all.

There was a gap between what the Congress expected of Rahul Gandhi, and what he actually wanted to, and could, do. This would set the stage for an increasing disconnect in the relationship between the party and him; a tension and distance that would play out at different points in Rahul Gandhi's political career over the next few years. It would be apparent in his ideas to build a new Congress organization by rejuvenating the IYC and NSUI. The idea behind the efforts to 'democratize' the two bodies was noble; but it was made in complete ignorance of the historical circumstances and political imperatives that had shaped the Congress in the past. One of Rahul's chief ideas for the revamp of the IYC and NSUI, which he undertook from September 2007 onwards, revolved around ending the role of family connections in appointments and promotions in the two organizations. He did not realize this would be an up-hill battle in a party controlled by his own family at the top and populated by political families at different levels of the party structure. However, in 2006, the disconnect between the Congress and Rahul would form the backdrop against which the UP Assembly elections of 2007 were fought – and lost – by the Congress.

Until the 2007 UP elections, Rahul Gandhi didn't expressly take on the job of directing the Congress' 'turn-around' in the state. It was gradually that he came to associate himself with the planned revival of the Congress in the UP.

Rahul intended to 'educate' himself and young workers about the situation on the ground in Uttar Pradesh before the party embarked on re-conquering power in the state. Since 1989, Congress had steadily lost ground in UP. It slid from 94 (out of 425) seats and vote share of 27.90 per cent in 1989 to 25 (out of 402 seats) with a vote share of 8.96 per cent after the 2002 polls. This is why he sought out academics to discuss the state of the party and gauge the strength of his competitors in UP.

An opportunity to test these ideas unexpectedly presented

itself in April-May 2006. Sonia Gandhi was slated to contest a re-election from her parliamentary constituency, Rae Bareli, in the wake of the office-of-profit controversy. In March 2006, when the Opposition charged the Congress-led government with bringing an ordinance in Parliament to protect Sonia Gandhi's position as the chairperson of the National Advisory Council she resigned from the Lok Sabha, gave up her official posts and stood for re-election.

The episode began as an insignificant bout between a small, Kanpur-based Congress leader, Madan Mohan Shukla, and Samajwadi Party MP, Jaya Bachchan.

Jaya Bachchan's disqualification from the Rajya Sabha for holding the post of the chairperson of the UP Film Development Corporation, prompted a rash of disqualification petitions to the Election Commission. The Constitution prohibits lawmakers from holding 'offices of profit' under the Central or state governments, though there are some 'offices' that are exempt by law from this provision. The Jaya Bachchan case opened a political Pandora's box. Many high-profile MPs could lose their seat for holding 'offices of profit', none more high-profile than Sonia Gandhi.

Sonia was chairperson of the quasi-government, in-house think-tank that functioned under her, and aimed to direct and oversee the Central government's social sector agenda. She enjoyed the rank of a Cabinet minister[4] in the Central government, and, unfortunately for her, there was ambiguity over whether or not the NAC was exempt from the ambit of the 'office of profit' law. Though the Congress contended that it was essentially an 'advisory' post, her disqualification could not be ruled out. As *India Today*[5] reported, Opposition parties had raised the fact that a Lutyens bungalow – 2 Motilal Nehru Place – was allotted to the NAC along with financial allocations in the General Budget. The Congress was in the midst of a political crisis it did not see coming. The UPA government started seriously exploring the option[6] of bringing an ordinance in Parliament to exclude the NAC from 'offices of profit'. However, the Opposition sensed an opportunity to hit the Congress where it hurt most. It attacked both the government and Sonia Gandhi. L K Advani of the BJP, the then leader of the Opposition in the Lok Sabha, alleged[7] that the government was bringing an ordinance to save all MPs who stood to lose their seats with the sole aim of protecting Sonia. His counterpart in the Rajya Sabha, Jaswant Singh (BJP), questioned: 'If somebody is likely to get caught in a fire, why is the Parliament being made a victim?'[8]

Denying the Opposition a moral victory, Sonia Gandhi resigned from her position as chairperson of the NAC as well as her membership of the Lok Sabha from Rae Bareli. The decision was taken in consultation with Rahul and Priyanka. The Congress hailed it as her second 'renunciation', the first being her act of turning down the PM's post after the 2004 elections, in which the Congress-led UPA coalition came to power.

The Gandhi family decided that Rahul, and not Priyanka, who usually handled her mother's election campaigns, would be in charge of the Rae Bareli by-election. It was possibly a move to raise his profile in UP, a year before the Assembly polls. It would provide a safe debut for him since there was never any doubt about Sonia's win in the constituency. The only thing in question was whether she would exceed her previous victory margin. If Sonia did that, the Congress could claim that her second act of 'renunciation' had been vindicated.

Therefore, the by-poll was about salvaging Sonia's pride.

≈

The Rae Bareli election was scheduled for 8 May 2006. The Samajwadi Party fielded a political non-entity, a backward-caste nominee named Raj Kumar Chowdhury, who happened to be a key Kurmi community leader and Beni Prasad Verma's (now in the Congress) son-in-law. Uma Bharti backed Apna Dal's Prabha Singh, a candidate who, like Bharti, belonged to the backward Lodh community. The BJP nominated firebrand speaker and religious hardliner Vinay Katiyar, a Kurmi, who had attacked Sonia over her 'foreign origins' in the period before the 2004 elections. The BJP's move to field Katiyar was prompted by its fear of losing ground to Uma Bharti.

The Congress went on a publicity overdrive. It was an election in which its president's honour and prestige were on the line. The nation watched the event. The constituency was plastered with election posters of the entire Nehru-Gandhi clan, living and dead, from Feroze and Indira Gandhi, to Rajiv, Sonia, Rahul and Priyanka and even her husband Robert Vadra. *Rishta bada purana hai/ bahu ko bhari maton se jitana hai* said one such poster[9], talking of the 'very old' relationship between India's first family and Rae Bareli.

The posters were intended to wring out emotional responses. They talked about Sonia's saintly virtues of 'sacrifice' and 'service'. One said: *Aap ke liye seva hi taaj hai/ hamein aap par naaz hai* (For you 'service' is the only crown, we are proud of you). Another said: *Tyag, tapasya aur kshama dan, Soniaji ki yehi pehcchan* (Renunciation, ascetic fervour, and forgiveness, these are the qualities of Sonia). Then there was an appeal to create a 'world record' for an election win: *Humne yeh pran thana hai/ vishwa record banana hai*[10].

Amidst this emotional, old-style election festival, Rahul came across as an adherent of the 'professional' school of politics. Such tactics had rarely been tried before; senior Congress leaders looked at the by-election as a one-day cricket match against a minnow team, where the captain asked the pinch-hitter to open the innings. It was a risk, but there was little danger involved, at least politically.

Rahul was helped in his role as the chief campaign manager by Kanishka Singh, who had become his chief aide. Others such as Manoj Muttu, who were part of Rahul Gandhi's Amethi team, assisted him in his maiden electioneering venture.

Team Rahul set up its 'control room' at the Congress district headquarters. Detailed election management discussions became the order of the day. Asked by a journalist whether he had set a target in terms of vote share in the elections, Rahul replied: 'We don't really have a target. We're just trying to make sure that the maximum number of lower-level workers – junior workers – are involved in the process.' He reiterated this point to another journalist that he did not set targets for 'public consumption'. All that he wished was to involve workers at each level – from the district down to the block and the booth level. 'We've told our booth workers it is their responsibility to win the elections . . .'[11] he said, and later added, 'The organization is back in the hands of the party worker'[12].

Rahul wanted the organization to act as a permanent after-sales force on the ground for Brand Congress. That meant that not only would the workers act as facilitators during voting and to make sure that the voters faced no problems in casting their ballot, but they would be involved with the ongoing welfare programmes in the constituency. 'They (party workers) will not be forgotten once the elections are over and will be deployed for the party's development schemes later on,'[13] he said. This idea would later take shape as the 'aam aadmi ka sipahi' (soldiers of the common man) programme within the Indian Youth Congress.

Rahul's planning was reflected in a series of chaupal sabhas or village square meetings and the launch of a jansampark abhiyaan or a mass contact programme. He travelled on several 'road shows' in his Toyota Land Cruiser across the constituency to address roadside meetings; the 'road shows' would, a year later, become the chief means of campaign for him in the 2007 UP Assembly elections. There were short journeys on foot into villages and even a hop on a bullock cart, which enthused both the press and the people. He covered all the five Assembly segments that fell under the Rae Bareli Lok Sabha constituency by the time the campaigning ended.

His speeches were short and functional; development cropped up as the buzzword in the short meetings. Typically, a speech would begin by invoking Indira's name[14] and talk about what Sonia had done for the constituency. Then, Rahul would lambast the ruling Samajwadi Party for not delivering essentials – employment, power, roads, and water – and claim that Sonia would provide support from Delhi for the development projects.

There was no mention of the office-of-profit controversy or Sonia Gandhi's 'sacrifice' that had been advertised by the Congress in its posters[15]. With the voter turnout assuming importance for the Congress, Rahul reminded people to cast their ballot early, in the first few hours of polling before the temperatures rose.

However, the speeches were never hits. Being wooden in his speech delivery, Rahul was unable to bring in the appropriate emotions to his utterances and, therefore, his punch lines fell flat. Therefore, he was rarely able to turn his speech into a two-way emotional connect with the crowds in the way that experienced public speakers do. His best moments came when he interacted directly with the villagers. His meagre public-speaking skills would be somewhat improved over the next few years when he participated in question-and-answer sessions in a village chaupal or college auditorium where he met students. After spending close to seven years in politics, it is only in the 2012 UP election campaign that he consciously worked on his oratory skills.

Even in 2006 it was apparent that Rahul fared better when it came to making one-on-one contact with the people rather than through public meetings. He set out on padayatras in the Rae Bareli by-election, traversing miles on foot. The kind of festivity and innate drama that a Nehru-Gandhi election in Rae Bareli generates can be gauged by the response that awaited him during these trips to the heart of the constituency.

In Maharajganj, where Rahul Gandhi undertook a padayatra down the Randhawa road, 'rose petals were showered on him by people who virtually mobbed him as he walked down the road'. In the Rahi block, where he spent a Sunday on 30 April[16], he 'spared a few moments for the village elders and women to listen to their grievances'. He 'showed keen interest' in the welfare of a physically and mentally challenged girl in Semra village; he told the father of the the sixteen-year-old Reena Kumari, afflicted by polio and cerebral palsy – 'I will send you a doctor to examine her'.

'Team Rahul' tasted its first success in the Rae Bareli elections. Sonia won by a margin of four lakh votes and nearly doubled her 2004 victory margin. It was touted as a huge success and the Congress intended to capitalize on the momentum to rev up its campaign for the 2007 UP Assembly election.

～

Although everyone credited Rahul for the Rae Bareli victory, there are other reasons that contributed to it. First, the

Congress already had a functioning organization in Rae Bareli and Amethi, unlike in other parts of Uttar Pradesh. The two seats had been with the Gandhis over the years. Rae Bareli was Indira Gandhi's constituency and before that with her husband Feroze. In the case of Amethi, Sonia became an MP from there in 1999 and the seat was passed on to Rahul in 2004. Priyanka Gandhi had campaigned in Rae Bareli during 1999 general elections along with Amethi when in a famous speech she attacked Rajiv Gandhi's old teammate and her uncle Arun Nehru for having betrayed her father. Nehru was contesting the election against Gandhi family loyalist Satish Sharma then. Therefore, Congress was present on the ground in the two constituencies unlike in other parts of UP where it may have withered away. As a result, Rahul's job was easier and essentially one of planning. Second was the Priyanka factor. She was present during the last few days of the campaign as a poll agent. According to eyewitness accounts, she was largely responsible for overseeing the process to get people out of their houses and vote. The third factor was that this was a by-election to the Lok Sabha, and not a five-yearly election, with an emotive issue in the backdrop such as the office-of-profit controversy which would have then probably generated sympathy for Sonia among the voters.

Therefore, while Priyanka said this was only a small job compared to what Rahul could do for the Congress, it was an easy task. But one has to credit Rahul since he took up the job seriously and went into the nitty-gritty of planning and execution. But would these qualities, minus the essential skills to woo the voters through speeches and charisma, be enough for Rahul's success in 2007?

8

THE BIG BATTLE –
UTTAR PRADESH ASSEMBLY
ELECTIONS, 2007

About three months before the Uttar Pradesh election kicked off in April 2007, a senior Congress leader, who was part of the inner council of the Gandhi family and a leading general in the party's political army in UP, invited several political journalists for lunch at his Lutyens bungalow in Delhi.

The house was unimpressive. Cauliflowers grew in the bright garden patch outside. Inside, the rooms were somewhat dark, cluttered, and constricted. But the meal was sumptuous and the host's living room teemed with journalists by the time lunch was done. Conversation turned to UP. He was asked about Rahul Gandhi, who was deemed to play an important role in that election. Someone asked him about Rahul's expectation, another probed him about the electoral target that Rahul had in mind. The answer was a revelation.

'He is prepared for a battering,' the leader confided. Rahul had made it clear he wanted the party to give its best shot. If it failed subsequently, it was all right by him. Rahul wished to use the 2007 elections to study the various problems in the state, and come up with a winning strategy for the 2009 Lok Sabha polls.

Despite the Congress functionary's attempt to underplay the link between Rahul's future and the UP elections, there was no questioning that a lot was at stake for Rahul. He would be judged on his charisma, leadership abilities, and political acumen. If the Congress managed to better its tally significantly – there was still no question of it forming the government or emerging as the main Opposition party – he would become a force to reckon with in national politics.

If he failed, the BJP and other political parties would portray him as unworthy of the mantle reserved for him solely on the basis of his lineage. The Congress would find itself hard pressed to continue its projection of him as a future PM, or a leader of stature.

Disastrously, for both Rahul and the Congress, he made no impact on the party's performance – the Congress tally dropped by three seats from 25 to 22, and its vote share came down. There was a consensus in political circles that he was politically naïve and immature after a series of gaffes about the demolition of the Babri mosque and India's role in the formation of Bangladesh. During the campaign, he said had anyone from the Gandhi family been active in politics in 1992, the Babri Masjid would not have been demolished. On Bangladesh, he spoke about the 'division of Pakistan' as one of the definitive things his family had achieved for India.

'Basically what happened was that we don't have an organization there. That's the long haul. We have to build that. And we are going to do that,'[1] Rahul told reporters outside Parliament a few days after the results came out on 12 May 2007.

He may have identified the absence of an effective organization as the reason for the Congress' poor performance, but he should have known it all along. More important, the strategy to play the dynasty card, by designating Rahul as the chief campaigner, and the invocation of the 'development' plank as a counter to caste-and-community based politics, didn't work. It was supposed to be a game changer, a word that Rahul uses frequently. It turned out that the Congress was no longer in a position to attract any of the electorally-decisive vote blocs in UP.

To understand why Rahul failed, it is important to understand the implications of the above-mentioned reasons.

How Congress Lost Ground in UP

The Congress dominance in UP came to an end after the simultaneously-held Parliament and Assembly elections in 1967. The anti-Congress coalition, under the leadership of Charan Singh, was formed in the backdrop of the Socialist Ram Manohar Lohia's call to install Samyukt Vidhayak Dal (SVD) governments in North India. Lohia's credo at that time was ousting the Congress, which had been in power for the past thirty years, by getting all non-Congress parties to join hands.

After the 1967 rout in the north, the Congress suffered its second big setback in the 1977 Parliamentary elections held at the end of the Internal Emergency (June 1975-March 1977). The Janata Party and its allies won a huge majority in Parliament and formed a coalition government. The extent of the Congress' defeat in North India became evident when the results for UP came in. The party drew a blank in UP, losing all the 85 seats, including Indira Gandhi's Rae Bareli constituency. However, the party managed to retain its core vote banks among the upper castes (mainly Brahmins), Muslims, and Dalits[2].

The fractures in the traditional vote banks became apparent in the 1989 general elections. The Congress, led by Rahul's father, Rajiv Gandhi, was pitted against Janata Dal a confederation of anti-Congress forces including the Lok Dal[3] and Janata Party. V P Singh led JD after he had emerged as a key anti-Congress icon. He took on Rajiv over corruption, primarily over the allegations of kickbacks paid to middlemen in the purchase of the Swiss Bofors guns and other scandals such as the HDW submarine deal. The JD according to some political analysts was the 'culmination of the Lohiaite agenda initiated during the late 1960s'[4].

JD trounced Congress; the latter won 15 out of 85 Lok Sabha seats with a vote share of 31.77 per cent, and 94 out of 425 Assembly seats with a vote share of 27.90 per cent. In comparison, JD won 143 seats (17.79 per cent) and 208 seats (29.71 per cent), respectively. Mulayam Singh Yadav became the chief minister of UP; he later formed the Samajwadi Party (SP) in 1992 which 'retained and even expanded'[5] the support base of the original JD, which had disintegrated by then. The emergence of JD defined the 'backward' political space, which for long had been the crucible of anti-Congressism in North India.

In the 1989 Assembly elections, the Bahujan Samaj Party (BSP), a new political outfit, secured 9.14 per cent of the vote, and signalled that the Dalits had moved out of the Congress fold. 'The emergence of the BSP . . . marked the beginning of the decline of the Congress party in the region.'[6] In addition to the rise of JD and BSP, there were other parallel trends that led to the Congress' rapid slide in the first half of the 1990s.

The upper castes – the Brahmins and the Thakurs – migrated to the BJP in the era that came to be marked by what is known as Mandal-Mandir politics. The Brahmin-Dalit-Muslim combine, the bulwark of Congress voters, was fragmented. The Brahmins and Thakurs joined the BJP for several reasons that included the Ram Mandir agitation and the fall-out of V P Singh's decision to implement the Mandal commission report, which recommended reservations for OBCs in government service, promotions and educational institutions.

As a result, the communalization of politics whipped up Hindu sentiments over the building of a Ram temple in Ayodhya and L K Advani's rath yatra, and allowed the BJP to reposition itself as a player in UP. From 57 seats with 11.61 per cent vote share in the 1989 Assembly elections, its tally rose to 221 seats (31.45 per cent) in 1991. In the Lok Sabha elections the same year, it won 51 seats (32.82 per cent). This trend peaked in the 1998 general elections, when the BJP won 57 seats (36.49 per cent). The BJP had anyway replaced the Congress as the political player in UP by the 1996 Lok Sabha elections[7].

The third aspect of the Congress' degeneration in UP had to do with Muslim voters. Rajiv's decision to perform the shilanyas of the proposed Ram temple at Ayodhya in 1989 created resentment among Muslims. This set off a disenchantment process that culminated with the Muslims deserting the Congress after the demolition of the Babri mosque in 1992. Though the demolition was carried out by Sangh Parivar elements, the Congress was blamed as it happened during its tenure at the Centre with P V Narasimha Rao as prime minister. Rao was seen as responsible since he didn't act to stop the demolition of the mosque, even though Central paramilitary forces were stationed outside Ayodhya on 6 December 1992 in anticipation of things getting out of hand. The BSP had a steadily increasing graph through the 1990s. It won 67 seats and polled 11.12 per cent of the votes in the 1993 Assembly elections. That figure had gone up to 19.64 per cent, though it won the same number of seats in 1996. In the elections prior to 2007 – the 2002 Assembly polls – BSP's vote share went up to 23.06 per cent and it won 88 seats.

The Congress' vote share declined. In 1989 it had 27.90 per cent, which dropped to 15.08 per cent in 1993, and touched a low of 8.35 per cent in 1996. In the 1998 Lok Sabha elections, it won no seats in the state. After the 2002 Assembly elections, its vote share stood at 8.96 per cent and it had 25 of the 402 seats. The Congress had been reduced to a non-entity in UP politics. It had been unable to adapt itself to the new realities that cropped up as a result of the 'collapse' of 'the old socio-political structure controlled by the upper castes'[8].

On the organizational front too the Congress had been weakened through the 1990s and the 2000s, though the process began much earlier. In 2007, the Congress had no prominent state-level leader, or any leader of standing from among the social groups that had been with it earlier. It had become dependent on the Gandhi family to provide it a face in UP. 'It was the centralization of power in the hands of Indira Gandhi during the 1970s that was arguably the most important factor in the disintegration of the Congress party machine in Uttar Pradesh.'[9]

Political scientist James Manor argued that until the 1960s, the Congress was a party that functioned as a 'loosely integrated machine'[10] that was the world's 'largest and most formidable agency for distribution of patronage and extraction of loyalty'[11]. It had strong factional leaders at the state-level who took diverse social groups along[12]. As a result, Congress could woo the lower-caste groups, including Dalits. Though there was a parallel grouping of the intermediary and backward castes around the Socialists[13] and Lok Dal, the Congress remained the predominant political force till the late 1960s.

However, under Indira Gandhi 'the old Congress machine crumbled during the 1970s . . .'[14]. Manor wrote that Indira's efforts to centralize power in her own hands led her to 'abandon the principle of representation for the selection of personnel at every level of the party'[15] and after 1972, 'Congress committees and party offices, both great and small, were filled by appointment rather than by election'.

The Congress' semi-official *A Centenary History of the Indian National Congress*, released at its 85th plenary held in 2010, said that Indira Gandhi's 'intervention' in UP's politics was the main reason for the decay of the party organization. 'While earlier factions (of the party) attempted to be inclusive of various religious, caste, and regional groups, from the 1970s, they became largely caste or religious lobbies due to the growing intervention of the Central government into UP's politics and the related decay of the Congress machinery.'[16]

Professor Sudha Pai, who is one of the people Rahul sought out to understand UP politics, put forward the view that the 'high command' felt that a strong organization with influential leaders in a electorally significant state such as UP would be 'difficult to manipulate'[17] and therefore it made 'no effort to resurrect the apparatus after it was repeatedly damaged in the late 1960s due to the split (in the Congress) and then the Emergency in 1975-1977'[18].

Rahul's speech at the party's 82nd plenary in Hyderabad in 2006 reflected the influence of this strain of analysis. 'We have failed in those very states where we stopped battling for the people and addressing their needs and their problems . . . We failed because we had lost the ability by which we could bring forward the true worker of the party.'[19]

Even as he talked about rebuilding the party in UP, he asserted he did not agree with the prevalent view that 'regional parties who practised caste-and-religion based politics were responsible for the Congress' failure' in UP and other states. It appeared that he wanted to turn the clock back and take the party to the era when it used to be a 'catch-all voters' formation. What Rahul suggested was short of impossible, at least in the short run. Caste-and-identity politics could not be wished away. Politics had moved on from the pre-1970s era. It would be difficult to re-emerge as the party which represented a crosssection of interests in society, especially among the lower castes.

It was not as if Rahul did not grasp this point. When asked during the 2006 Rae Bareli election campaign 'how important a factor was caste (in terms of getting the right caste equation to win elections) in UP', he replied: 'I think caste is a factor. But more important than caste is developing leadership among different areas of society.'[20]

However, Rahul Gandhi's attempt at building up a new leadership in the Congress through the Youth Congress and as a replacement for the old, defunct party did not yield results even five years after the 2007 UP elections. Just as he had done after the 2007 polls, Rahul identified a lack of organizational structure as one of the main reasons for the Congress' dismal performance in UP in the 2012 Assembly elections. Rahul was responsible for putting that organizational structure on the ground in the five years he had on hand. The Congress' showing in the 2012 UP polls has revealed Rahul's organization-building attempt as ineffective. His work in the

Youth Congress and why it has failed to do what it set out to do is examined in more detail in the next section.

～

Prior to the 2007 election, Rahul's ideas about regenerating the organization in UP were not implemented in the year or so before the polls. In early 2005, he had participated in two chintan shivirs (brainstorming sessions) held at Chitrakoot and Gorakhpur which were meant to be training camps for the youth in the state unit. They were followed by a round of organizational restructuring in early 2006. The UP Congress was carved up into eight zones, each representing a region of the state, and a coordinator was appointed for each zone. These 'zonal chiefs' reported to both the UP Congress Committee (UPCC) chief and AICC general secretary in-charge of the UP, but also interacted with Sonia and Rahul directly. The zonal chiefs were asked to identify potential candidates for the Assembly elections[21].

The Congress began the process of candidate selection in late 2006. Rahul was involved in the screening process[22]. He had information about each constituency, the caste-break up of the voters, and the prospects of the Congress. His influence was evident as younger faces got the nominations. For instance, Yusuf Ansari, a London School of Economics graduate in his late twenties, and a great grandson of the legendary Congress President M A Ansari, contested from Mahmudabad.

On the question of alliances, the Congress was guided by Rahul. He had publicly termed the alliance with BSP in the 1996 Assembly election as a 'sell out'; he blamed it for the destruction of the party in UP. However, this was criticized as, by then, the Congress had still not negotiated an alliance with Ajit Singh and/or V P Singh's Jan Morcha. Congressmen believed the statement was premature; BSP was likely to emerge as the single largest party, and they wanted to leave open an opportunity to ally with Mayawati and use the seats they won as a bargaining chip.

Therefore, in 2007, Rahul was not tuned into the caste arithmetic. (However, this non-aligned policy paid off in the 2009 Lok Sabha elections, when the Congress won 21 out of 80 Parliamentary seats.) But then, politics is about aligning one's strategies and tactics to the changing political equations.

The Campaign

The 2007 elections were, in retrospect, historic because the BSP, a predominantly Dalit outfit, managed to capture power on its own, bucking the trend of coalition governments. It reinvented itself as a party that sought Brahmin support and gave a number of nominations to high-caste communities. It was an audacious move; the essentially Dalit party had fought previous elections on an anti-upper caste plank. The party made attempts to woo the Muslims; it gave tickets to 61 Muslims. The BSP aimed at and succeeded in recapturing the old Congress constituency and made a dent in the SP's popularity.

While these changes set in, the Congress campaign was all about Rahul. Only he and Sonia featured on the election posters[23]. The slogans too talked of change or badlaav that would be ushered in by the Congress' new young leader. The posters showed a beaming Rahul waving or with his hands folded in a namaste, and reminding the people that 'change is in your hands' (*badlaav aapke haath mein hain*). It was also a way to remind the people of its winning slogan in the 2004 general elections where it pledged that the Congress' hand was with the common man (*Congress ka haath/aam aadmi ke saath*).

In one poster that depicted a group of outlaws with rifles and lathis, a couplet set out the message that UP's electorate was in the mood for a change. It said, 'You have given everyone a chance/ but it has never been as good as when the Congress was in power' (*Sabko azma liya/ Iss sab se achcha to Congress ka zamana tha*). In other posters, the Congress spoke of its fight for principled politics, struggle for UP's pride and respect, and dreams of the youth, a segment that the party tried to target through Rahul.

Since the Congress' result hinged on Rahul Gandhi's ability to convince voters to take him on his word, his presence would have to be an overriding factor. He covered as much of the state as he could by road. His team planned out the 'road shows'. Old family loyalist and Rajiv's flying partner, Satish Sharma, chaperoned Rahul around.

Rahul undertook seven 'road shows', one for each of the seven phases of the mammoth UP elections. He kicked off his campaign on 18 March 2007 from Ghaziabad in Western UP, right on the border of Delhi and travelled[24] to Meerut, Muzaffarnagar, Bareli, Deoband, Lalitpur, Jhansi, Aligarh, Shahbad, Sitapur, Bahraich, Mujaina, Amethi, Lucknow, Varanasi and Gorakhpur among other places. He was on the road for twenty-nine days and averaged six election meetings daily according to a report in the *India Today* magazine[25].

Rahul was finally being discussed as a 'factor' in the elections, thanks to the media attention. Rahul attracted crowds wherever he went. He would be mobbed by local Congress leaders, many of whom were accompanied by young men on motorbikes eager to get a glimpse of the fair-skinned, good-looking 'future PM of India'.

In Khurja[26], a town on the outskirts of Aligarh in Western UP, famous for its ceramic ware and pottery, a group of youngsters waited for his convoy at the edge of a garbage-strewn road. Twenty-four-year-old Javed Hashmi said he was a 'fan' of Rahul Gandhi. Another claimed to be a 'supporter' but admitted he did not vote for the Congress, which produced titters from his friends. While Hashmi, a traditional Congress supporter, said he wanted Rahul Gandhi as the PM, Naser Ali, a SP voter, was sceptical if Rahul would get the votes. However, he said that 'only the youth can understand the youth'.

During the road shows, Rahul began typically with a visit to the local temple. In Khurja, for instance, he paid obeisance to the local goddess – Khurja Maiyya and emerged out ready for battle with a tilak on his forehead and the chunri (a piece of red cloth associated with goddesses in North India). The tilak-laden young scion with garlands around his neck would canvass by sitting on top of his vehicle and wave out to the people gathered at the roadside. He would have garlands and flowers thrown at him and would occasionally throw them back at those cheering him. The routine would continue until the next village stop where he would address small gatherings of people. The road shows would continue late into the night in the bigger towns where Rahul would stay for the night.

The backend of the road shows and overall campaign was managed by his core team who would give him feedback on what to say at each local stop. There was no in-depth consultation with the state leaders. In fact, senior leaders did not accompany him. However, local candidates would at times be at his side during his road shows or his stops at the homes of prominent village leaders.

Kanishka Singh and Sachin Rao were firmly in the 'RG' core team by then. Kanishka accompanied Rahul on the road shows. Sachin manned Rahul's office in Delhi. In charge of media management was Pankaj Shankar, a documentary film-maker and journalist. He had made a film on the 2002 Gujarat riots, *In the Name of Faith*, and joined Rahul after a stint with Doordarshan, the state-owned TV channel.

Rahul was never comfortable with speeches, neither in 2007, nor earlier, nor later though he worked on his public speaking through the UP 2012 election campaign. In April 2007, speaking at a rally in Iglas[27], a non-descript agricultural town about 25 km away from Aligarh towards Mathura, he seemed in such a rush to get over his speech that he forgot to ask the people to vote for the Congress candidate, Rakesh Choudhary, the wife of the sitting MP from Aligarh, Virendra Singh. On being prodded by Virendra Singh, Rahul obliged, but it came across as an afterthought. The speech at Iglas followed the unchanging template, with minor variations, that Rahul repeated at all his public meetings. There was no spontaneity and he struggled with Hindi.

The speeches began with an invocation to the old glory days of UP. 'There used to be a time when UP used to show the way to the entire country. In our fight with the British, UP showed the way . . . After that when the work of development began, UP was at the forefront of this effort. UP used to run ahead of the other states,'[28] he said. Then he pointed to the contribution of Indira Gandhi, and what she had done for the poor in UP.

Typically, the Opposition parties were painted as the villains. 'In the last fifteen years there has been a change here. The parties which came here subsequently (after Indira) divided you. Some divided you in the name of religion, some in the name of caste. All of them exploited you. They came to power, but they betrayed you. They left you exactly where you were.'[29]

In another speech he said, 'UP has not progressed the way it should have, while the rest of India has gone ahead. Wherever I go, Haryana, Punjab, Delhi, Bangalore, Maharashtra, I meet the youth of UP, they work there and help in taking those

states ahead. There is nothing lacking with the people of UP
... But their hands are tied. They are tied for one reason
alone, because your government and your parties have tied
your hands. They have tied your hands by not bringing
development here.'

At another place, the routine was the same. '. . . The amount
of electricity that used to be produced here fifteen years ago,
(even) that much electricity is not produced now. The same
roads that were built fifteen years ago are being used even
now though they are broken. There is no evidence of education
and healthcare (facilities). On top of all of this there is
unemployment, goondaism, atrocity, and corruption.'[30]

As an alternative, he promised personal intervention. 'I
have not come here to fight an election. I don't like doing
short-term work. I have come here for the long haul. And I
have come here for one reason alone – to bring vikaas
(development) and to bring badlaav (change). So I have not
come here for a round of electioneering and then to return to
Delhi.'[31] He invoked his family's standing to make his promises,
to improve UP's backward condition, sound credible. 'The
leaders here in other political parties and the youth of this
state should understand one thing very well. I come from a
family, which does not go back once it has made up its mind
about something.'

There was a strong overture to the youth to 'think anew'
and reject the old politics of caste and community. 'If you
want to bring about change, then the youth of UP can bring
about this change. And the youth of UP can bring about this
change only when they think and work in a new fashion. If
you get divided (along caste and community lines) like you did
earlier, you will remain exactly where you are.'[32]

At the same time, there was an invitation to the young
voters. They would be given a place in the Congress

organization, wherever possible. 'It is my thinking that it is necessary to open the doors of the Congress party to the youth. And wherever I can induct the youth of UP into this party, I will do so. Because I believe that if anybody can bring change to this state, it is the youth of Uttar Pradesh.'[33]

When he was asked by a journalist during the campaign whether he had a 'plan' for the youth since he had talked about them, Rahul replied: 'First from a political point of view, it is using the youth in the political organization . . . Of course after that there are different sorts of economic and other issues.'[34]

Looking at Rahul's election strategy in 2007, a few ideas emerge. The first was his attempt to run down regional parties as narrow political forces whose appeal was limited to 'caste' identities, or who peddled 'communal' ideas. The Congress did neither; it only worked for the poor. The second idea was fighting elections on the development plank. The third idea was to reach out to the youth and urge them to 'think afresh and act differently'. It was an attempt to connect with the people who were more likely to share Rahul's ideological discomfort with caste-and-community based parties as well as appreciate his line that while the rest of India had progressed, UP had been left behind. It was a call to them to join the Congress.

Why Didn't the Strategy Work?

Rahul's approach to politics was chiefly inspired by organization-building ideas, which can be traced back to his professional stint as a business strategy consultant. When speaking the language of politics, so to speak, during the vote-seeking exercise, he failed to articulate specific ideas or a stance that would instantly draw the people to the Congress.

Though there was a freshness about Rahul, there was nothing solid about what he offered the voters. His call for change sounded like he was addressing the converted – and there were not many Congress converts left in the UP of 2007. He failed to paint the Congress as a successful alternative to the other parties he disparaged. He spoke in general terms about the dearth of basic amenities such as water, roads, electricity, schools, and hospitals. He did not target the incumbent SP and spell out the Congress' priorities. He wished to infuse fresh blood into the organization, but he did not lay out a long-term, or short-term, economic programme for the youth.

He conjured up a golden age for UP under the Congress, which he claimed had been lost under subsequent non-Congress governments. The historical vacuum in which the argument was made was not easy to swallow since Congress had been the pre-eminent political force in India and Uttar Pradesh for a very long time. So, it was to be blamed as much as the others for the lack of amenities. His only guarantee was that he was from the same family as Nehru, Indira and Rajiv and therefore the people should place their trust in his ability to deliver the goods. This was a particularly difficult proposition since the Congress had ruled out Rahul's name for the chief ministerial spot.

He was not a natural politician; he could not go out and be as charismatic as his grandmother or recreate the excitement that surrounded his father's first prime ministerial campaign in 1984. Part of the reason was that the aura of the Nehru-Gandhi family was no longer as potent as it was until the 1980s. The other part was his lack of talent as a public speaker.

Many a time, his political naiveté could not be camouflaged. While on his way to the Islamic seminary at Deoband, he said: 'Had anyone from the Gandhi family been active then (in

1992), it (the demolition of the Babri Masjid) would not have happened at all. I have heard my father telling my mother that he would have stood in front of the masjid to protect it.'[35] The Congress' rivals immediately questioned the statement, and pointed out that it was Rajiv who had ordered the shilanyas ceremony.

The Samajwadi Party leader Mohan Singh said 'the foundation for the demolition of the mosque was laid during the Rajiv (Gandhi) era while what was witnessed during the (P V Narasimha) Rao regime was its after-effect'. Left parties, who were then supporting the Congress-led UPA government, were forced to mouth their disapproval. 'We believe that the government at that time (1992) could not carry out its responsibility in the manner in which it should have done. There is no point in raising this historical question now,'[36] said Communist Party of India (Marxist) polit bureau member Sitaram Yechury.

Speaking in Badaun on 14 April 2007, Rahul talked about how his family had seen through to the end whatever task they had taken up. 'I belong to the family which has never moved backwards, which has never gone back on its words. You know that when any member of my family has decided to do anything, he does it. Be it the freedom struggle, the division of Pakistan, or taking India to the 21st century.'[37] The Pakistan establishment was up in arms over this remark. The BJP also lashed out at Rahul.

'The recent remarks of Rahul Gandhi . . . expose his limited family world vision. His statement that the freedom struggle is the achievement of his family is an insult to the great freedom struggle . . . His assertion that the division of Pakistan was also his family achievement is also absurd and has proved a diplomatic disaster. The Congress may defend him but let the Ministry of External Affairs validate his statement. His earlier statement about demolition of the disputed structure in Ayodhya also betrays the same mindset,' BJP spokesperson Prakash Jawadekar said in a statement[38].

A cable from the US' New Delhi embassy dated 23 April 2007 which focused on Rahul's 'political gaffes'[39] noted that he had made an 'uneven start to his active political career . . . Congress insiders complain that he is a neophyte who does not have what it takes to become prime minister. Their hopes have now shifted to yet another member of the Nehru dynasty, Rahul's sister Priyanka, as they await her entry into politics.'

When the votes were counted, it was apparent that Rahul's campaign in UP made little difference to the fortunes of the party. Mayawati's BSP managed an absolute majority on its own with 206 seats in a house of 402. The Congress won 22 seats and its vote share stood at 8.61per cent. Both its seats and vote share had slipped from 2002.

Criticism was levelled, though in hushed whispers, against the new team that supported Rahul and its excessive dependence on computers and data. The Congress condemned the 'computer whizkids'[40] again for having let down the party, as they did for the group that had gathered around Rajiv during the 1980s. Then, the professionals, Arun Singh, Arun Nehru and others, were given the same nickname because of their emphasis on data and use of computers and a 'technocratic'[41] way of dealing with politics.

The fact that Rahul had taken total charge of UP led to a sense of heightened excitement before the polls. By the time the elections came around in March-April 2007, it had touched fever pitch. Rahul was seen and projected as the party's saviour by many UP Congress leaders. The aura shrank after the election results. His vulnerabilities were out in public. He was not the one-stop-solution to the Congress' problem. He was unwilling to connect with the ground realities of Uttar Pradesh politics, and sounded amateurish in his political statements.

PART THREE

IYC AND
NSUI REVAMP

9

A 'NEW BRAND' OF POLITICS

Rahul Gandhi assumed the role of the Congress' chief campaigner in UP during the 2007 polls due to his own special interest in the politics of the state. But the party failed to enthuse UP's voters. It stood fourth behind the BSP, SP, and the BJP winning a mere 22 seats with a vote share of 8.61 per cent. It actually dropped three seats from 2002, when it won in 25 constituencies and had a vote share of 8.69 per cent. Four months after the UP verdict, Rahul took his next step. The date was 24 September. It was a red letter day for Indian cricket, when a fresh-faced team led by the seemingly unflappable Mahendra Singh Dhoni lifted the first edition of the T20 World Cup in South Africa. An entire nation erupted in joy. The memories of the ignominious first-round exit from the 50-over World Cup earlier in the year, and nearly two disastrous years under Greg Chappell as coach, got erased in a flash.

For the Congress though, there was more reason to celebrate. That afternoon, an official press release announced the reconstitution of the Congress Working Committee and fresh appointments to the All India Congress Committee. It seemed like routine stuff in the Congress universe. The blandness of the press release was in keeping with the party's tradition. But there was a surprise tucked in – Rahul's induction into the CWC, the party's top executive body.

He was made an AICC general secretary in charge of the Indian Youth Congress and the National Students' Union of India. Congressmen and women burst crackers, distributed sweets, and thronged 10 Janpath[1], albeit somewhat less spontaneously than the cricket fans celebrating India's win. But, undoubtedly it was a special day for the Congress.

Rahul was taking the same route to the top of the Congress power structure that his father Rajiv Gandhi and his uncle Sanjay Gandhi had done in another era. Both made their respective political debuts with the youth wing of the party. Rahul had chosen the time of his elevation carefully. There had been rumours since mid-2006 that he would be made a CWC member and be given charge of the Youth Congress. But he chose to wait until he had fought the UP elections in 2007 and gained exposure to ground-level politics.

Back in 2005 he had told *Tehelka*, 'I will get into the CWC. I will take more responsibility in the party. After all I am in politics. But I have my own clear plans . . . I am not like the other politicians. I am not like those blokes who believe they don't have a job if they are not seen on television, or if they are not in the CWC or whatever else.'[2] He wanted to claim his inheritance; yet he didn't want a post in the government. The contradictory pulls coexisted in him.

This reluctance in Rahul to be politically active was partly due to his desire to learn, partly due to the feeling that he was not experienced enough to take on the job that had been earmarked for him[3]. Another reason why he secluded himself was that, like his father, he was not comfortable with the old way of doing politics. Even before he won his first election he spoke of wanting to 'create a new brand of politics'[4]. In his interview to *Tehelka* in 2005 he spoke of his idea of politics being 'very different from what is being done now'[5].

His father too had tried to bring changes in the Congress. Rajiv tried to promote younger and educated people and spoke of ridding the Congress of its 'brokers of power and influence' who, he said, dispensed 'patronage' and converted 'a mass movement (Congress) into a feudal oligarchy'[6].

Rahul would express similar ideas. In the speech he made at the Congress 82nd plenary session in Hyderabad[7] in early 2006, he pointed out that the party had become weak in states such as UP because it had 'lost its ability' to 'bring forward true workers'. He spoke of 'recognizing the anonymous mass of workers' in the party and giving them 'a voice in the organization'. He added: 'You know the difference between a true leader and a "neta". You are the first to know that leadership cannot be created, it has to be built slowly brick by brick.'

Both Rajiv and Rahul recognized that the Congress had become, as veteran journalist Harish Khare described it, a 'closed shop'[8]. With powers concentrated in the 'high command', the system has spawned 'loyalists' who wield power disproportionate to their political stature. They further their own interests by keeping out new entrants. This in turn has weakened the party. Whether in Maharashtra, Madhya Pradesh or Karnataka, the Congress has big 'leaders' but none capable enough to grab electoral success.

Rajiv attempted to correct the situation by holding internal party elections. Said Mani Shankar Aiyar, a close aide of Rajiv's, 'At the meeting of the extended Congress Working Committee on 4 April 1989, he virtually rammed through the Uma Shankar Dikshit report (on inner-party reforms).' A few months later, Rajiv's intention to hold internal elections was backed by others at the AICC plenary held in July 1989. 'However, the plans were postponed as the next general elections became imminent,' Aiyar said.

Rahul's approach was more structured than his father's. The son thought and behaved like a management strategy consultant. He thought of organization-building professionally, rather than approach it as a mere exercise to reform the party. Speaking at an AICC convention organized in November 2007 – held for all practical purposes to put a stamp of approval on his position as the next-in-line to the Congress' top job – he said that 'if we're truly to become an organization that represents the youth of this country; if we are to truly *develop leaders* of whom this nation is proud, we need to do two things. The first is to *build an organization* that *is open and relevant* to the broad range of Indians who believe in our values and seek to serve the nation. The second is to *build a meritocratic organization*. Young people bring tremendous passion and energy into our organization. We must see to it that they are *accountable*. It is our duty to ensure that their *progress is linked to their performance*.'[9] (Italics mine)

Rahul used his words carefully. He wanted the IYC and the NSUI to be professionally-run, modern organizations. His benchmarks to judge them would be the best business organizations in the world.

Kanishka Singh, a part of Rahul's A-Team, had made a similar case in the *Seminar* issue of December 2005. 'Our leaders are older than they ought to be. Our citizenry . . . is young. A severe and visible disconnect exists between the separate time horizons that each of the two groups are focused on and invested in.' He also wrote: 'If India is to leapfrog into the millennium we live in, we need to be proactive in demonstrating that political and organizational capital is being invested in the domain of future-oriented implementation.'[10]

Thus, the two organizations would serve as Rahul's lab for building a new Congress that would reflect his ideas and ideals in politics.

Immediately after he took over as an AICC general secretary, his makeover of his personal image began parallely. He positioned himself as a 'youth icon'. This was the natural extension of being a younger politician in a country with a young demographic profile. He cast himself as a representative of the poor and the underprivileged. This was the 'aam aadmi' aspect of Brand Rahul that grew out of his several visits to some of India's poorest states.

10

A STRATEGY CONSULTANT
GOES TO WORK

Manicka Tagore, the first-time MP from Virudhnagar in Tamil Nadu, defeated no less than Marumalarchi Dravida Munnettra Kazhagam's (MDMK) 'Vaiko', the firebrand, pro-LTTE veteran in the 2009 Parliamentary elections. At thirty-six, he is of average height, plump with a prominent belly, black hair and a thick black moustache. He was dressed like a new-age corporate executive – a pale violet checked shirt tucked into greyish-black trousers and topped off with a black sports jacket.

Tagore hails from Shivaganga in Southern Tamil Nadu, which is Congress leader and now Home Minister P Chidambaram's Parliamentary seat. His father was a Tamil school teacher. 'I got interested in politics during my early years and joined the NSUI. Rajiv Gandhi was my idol along with Rajesh Pilot,' Tagore recounted.

His fortunes changed with his decision not to join G K Moopanar's break-away group, the Tamil Maanila Congress in 1996. 'You can call it luck or anything else,' he admitted and acknowledged it was his decision to stay on with the Congress that finally led to his induction into Rahul's team. Just to buttress his loyalties, the wall behind him had a picture of a smiling Rahul, framed in the orange, white, and green of the Indian flag.

Tagore is among the group of leaders being groomed by Rahul to play a bigger role in their respective states. This group includes Jitendra Singh (Rajasthan), Meenakshi Natarajan (Madhya Pradesh), Ashok Tanwar (Haryana), Ravneet Singh 'Bittu' (Punjab), Vijay Inder Singla (Punjab), Mausam Benazir Noor (West Bengal) among others. They became first-time Lok Sabha MPs in 2009 after being given nominations at Rahul's behest.

Tagore became a national general secretary in the NSUI in 1998 and was put in charge of the Delhi University Students' Union (DUSU) elections between 1999 and 2002. 'My work in the DUSU elections showed the leadership what I was capable of,' he said. After that, he was promoted to the IYC as a general secretary.

He was in the Youth Congress when Rahul took over in 2007 and was among the older lot of promising leaders drafted by 'Team RG' to rebuild the organization. His work got him a nomination from Virudhnagar. 'I never asked for the seat,' he said, talking of the new 'culture' of merit under Rahul.

But it was not always like that. 'We came into politics under the appointment system. You had to be a loyalist, or you had to work very hard and hope to be recognized, or you needed to have money, or be the son of a senior leader to get a post in the Youth Congress in those days,' he said.

Through the 1990s and 2000s, the IYC and NSUI were moribund organizations. The Congress' factional chiefs cornered posts to dole them out to their supporters. 'If you went to the Youth Congress office in Delhi before the merit system was introduced, you found men with thick gold chains, leaning against their big cars, sipping tea and gossiping in the evening. Once a year, they would go to Jantar Mantar (where protests are held in Delhi) and participate in token agitations. They would have their pictures clicked and displayed at the IYC office. There was nothing much going on,' said an IYC functionary.

Even Rahul recognized this when he took over. He complained to his mother that she had given him a 'dead organization' to run, said a source in Rahul's extended Youth Congress team. Still, as Tagore said, Rahul decided to talk to a crosssection of workers to understand how to improve the condition of the two organizations. 'What he heard from them was that nobody had an assured future; there was a custom of parachute landings by which those with family connections were given posts; and that in all there was no value at all for work.'

Rahul put forth the idea of 'bringing democracy' into the IYC and the NSUI to tackle some of these problems. In his meetings with JNU professor Sudha Pai and other academics, it may have got a push. Pai recalled that when she told young Congress workers in Chitrakoot that Indira Gandhi was responsible for the poor condition of the party in UP because she had dismantled its organizational machinery, Rahul did not object. The idea was also raised at the meetings of an AICC committee named 'Group on Future Challenges', which was formed after Rahul became a member of the CWC. The group was seen as his think-tank for party reforms and, in 2008, came out with a report on it.

However, it was not pushed down the throats of IYC and NSUI. There was still a consultative process and, according to Tagore, the matter was discussed with the top office-bearers of the two organizations. The idea 'evolved' out of this. Former Youth Congress President Ashok Tanwar, and another leader, who did not want to be named, corroborated the consultative mechanism.

Tanwar said that the senior leaders of the two bodies debated the matter 'democratically'. At the end of the discussions, Rahul asked which was a better system – the election system or the nomination one – to appoint the office-bearers? A show of hands revealed that the majority overwhelmingly favoured elections.

Tanwar, an MP from Sirsa in Haryana, has an MA and MPhil in history and a PhD from Delhi's Jawaharlal Nehru University. He was the president of the NSUI between 2003 and 2005. When Rahul was made an AICC general secretary, Tanwar was the Youth Congress president. What helped him forge close links with Rahul were his political networks and credentials as a Dalit politician. Tanwar said that when the decision to introduce elections in the two bodies was made, 'the hows and the whys' of the exercise were not clear. Rahul employed a management consultant and roped in other 'experts' to get those answers.

Project 'Vistar'

Rahul turned to G K Jayaram, a management consultant, who had worked in the US with consulting firms such as Arthur D Little and Coopers and Lybrand, and set up an in-house training facility for Infosys, one of India's biggest IT services companies. Jayaram was the founder of the Bangalore-based Institute of Leadership and Institutional Development (ILID), which describes itself as a 'not for profit organization that caters to the leadership and institutional development needs of social organizations'. It states it is an 'umbrella organization that helps social entrepreneurs improve and innovate to deliver the best results possible to the poor and the disadvantaged'.

ILID has worked with NGOs in and around Bangalore,

and consulted businesses aimed at the 'Bottom of the Pyramid' sector. Among its clients are the Rajiv Gandhi Foundation and the Rajiv Gandhi Institute of Contemporary Studies. Its work with its clients adopts the 'VISTAR' approach developed by it. VISTAR or 'transformation' was how the restructuring of IYC and the NSUI came to be known internally. Rahul used ILID to set up the IYC and NSUI's in-house training centre, the Jawaharlal Nehru Leadership Institute (JNLI).

Jayaram refused to talk about his work with IYC and NSUI citing confidentiality: 'I am a consultant and I have worked throughout the world. It wouldn't be ethical for me to talk about my client's work unless they have explicitly agreed to such disclosures.' However, ILID's website describes VISTAR as a roadmap for organization building that consists of 'Vision, Strategies, Structure, Action Plans and Review'[1]. It is aimed at creating an overall diagnostic, planning, and execution blueprint for organizations and to maintain a sustained effort to achieve optimum results. 'ILID consultants work to infuse professionalism, result-orientation and corporate pragmatism into NGOs,' the organization says of itself. It could have added political parties to the NGOs.

Rahul was immersed with the work ILID did for IYC and NSUI. 'He devoted time. He was completely into it for two or three months as the organization was being conceived and developed,' a leader who worked with Rahul said. He said the most important idea at that time was to 'systematize and standardize' practices within the organization. 'How the energy of the cadre is systematically channelized that was the question before us.'

The 'Toyota Way'

Rahul, his team and ILID wished to develop the right 'process and systems' which would make standardization possible.

This philosophy was at the heart of the 'Toyota Way', a series of best practices used by the Toyota Motor Company of Japan, which emerged as the world's number one car maker between 2008 and 2010, leaving behind other global manufacturers like General Motors (GM) and Ford. (In 2011, however, Toyota was relegated to the number three position.)

The management philosophy, popular till the mid-2000s, grew out of the Toyota Production System (TPS), and consisted of a set of production practices used by the company. TPS and the 'Toyota Way' principles were credited with Toyota's spectacular success as it grew from being a small Japanese car-maker to one of the world's largest automobile companies.

According to Dr Jeffery K Liker, the author of the *The Toyota Way*, one of the most authoritative books on the subject, its core principle was that 'the right process will produce the right results'[2]. It aimed to do this by eliminating 'waste' in the production process to almost nil. It held that 'standardized tasks are the foundation for continuous improvement and employee empowerment'[3].

The Toyota Way spoke of making decisions slowly by consensus, by thoroughly considering all options and then implementing these decisions rapidly. The principle is called *nemawashi* in Japanese. Liker says: '*Nemawashi* is the process of discussing problems and potential solutions with all of those affected, to collect ideas and get agreement on a path forward. This consensus process, though time-consuming, helps broaden the search for solutions, and once a decision is made, the stage is set for rapid implementation.'[4]

Nemawashi is what Rahul used to find a solution to revamp the IYC and NSUI. A Congress functionary who has worked with Rahul said the Nehru-Gandhi scion was a convert to the merits of the 'Toyota Model'. The leader said Rahul talked of how the 'Toyota model' might help bring down errors to one per cent. He also sent his team members to Toyota's facilities to get first-hand knowledge of how TPS worked. 'I told Rahul I was travelling to Japan. He immediately wanted to know whether I planned to visit the Toyota factory,' recalled the leader.

Therefore, the 'Toyota Way' is a rough guide to Rahul's revamp of the IYC and NSUI. As we follow the IYC and NSUI overhaul over the next few pages, the parallels will crop up at various places. The overt-emphasis on business management ideas and standardization to shape the IYC and NSUI would become the hallmarks of the new organizations.

There was, however, one crucial chink in the strategy. Rahul and his team did not question how a political party could be treated like a business organization or an NGO, and how could the best practices formulated for the latter two be applied to the first. Such issues would later emerge as weaknesses of the new system. The new-look IYC and NSUI would be divorced from ground-level politics.

Talent Hunt

Until the new system was devised, an interim arrangement was required. The first task was to identify young leaders who could conduct internal elections. It was also necessary to find suitable replacements for IYC and NSUI state presidents. Thus, Team Rahul launched, what became known in Congress circles, as a 'talent hunt' in 2008-09 to spot young and talented workers.

Rahul Gandhi said at a press conference in Thiruvananthapuram in October 2009: 'The idea behind the talent search is and still remains . . . that democratic elections take time. They require an institutional set-up to deliver them effectively. They demand a machinery to deliver it . . . In our

Tamil Nadu election, there were around 600 Youth Congress members working to deliver that election. So, the idea of talent search is that in that intermediate period, until we are ready to start that election process, we should find talent.'[5]

Senior AICC general secretaries, MPs of the Congress 'youth brigade' such as Sachin Pilot and Sandeep Dikshit, and the members of Rahul Gandhi's team were asked to interview 300-400 people from each state. For smaller states such as Delhi the group was pared down to sixteen from about 250 participants. The number was higher for the larger states. A Congress leader, who appeared for the interview, said the panel that questioned him included Jitendra Singh, and AICC general secretary and CWC member, B K Hariprasad. At the initial stage, the panel was interested in general information. 'I was asked about my work experience in the Congress and what ideas I had for the Youth Congress,' the functionary said.

At the next stage, when several candidates had been eliminated, the other core members of Rahul's team – Kanishka Singh, Sachin Rao, and Meenakshi Natarajan – joined the exercise. Group discussions (GD), which lasted two to three hours, were held which Rahul attended. 'It was a fantastic opportunity. It felt like we had been given licence to breathe fresh air. Each of the participants wanted to grab the opportunity. After all it was a chance to speak your mind in the presence of Rahul Gandhi,' said this candidate. The topics covered included 'how important is money in politics' and 'how can you mobilize the youth', among others.

After the GD, six people were chosen for interviews conducted by Rahul. 'I was asked why the Congress was not able to do people's politics,' the candidate said, and Rahul explained that he meant the activities that NGOs such as Aruna Roy's Mazdoor Kisan Shakti Sanghatan (MKSS) did in areas such as monitoring of NREGA. Rahul's point was that the Youth Congress should get involved in activities that were not necessarily 'vote pullers'. He felt that there was no need to get extremely competitive, and what mattered most was to be among the people.

The Congress leaders enjoyed being part of the process, but came back with the impression that Rahul had devised a system designed to find candidates for 'Ivy League colleges' rather than political workers.

11

'TRANSFORMATION'

The ILID worked with the IYC and NSUI to 'unleash the energy of the Indian youth and open the doors of politics to them,' G K Jayaram told *Forbes India* magazine in 2011. The brief that Jayaram got was the same Rahul Gandhi articulated at the Hyderabad plenary of the Congress in 2006. 'We must embrace the young of this country; we must use this organization of ours to unleash the immense energy to build a better India,' Rahul said. In the same speech he spoke of 'open(ing) the doors of the Congress party to . . . thousands . . . millions of Indians'.

The 'transformation' exercise in the IYC and NSUI would have three aims. Firstly, to build an 'open organization' by which he meant there would be no entry barriers. Its leaders would be democratically elected rather than appointed or nominated and their progress too would be through democratic means.

'If I had not come from my family, I wouldn't be here. You can enter the system either through family or friends or money. Without family, friends or money, you cannot enter the system. My father was in politics. My grandmother and great grandfather were in politics. So, it was easy for me to enter politics. This is a problem. I am a symptom of this problem. I want to change it,'[2] he said at an interaction with girl students in Uttarakhand in October 2008. He was interested in attracting fresh people, those who were not part of the system and 'developing leaders' who would progress in the organization on the basis of their work and talent rather than by cornering 'posts and positions'.

It is possible that Rahul thought of the youth as a ready-made constituency. They had emerged as a dominant section of the electorate but were under-represented in politics. 'In India 70 per cent of the population is comprised of the youth ... Our political organizations are designed in such a way that the youth cannot enter them ... The most important job in Indian politics is to bring youth into politics. Seventy per cent of the population (the youth) doesn't play a role in politics,'[3] he said. He said his goal was to ensure that 'as many youngsters as possible ... enter politics'[4] and also that 'as many youngsters as who are capable and possible' become 'leaders' in the Youth Congress and the NSUI.[5]

Secondly, through the 'internal democracy' initiative, he wanted to provide the Congress with an assembly line of young political leaders. Some IYC and the NSUI leaders talked of the two organizations as a 'leadership-producing machine'. Speaking at a press conference held in Amritsar to launch the internal election exercise in November 2008, Rahul said: 'Every two years ... we'll give a list of Youth Congress leaders to the Congress and say that these are our elected representatives. These are the people who represent the youth in the Congress ... My vision for the Youth Congress and the NSUI is that these are organizations which will develop talent for the Congress party in the future, for the Youth Congress, and the NSUI.'[6]

Thirdly, Rahul wanted to position himself as a politician who stood for 'changing politics'. If a new generation of youngsters became part of the political system, it would not only help the Congress but it could also be instrumental in projecting Rahul as the man who had revolutionized politics in India.

The Youth Congress' principal planks to reach out to the youth was a chance 'to become a leader and choose your own leader' (*neta bano, neta chuno*). As he travelled to college campuses across the country, met prospective candidates, and interacted with professionals in Bengaluru and Ahmedabad, Rahul spoke of how the Youth Congress and the NSUI was the only political party in India which was trying to change politics itself. '. . . we're driving at . . . an organization that empowers the young of this country to fundamentally alter the politics of this country. I am passionate about it,'[7] Rahul said at a press conference in Bhopal in October 2010.

～

Team Rahul set up seven task forces to oversee each aspect of the new 'transformation' exercise. The Youth Congress and the NSUI call it the 'seven core pillars'[8] of the new organizations. Its wish list was the following: 'Open Membership', which would ensure IYC and NSUI were 'open to every youth in the country'; 'Internal Elections' held in a 'fair and transparent' manner; 'Training' to 'groom and develop youth leaders', provide them with 'political orientation', and 'develop their leadership capabilities'; 'Programmes' – the IYC's political programmes structured around monitoring of the Congress-led UPA government's social sector schemes; 'Performance management' or *Pehchaan* as a 'mechanism to identify and promote the performance' of its elected office-bearers; 'Financial self-sufficiency and Transparency' to work towards making each unit of the Youth Congress self-sufficient; and 'Ethics'which was an adherence to a code of conduct in public and private life to promote 'austerity and simple life' among cadres.

'Rahul ji was able to guide us through the process. He was a protective figure, allowing us to go forward with the idea even though we all knew that senior leaders would be disturbed by the exercise,' said Manicka Tagore, who was part of the team that studied the membership systems in other parties. 'We found that a party such as the BSP, which sought members from among the poorest of the poor charged a membership fee of Rs 15. We decided to do the same.' The Youth Congress membership fee was raised from Rs 2 to Rs 15.

Tagore justified the increase. 'Rahul ji has said that when I sit down, the system should not sit down,' Tagore said, explaining that Rahul felt the Congress may be willing to give funds to the IYC today as he was in charge but it may not always be the case. He emphasized at each point that Rahul was trying to build 'systems and processes' that would continue to do their job irrespective of the individuals in charge. This goes back to the idea of standardization in the 'Toyota Way'.

Internal Elections

The Youth Congress decided it was ready to hold its first internal elections by mid-2008. The process was handled by an independent NGO, Foundation for Advanced Management of Elections (FAME), started by former election commissioners K J Rao, James Lyngdoh, N Gopalaswami and T S Krishnamurthy.

Rahul explained why he felt it was necessary to seek the services of an outside agency. 'One of the things that we decided earlier on in the process . . . if we were to do an election that was fair, we needed to bring in an objective partner . . . (With the) Youth Congress doing their own elections . . . it would be a bit difficult for us to guarantee that the elections were 100 per cent fair . . . I sent some of the boys who work with me out and I said let us find the best authority who can help us do this job and we found the organization that Mr Lyngdoh and Mr Rao belong to, FAME. We felt that if there was a group of people who could help us in this task, who were credible, and who were unflinching in their resolve, it would be the people at FAME. And that is why we decided to bring them into our process.'[9]

When I met him, Rao, a former election commissioner known for delivering a free and fair election in Bihar in 2005, sat behind his cluttered desk in the Delhi Sealing Committee office at the capital's India Habitat Centre. Rao is a slim man, bespectacled and balding, with a simple bronze band on a finger on his right hand. He looks like someone's elderly, unremarkable uncle.

'Rahul Gandhi means business,' he told me as soon as the conversation began. He was all praise for the steps taken by the IYC and NSUI. However, he mentioned he did ask Rahul why he wasn't attempting the same in the Congress. Rahul replied that he was the final authority only for the Youth Congress and NSUI and that the party high command would decide on matters pertaining to Congress. 'He asked why political parties did not hold inner-party elections,' Rao recalled. 'I replied that it was because most parties were one-person organizations and they (the leaders) were scared to lose their power.' But Rahul went ahead as he was confident of building up his own support base in the Congress, Rao said. The former election commissioner was convinced Rahul would introduce elections even at its highest levels in the Congress.

It was in June 2008 that Rahul called up the former election commissioner Lyngdoh, now the chairman of FAME, and asked him whether the body could help with holding elections in the IYC and the NSUI. Lyngdoh directed him to Rao. At the meeting, Rahul was present with Kanishka Singh and Sachin Rao. FAME laid down the ground rules – no criminal would be allowed to contest the elections and any dispute regarding the elections would be settled by them. 'He (Rahul) thought about it for a few seconds and said yes,' Rao said.

There were several meetings, and Team Rahul presented the election model to FAME, which was only responsible for holding the elections. However, in the initial elections, eight FAME members were present even during the membership drive in Punjab, which was chosen as the pilot state for the internal polls.

FAME wrote to the state election commission for the use of the ballot boxes. Then they had to train members to be returning officers. '200-300 people were trained. They had to be taught how to open and close the ballot boxes, and seal them,' Rao said. Today, the Youth Congress has a department, the Central Election Authority, which is responsible for nomination, scrutiny and verification of candidates and for voting. The organization has hundreds of returning officers. This infrastructure grew over three years after the first elections in Punjab.

Tagore said Rahul could have selected Kerala for the first elections since it had a strong organizational base in place. He chose a 'tough terrain' because he wanted the system to be better and stronger in the long run. Rahul spoke about how he wanted the internal election 'process' to be 'credible, robust, and replicable'[10]. In the 'Toyota Way' one of the most important ways to build the 'right process' is to 'get quality right the first time'. Liker says: 'Build into your culture the philosophy of stopping or slowing down to get quality right the first time to enhance productivity in the long run.'[11]

In keeping with the structured approach Rahul followed in rebuilding the IYC and NSUI, Rahul's interactions with colleagues in the extended IYC and NSUI team showed him as someone who was 'very interactive and a great listener' but also 'very strict and no-nonsense'. A functionary who has worked closely with him said: 'He makes people come to the topic. He cuts them at the correct time (if they don't come to the point).' However, the source also described Rahul as 'very accommodative'. Speaking of the impression that has gained ground in the two bodies that only those who know English and are tech-savvy will be able to get through to Rahul, the leader said: 'He feels language should not be a barrier.' According to him, Rahul is 'a very good human being'. He spoke of the time Rahul had specifically checked whether he had been given a place to stay by the IYC. 'No Congress general secretary has ever asked me where I stay,' the leader said.

Another person in Rahul's team said he was 'warm . . . fairly talkative and joked quite a bit' but not the kind who would come up to his teammates and ask how they were doing and if everyone in their family was fine. 'Priyanka by contrast is someone who will ask you about your family . . . Rahul is very conscious that proximity to him should not be misused,' the leader said. This impression is common among those who know Rahul well. Another member of Rahul extended team said: 'Many of us have been working (for the IYC and NSUI) for years. But he is not the kind who will come up to us, back-slap us, and ask how we have been managing (to eke out a living full-time in politics).' He too felt Rahul stayed at a distance because he was conscious of people trying to misuse their closeness to him for personal gains.

The contest for the Punjab state president's post was held on 23 December 2008. As Rahul would tell the media, the membership forms were printed in the newspapers. Anyone under the age of thirty-five could become a member and contest the election as long as he or she was not a criminal. According to a website that is run by Rahul's office, www.pressbrief.in, the Punjab membership drive saw 3,50,000 youngsters join the party. '(This is a) ten-fold increase vis-à-vis the previous membership drive which yielded approximately 30,000 members,' the site said. The party computerized the database of all its members. The new members, who join the IYC and the NSUI get photo-identity cards with a membership number on them.

In the initial system (used in the first couple of states that held elections), block, district, and the state level elections were held. After the first few states, elections were held to elect committees in each polling booth, Assembly and Lok Sabha constituency and the state level. This was Rahul's vision to raise leadership from the grassroots. He aimed to empower the worker by democratizing the process of selecting higher office-bearers. There were reservations for Scheduled Castes (SCs) and Scheduled Tribes (STs), minorities, OBCs and women.

However, not everything went according to plan. Though Rahul himself camped in Amritsar to make sure the election lived up to the expectations of being the first free and fair one, the old Congress reared its head through the process. Ravneet Singh 'Bittu', the grandson of a former Congress chief minister, Beant Singh, became the first elected Punjab Youth Congress president. He had the backing of the former chief minister of Punjab, Captain Amrinder Singh. This raised questions about whether the elections had indeed ushered in internal democracy.

After Punjab, similar polls were held in twenty-two other states until November 2011. Punjab and Gujarat went for a second round of elections by March 2012. The Youth Congress' membership[12] count stood at 1,08,19,623 as on 7 November 2011. It had 87,42,081 males and 20,77,542 females. Among the elected office-bearers were 3,18,433 males and 84,106 females. The Youth Congress held a convention of about 7,000 elected office-bearers on 28-29 November 2011. The IYC session was called Buniyaad (foundation) and seen as the end of the first round of internal elections. It provided a platform from where Rahul declared that he had completed the process of initiating 'transformation' in the IYC, even though there were questions over how much change had been possible.

'Aam Aadmi ka Sipahi'

Apart from the restructuring of the IYC and NSUI, Rahul asked the Youth Congress to launch a programme to help build a cadre of workers at the village level. Known as the IYC's 'aam aadmi ka sipahi' outreach, it was launched in June 2008 and aimed at providing a constructive programme of work to new IYC recruits.

In Amethi, Rahul worked through NGOs to deliver services to the poor in areas such as education and financial inclusion through women's self-help groups. When he took charge of the IYC and NSUI in 2007, he wanted the two organizations to be involved with 'people's politics'. He felt political organizations should raise issues affecting the poor such as ineffective delivery of state-sponsored schemes.

'UPA's government schemes such as the NREGA, the right to information act (RTI), and Bima Yojana (an insurance scheme for the rural landless poor) did not reach the intended beneficiaries,' said one leader. So, an effort was made to identify three or four people in each of India's 2.5 lakh villages. The idea may have been to provide the Congress with the one thing it lacked vis-a-vis BJP – a committed cadre which could penetrate to the lowest levels of the political structure and act as a channel of communication with voters.

'We had almost 60-70 per cent of the exercise complete,' said the leader. The Youth Congress worked closely with Nikhil De of MKSS. There was a five-day training for the 'aam aadmi ka sipahi' held at Hyderabad in September 2008.

The idea was right out of C K Prahalad's seminal management study, *The Fortune at the Bottom of the Pyramid*. The book spoke of how business organizations stood to profit by targeting the poorest of the poor or those who were at the bottom of the economic pyramid. One of the case studies in the book was on ITC's e-Choupal initiative. The case study was co-authored by Rahul's aide, Sachin Rao, who worked under Prahalad's supervision during his MBA project at the University of Michigan. 'Bottom of the Pyramid' was an approach that found wide acceptance among businesses in the first decade of the twenty-first century. Just as many Indian businesses succumbed to the idea, India's largest political party found itself at the altar of Prahalad. If it was the Nano for the Tata Group, affordable five rupee cola bottles for Coke, and miniature Re 1 sachets of everything that Fast-Moving Consumer Goods (FMCG) companies could manufacture (from shampoos and talcum powder to toothpaste), it was the 'aam aadmi ka sipahi' for the Congress. It was a system that was aimed at creating a local entrepreneur, the sipahi on the ground, who could network with the constituency which 'Brand Congress' wanted to capture.

In 2000, Hindustan Unilever Limited (HUL), India's largest consumer products company, launched Project Shakti, initially in Andhra Pradesh and expanded it to several states. The project aimed to increase its market share by selling products in India's small and far-flung villages. It wanted to reach millions of potential customers in areas where there was no sales distribution network, no advertising coverage and poor roads and transport[13]. HUL tapped into India's expanding network of women's self-help groups which facilitate rural women with no access to banks to save and borrow from each other. It identified women in each village who could become micro-entrepreneurs or direct-to-consumer sales distributors.

Project Shakti according to HUL was a great success and represented a 30 per cent increase in rural population that was reached by the end of 2004. The company website says HUL reaches three million households monthly through the Shakti network and the project contributes to 10 per cent of HUL's rural turnover nationally[14]. Through the 'aam aadmi ka sipahi' initiative, the Congress might have hoped to reach millions of voters it had lost due to the fragmentation of voters over the decades, as well as new ones.

However, the Rahul initiatives encountered several problems. First, there was a clash between the state governments where the Congress was in power and the IYC's 'aam aadmi ka sipahi'. Rahul, who knew of the potential conflict, rationalized the exercise. The issue came up at a meeting of Youth Congress activists. Rahul, with his penchant for using the white board to illustrate his point of view, drew two circles on a piece of paper. 'He told us that one stood for the Congress and the other for the common man,' said one leader. 'He then asked us whom we wanted to work for, the Congress or the common man,' he added. When all of those present at the meeting replied that they wanted to work for the common man, Rahul told them to go ahead and not fear the repercussions. However, in Congress-ruled Assam which was the pilot state with about 7,000 to 8,000 recruits under the programme, the Youth Congress activists took up the issue of irregularities in the state Public Distribution System (PDS). This led to friction between the Youth Congress and the state Congress leaders. But there was no clear support from Rahul or his team for the 'aam aadmi ka sipahi', a source said. The programme drew flak from within the Congress party for being overtly NGO-ish in scope. 'One senior Congress leader took us into a room and gave us an earful for treating a political party like an NGO,' a source involved with the exercise said. The 'aam aadmi ka sipahi' programme was finally merged with the IYC's regular programmes in 2009. The 'sipahis' identified in each state were inducted into the organization in different capacities for helping with the 'transformation' process.

The IYC now describes the aam aadmi ka siphai as its 'common programme'[15] for all its workers. Though the programme is still centred on the idea of monitoring the implementation of the UPA government's social sector schemes, it is now a political programme of the IYC. As part of it, the IYC has decided to use the Right to Information (RTI) extensively to expose corruption in the delivery of Centrally-sponsored schemes. This was done by the IYC in UP – with Rahul leading the charge – to expose alleged corruption in the Mayawati government's implementation of the National Rural Health Mission (NRHM) scheme in the run up to the 2012 UP elections. The Congress used RTI to seek details of funds received by the state government from the Centre and the expenditures undertaken by the UP government under the NRHM. It particularly sought details of the implementation of the Janani Suraksha Yojana, a Central scheme which aims to promote institutional delivery among poor pregnant women. It identified graft in the payment of

Rs 1,400 meant for the pregnant women after IYC undertook a social audit of the scheme in twelve districts of the state. Rahul referred to the findings from the RTI applications during the 2012 UP campaign, sarcastically remarking that there were women in UP who were giving birth to a child each week and delivering fifty-two children a year. It plans to use the RTI to check on the implementation of other Centrally-sponsored schemes such as the NREGA too.

Training

To train its elected office-bearers and create trained political professionals, Rahul set up a dedicated training institute on the same lines as big corporate organizations such as Infosys. The Jawaharlal Nehru Leadership Institute (JNLI) was set up in 2008 with Jayaram as its 'chief mentor'. He declined to answer questions about whether or not JNLI was part of the Congress. However, a Congress leader in the know said JNLI would become a part of the Congress in the future though it operated independently now. ILID lists JNLI as one of its clients. Its website states that it was set up to 'train young political leaders in a holistic manner to serve the society'. It adds that JNLI trains IYC office-bearers at the state, Lok Sabha, Assembly and Panchayat levels.

IYC has its in-house trainers from the JNLI. The party is in the process of identifying 1000 'master coaches' at the Lok Sabha Youth Congress committee level who will be trained by JNLI. Their job will be to train office-bearers at the lower levels. Other than holding workshops, JNLI is involved with the training of returning officers in the party (the IYC has about 2,500 returning officers, according to one Congress leader's estimate) who have to pass a written exam to qualify. During the 2012 UP campaign, they were involved with the training of booth-level polling agents. The IYC with help from JNLI conducts targeted training workshops for Dalits and women office-bearers.

Training typically means corporate-style training, one former Youth Congress leader said. The participants would be at a round table while professional trainers from JNLI conducted the programme. Among those who are part of the JNLI's team of trainers are Jayaram; former Youth Congress president of Karnataka, Krishna Byre Gowda, who is the son of veteran Janata Dal leader C Byre Gowda, and an MA in international affairs from the School of International Service, American University, in Washington DC; and outside experts such as Vijay Mahajan, a pioneer of the micro-finance industry in India and founder and chairman of the Basix Group.

'Many of the elected office-bearers are young adults, they are even younger in the NSUI,' Mahajan said, and added that unlike the BJP or the CPM, the Congress did not have a set ideological prescription. Therefore, it was the job of the trainers to make people coming into the organization ready for their work in their respective constituencies. The IYC recruits would be tasked with overseeing the implementation of Central government programmes in their regions.

Speaking at an interaction with young professionals in Ahmedabad in February 2009, Rahul said: 'Once we have candidates who have won elections, we will give them a particular set of training . . . What does it mean to be a public representative, what are the type of issues that are important, how do you raise issues, what is the difference between local issues and national issues. So general training on what it means to become a public representative. For example, even myself over the last five years, I have learnt a lot about what it means to be an MP. A new MP doesn't normally have that type of training.'[16]

The IYC's training programmes are called 'Yuva Drishti' camps and are held at various levels. The sessions are usually three to five days long. Other than Congress-related information, the camps focus on the importance of teamwork and time management. The elected office-bearers are trained in the use of 'Pehchaan', a web-based mechanism which functions as an intra-net for IYC and NSUI members and is meant to help in their performance assessment. It is introduced as Facebook for the IYC and NSUI members. They are taught how to design political programmes, and how to plan activities in their respective areas all of which have a standardized format developed by the JNLI. That the IYC and NSUI aim for a high level of standardization is evident in a training manual prepared by the organization with inputs from its own trainers and the JNLI.

The manual has a section on the importance of teamwork ('Team is more than the sum of its members'); there are guidelines on 'how to run your committee' and 'roles and responsibility of office-bearers' (advice on conducting meetings and detailed guidelines on 'functional roles' and reporting instructions); there is one section on 'conducting meeting effectively' which ironically for a political party starts off by saying 'you will be spending a lot of time in meetings'. It gives the format of field visit reports to be filed by its office-bearers and has a case study of a NREGA campaign design broken up into eleven stages for easy use by IYC leaders.

There is a 'padayatra work plan' which spells out the exact method and specifications of how the agitation method should be used by IYC members. The training manual gives the new generation of Congress leaders specific directions on the number of hours they should be spending on the road each day ('cover 20-25 kms a day in two slots of 3-4 hours of padayatra'); it details the preparations that need to be made before the actual padayatra is carried out including the formation of an agrim toli (advance party which the manual specifies is supposed to move three hours ahead of the padayatris to make prior arrangements and mobilize crowds) and identification of 'start-to-end padayatris' (who are supposed to represent various regions and communities of the state according to the guidelines specified). There is a model padayatra proposal that asks the state units to give detailed information about the padayatra plan, including the names of the organizing committee members, the issues identified, the start-to-end padayatris, the agrim toli, and the padayatra route with the map. This proposal has to be sent to the Delhi leadership for approval only after which the padayatra can be undertaken.

The prototype of the professional politician that JNLI is creating is the way forward in the Congress. Mahajan said Rahul himself was a representative of this generation of politicians who was more 'organized and result-oriented' and exposed to more effective ways of working. He would like these ideas to be reflected in the organization that he was building.

It has helped individual Youth Congress leaders, especially those who came into Rahul's team through the 'talent hunt' route. Their communication skills have improved considerably, they are confident, and appear to have a sense of purpose. Within the Congress, where power flows from the 'high command', it is a matter of prestige to be connected directly with Rahul's pet project. The training process has helped create and reinforce the IYC and NSUI's organizational culture – an important aspect of the Toyota Way.

However, it is difficult to see how this translates into developing political skills. Learning the four compartments of the 'Johari Window', a management tool that is used for self-exploration in order to develop leadership skills, can only go so far in preparing a person for political life. In any case, it is difficult to imagine people who have 'managed elections' – shorthand for money power and clout – to see the merits of professional training. Basing all political activity on the monitoring of the state-sponsored schemes displays a limited conception of politics, especially for a youth organization.

In its emphasis on standardization, the IYC and the NSUI seem to be missing the point that the benefits of a systems and process-driven approach has its limits when it comes to people-centric organizations. In fact, over-emphasis on systems and process is one of the biggest criticisms against manufacturing practices such as the TPS. There cannot be a rule-book for producing political activists or activities because the dynamics of each state and region vary considerably. Therefore while it might be possible to run a McDonald's style franchise chain with a manual on Standard Operating Procedures (SOP), producing political leaders on the assembly line is bound to fail, sooner than later.

Performance Management

When Rahul spoke of 'internal democracy' in the IYC and NSUI, there were two parts to the exercise. The first was to hold free and fair elections and the second was to ensure that promotions were 'based on democratic norms'. It was to address the second aspect that he set up a task force on 'meritocracy' at the beginning of the restructuring exercise. This would be later converted into a mechanism for 'performance management' within the two organizations.

It was hoped this would ensure that promotions – or getting party posts and election nominations – was not based on ad hoc criteria but happened on the basis of a political worker's performance within the organization. This is what Rahul had meant when he said at the 2007 AICC[17] convention that it was the duty of the Congress to ensure that the 'progress' of young people coming into the organization was 'linked to their performance'. It was also a way to ensure a measure of accountability for political leadership in the two organizations.

'We're making a number of criteria on which we can easily measure the person (a new recruit to the IYC and NSUI) . . . How close is that person to the common man. How much time does he spend with the people he represents. What is the performance of the party in his polling booth . . . you can be a very big leader but if you can't win a single polling booth, then what's the point . . . We are trying to bring measurement into political leadership. Today there's no measurement in political leadership,'[18] Rahul said at the interaction with young professionals in Ahmedabad.

There was a reporting process initiated from its earliest days. The IYC's state units sent or emailed reports to the main office in Delhi after collating information from the Youth Congress office-bearers at the lower levels. The reporting culture was far more systematic and rigorous than what existed in the main Congress party.

Over time, the process of reporting was expanded to include the idea of self-reporting. The web-based Pehchaan platform was set up. The Buniyaad convention's organization resolution described Pehchaan as a 'mechanism to identify and promote elected office-bearers (EOBs) at every level'. It said each elected office-bearer would have an opportunity to let the senior leadership and peers know about his or her activities. 'Every EOB is allotted a unique ID and password and given the opportunity to share their work and connect with the organization at various levels,' the resolution said.

Its elected office-bearers, returning officers, and master coaches can update personal and official information; 'showcase' their 'political journey to the leadership'; connect with their peers across the states; seek appointments, and download visiting cards and letterheads through Pehchaan. It said they would be able to get 'political recognition' in a 'transparent, free and fair manner' by establishing their political identity, keep the 'leadership' abreast of their profile and political inputs. 'It provides the organization the means to recognize every individual in a systematic way,' the IYC says of the web-based tool.

The IYC tied up with Google to provide it with a communications platform using cloud computing technology. The IYC's applications on Pehchaan such as email, chat and other apps were provided by Google. The organization said in its July 2011 newsletter that it planned to move 28,000 of its elected office-bearers and volunteers on to the Google platform to help them 'carry our various development programmes at grassroots level all across India.'

The problems that bogged down 'aam aadmi ka sipahi' plagued 'performance management' as well. A political party is not a corporate organization. It is debatable whether the performance of a political leader can be assessed through the tools used by the IYC and NSUI. Election nominations are typically distributed on a number of factors ranging from right parentage, to money and resources, and clout with influential voter blocks. How would a corporate-style performance management system be able to capture all of this?

As one leader explained, performance management went only that far in influencing the selection of candidates. 'What is the nature of politics in this country, and is the IYC suited to its needs in terms of the systems and processes it follows?' the source asked. It makes people question a system that claims to be transparent and meritocratic but does not follow through on its promises.

Since Rahul advertised the entire process as a chance 'to become a leader and choose your own leader', he raised the aspirations of the members. But since there aren't enough opportunities to go around among all the young people entering the system or it requires them to raise substantial financial resources independently to fight the polls, it has upset many who could not progress in the organization. This has created frustrated young political workers who are unlikely to be of help in the Congress' electoral projects. The fact is that it is not the job of political parties to provide all the youngsters with a career option. 'Many young people join the IYC right after finishing their education. They don't have a career. This makes them uncertain about their future. However, once they are in the IYC system they find the uncertainty increasing,' an IYC source said.

Another IYC leader defended Pehchaan as a tool to introduce 'checks and balances' in the system. The leader said that established Congress leaders used the IYC and the NSUI as 'launch pads' for their sons and daughters. However, if tickets were distributed on the basis of performance, it would dissuade them from taking their place in the new establishment for granted. They would have to work to get ahead like the rest of the members. However, it is a political and organizational decision whether the Congress decides to expand its base beyond the political families and cliques that have come to dominate it.

NSUI

The bland and characterless NSUI office, situated inside the IYC campus in Delhi's Raisina road, was in sharp contrast to its young and with-it office-bearers. It was full of the bustle of young men and a few women. The boys were dressed in tight tapered jeans and fashionable pointed leather or faux-leather shoes. They wore sweaters or jackets that had hoods attached to them and sported gelled, spiky hairstyles. This could have passed for a students' union office on a college campus, were it not for the air of official purposefulness that hung around the place.

Roji John, the young national vice president of the NSUI, hails from Eranakulam in Kerala where he joined the Kerala Students' Union and rose through its ranks. Roji said NSUI was the 'only real student organization in the country'. 'Earlier there was no record of the members or the office-bearers. There used to be a lot of non-students in the organization. There would be a lot of older people, those in their 30s and their 40s. It is now a purely student organization with an upper age limit of twenty-seven years,' he said.

The walls had old posters of Rajiv Gandhi with the words 'I am young and I too have a dream' written in Hindi on them. In addition, there were pictures of Sonia, Rahul and Priyanka. NSUI has travelled a long way from the time it was under Rajiv. It had close to 25 lakh members spread across 15,000 colleges as of March 2012. In the NSUI, internal elections bring in elected members at the college, district, and the state level. There are reservations in the committees at the each of the levels for women. SCs and STs have reservations at the district and the state levels.

Roji says the student organization has completed its first round of organizational elections in all states and a second round of elections is taking place in about eighteen states. The process began in end-2008 with the first organizational election held in Uttarakhand. The NSUI is planning to hold a big convention of the kind that the Youth Congress did with Buniyaad.

NSUI has not been given the same priority accorded to the Youth Congress within Rahul's dispensation. Certainly, the objectives of the Youth Congress and the NSUI are different. 'We are different from the IYC. We believe that there is no need to develop student leaders into politicians. We want to develop leaders at the student level. It is an opportunity for them to develop their leadership abilities. Whether they wish to continue in politics or not is up to them,' Roji explained.

One of the things that Rahul has spoken about often is the stigma attached to politics among large sections of the educated youth. NSUI's attempt seems to be to market its membership as an opportunity for general leadership development rather than advertise it as the first step into politics or a political career like in the IYC. The NSUI's track-record under Rahul has been mixed. In 2010, for instance, the BJP's youth wing, the Akhil Bharatiya Vidyarthi Parishad or ABVP, did better than NSUI in university elections in Kerala, Rajasthan, Vidharbha, and Madhya Pradesh. It also lost the prestigious DUSU elections. The year 2011 was better. NSUI's Ajay Chikara won the DUSU president's post though the ABVP captured the other three top posts. Delhi chief minister Sheila Dikshit marked the win with a big celebration which was attended by Rahul. The body did well in university elections in parts of Gujarat and Orissa and won student polls in North Bengal after a gap of forty years. It did well in Congress-ruled Assam and Rajasthan. 'We are very happy with the overall performance of the NSUI, though there are some states where we need to pick up such as in Himachal Pradesh,' Roji said.

12

WITHER 'TRANSFORMATION'?

On 28 and 29 November 2011, Delhi's sprawling Japanese park in its western suburb of Rohini was converted into a tented city to host over 7,000 Youth Congress delegates from across India. On Delhi's roads and flyovers it was difficult to miss posters of Rahul Gandhi advertising the convention. The meet was named Buniyaad: perhaps to signify that the IYC had built the 'foundations' of a new organization.

Buniyaad was meant to brand Rahul's restructuring exercise as a success and set the stage for him to move on to bigger things. Rahul had shifted his focus to UP, where Assembly elections were due, by mid-2011. The Youth Congress show was possibly meant to neatly round-off his stint with the IYC and NSUI, a project on which he had spent the bulk of his time in politics between 2007-11. Amongst those who spoke at the convention were Sonia Gandhi and Prime Minister Manmohan Singh.

In his opening speech at the Buniyaad convention, Rahul Gandhi patted himself and his team on the back. 'There is not a single political organization which has been built like this. We have made a system which can conduct free and fair elections. Our opponents in Punjab have accepted this fact,' he said. He spoke of how the system would create a 'chain' of new entrants into the party. '. . . after you, new boys will come and gradually the doors of politics will open up,' he said.

He pointed out that in other organizations people were 'nominated' to posts unlike in the IYC and NSUI. He said in the earlier system 'relatives and kin' would get the 'upper hand' and 'friendship and acquaintance' worked. 'We are trying to change this. In this gathering there are thousands of workers who don't have anyone in politics. But today your roots are in the Youth Congress,' he said.

Contrary to Rahul's projections, though, that in itself has not brought 'transformation'. The results from the first round of elections show that the relatives of established Congress leaders or their 'loyalists' dominated the new system. The results are proof that the new system has been unable to create a level playing field for those outside the system to contest and win elections and therefore progress in it.

Connected to this are two other issues. There is doubt over whether the new system, conceived as a 'leadership-building machine', has been of any help to the Congress' electoral projects so far. Third, Rahul's branding as a youth icon has had limited traction with young voters.

Before we look at these three individually, it needs to be stated that these are broad trends rather than a definitive analysis of whether it has been a success or a failure. The experiment is at a nascent stage and the results will concretize only after a few more rounds of internal elections. Leadership building is a slow process. IYC estimates it will be at least ten years before a new state-level leadership emerges from its ranks. Moreover, the new system is still being fine-tuned.

Level Playing Field?

The results of the first round of internal elections show that in a number of states, the polls were won by the close relatives (in most cases, sons) of senior Congress leaders. If it was Beant Singh's grandson, Ravneet Singh 'Bittu' in Punjab's first round, former Congress minister Santokh Chaudhary's son, Vikramjit, was elected as the Punjab Youth Congress president in December 2011. In the eight-member committee that took office under Vikramjit, there were three sons of former ministers and two of sitting MLAs[1].

In Haryana, Chiranjeev Rao, son of senior minister Ajay Singh Yadav won the polls. In West Bengal, Mausam Benazir Noor, the niece of the veteran Congress leader and former Union minister, the late A B A Ghani Khan Chowdhary was the victor. In Uttarakhand, Anand Singh Rawat, son of Union minister Harish Rawat won the post. In Himachal Pradesh, another Union minister, Virbhadra Singh's son, Vikramaditya, polled most votes in a controversial election. However, the Foundation for Advance Management of Elections has recommended that the last election be declared null and void[2].

Maharashtra witnessed a clash of major proportions. Sangli strongman and state minister, Patangrao Kadam's son, Vishwajeet, took on Satyajit Tambe, the nephew of another senior leader, Balasaheb Thorat, who hails from Ahmednagar. Also in the fray were Kunal Raut, son of minister Nitin Raut, and Rahul Pugalia, son of former Congress MP Naresh Pugalia. The much-hyped contest was won by Vishwajeet, though all the four political heirs made it to the Congress' state Youth Congress committee. In the system used by the Youth Congress all the top candidates become a part of the committees that are formed after the elections. Some feel such a system puts rival factions together in the same team and weakens the winning candidate. He or she is not able to form his own team and build a support base on the basis of the election victory.

In states where the relatives of senior leaders have not won directly, top leaders of the Congress manipulated the system to ensure that their supporters became presidents. In the first round of elections in Gujarat, the winner was Indravijay Sinh Gohil, an education baron who is considered close to Shaktisinh Gohil, the leader of the Opposition in the Gujarat Assembly. In Tamil Nadu, M Yuvaraja, a member of Union minister, G K Vasan's, faction won the polls. The Tamil Nadu elections, which saw a record 12.92 lakh members joining the organization, also made news for the alleged massive use of money power by the top contestants.

In Chhattisgarh, Rahul Gandhi's team member Jitendra Singh spoke to Congress strongman Ajit Jogi's son Amit to dissuade him from contesting the elections. He was the prime accused in the murder of a state NCP leader and had been arrested by the Central Bureau of Investigation (CBI) twice. Though 'Team Rahul' managed to stop Amit from contesting, it could do nothing about the post being won by his supporter, Uttam Kumar Vasudeo.

In Jharkhand, Manas Sinha, a youth leader who had the support of Union minister Subodh Kant Sahay, became the president. Priyavrat Singh, a supporter of former chief minister Digvijay Singh was elected in Madhya Pradesh. Kerala saw a tight contest between Ommen Chandy's 'A' group which supported the candidature of P C Vishnunadh and Pradesh Congress Committee (PCC) chief Ramesh Chennithala's nominee M Liju, who was also backed by all the other factions in the state now known as the expanded 'I' group. Vishnunadh won the contest.

In Goa, the Youth Congress managed to score a victory on

the image management front by debarring veteran leader Churchill Alemao's daughter Valanka from contesting the top post on grounds that she had resorted to unethical means during the campaign. The matter had seen political tempers rise in Goa with the powerful Alemao brothers threatening to resign from the Goa government. The dispute was resolved after the Alemao brothers were called to Delhi for a meeting with Sonia Gandhi's political secretary Ahmed Patel. The Goa polls were won by Pratima Countinho, a rival of Valanka's.

The Youth Congress has also been unable to keep away criminals or those with dubious antecedents. UP and Bihar, among other states, have a number of office-bearers with criminal backgrounds. This is despite the Youth Congress announcing up front that it intended to debar criminals from contesting the elections.

The results indicate that senior leaders have used the Youth Congress to extend or defend their turfs. By getting family members into the Youth Congress, they attempted to get a foot into the new Congress under Rahul.

Rahul and his team responded to these allegations by claiming the problems would iron themselves out after two or three cycles of the election process. 'A new generation is being created there (at the panchayat level). Lakhs (of youngsters) . . . are getting elected and entering into the system. In the beginning, there will be problems at the higher levels. When we look at our organization, when we recognize people in the organization, we look at the whole organization,' he said at a press conference in Aurangabad in January 2011.

Rahul cited the example of Kerala, where in the panchayat elections held in 2010, the Kerala Pradesh Congress Committee (KPCC) decided that 50 per cent of the seats would be reserved for candidates under the age of forty. It was an idea that was close to Rahul's heart. 'Thousands of young boys and girls stood in these elections. And the young people from our organization who stood ... new youths, with no connections, 90 per cent won ... Changes in the political system are coming from below.'

Though Rahul spoke about the success of Youth Congress and NSUI candidates in the panchayat elections in Kerala, the state does not correctly reflect the condition of the Congress organization across India. In fact, due to the existence of strong state-level leaders, the Congress organization in Kerala, including the Youth Congress and the NSUI, is among the more robust in the country.

The Tamil Nadu elections, both to the Assembly (May 2011) as well as to the local bodies (October 2011), proved that even if the Youth Congress notched up impressive numbers during the membership drive (an achievement that Rahul cited ad nauseum during his promotional visits to all other states where elections were to be held) the system was simply not effective when it came to converting these members into workers who would galvanize voters during the polls. In the local body elections held in Tamil Nadu in October 2011, the Congress performed miserably close on the heels of the drubbing it received in the Assembly elections held in May.

In the local-body elections, the ruling All India Anna Dravida Munnetra Kazhagam or AIADMK emerged with a crushing majority. The Congress was among the worst losers, with the party cornering a mere 751 out of the total 20, 604 posts for which elections were held. At the panchayat union level, the elections closest to the ground fought on a party symbol, the Congress could make just 154 ward members out of a total of 6,470.

In the Youth Congress system, those who wish to become office-bearers need to 'make members' who will in turn vote for them. The membership fee for the Youth Congress is

Rs 15 with a reduced fee for special groups pegged at Rs 5. The nomination fee for contesting elections varies but in most states it is Rs 100 at the booth level, Rs 1,500 at the Assembly level, Rs 3,000 at the Lok Sabha level, and Rs 7,500 at the state level. For special groups, namely, women, Scheduled Castes and Scheduled Tribes, and Below the Poverty Line (BPL) members, the fee is cut by half. Only those who have a corpus of about Rs 5-10 lakh can aspire to win the Assembly-level Youth Congress elections, one IYC office-bearer from Bihar, who did not want to be named, said.

At the higher levels, such as that of the state president, the stakes become even higher as the person who is contesting needs to have the clout to transport and arrange lodging and boarding for all members who will vote for him in the place that voting is supposed to take place, the office-bearer said. The money required to fight IYC elections at the higher level varies according to the socio-economic profile of states. The amount of money spent in states such as Bihar is still modest compared to the Rs 2 crore spent in Tamil Nadu for the position of the Lok Sabha Youth Congress president's post, according to the figures of a party insider.

In response to these allegations of money playing a big role in the elections, the system was modified in such a way that now booth-level elected office-bearers directly elect those at the Assembly Youth Congress committee, Lok Sabha Youth Congress committee and State Youth Congress committee levels. However, this has not really meant that big leaders cannot manipulate the system. In fact, one ex-Youth Congress leader admitted that it is only the senior leaders who would have the clout to 'manage' the elections from the lowest levels. Even in such a system it is difficult to imagine common people coming into the Congress party at the grassroots and rising through the ranks because at the higher levels, the election system would make it impossible for those without sufficient resources to rise to the top.

The Youth Congress' system, with its heavy emphasis on corporate-style training and performance measurement mechanisms has not been able to tackle what is a fundamental problem in the Congress party and not the Youth Congress and NSUI specifically. Harish Khare, while making a case for organizational elections in the Congress party wrote in *The Hindu*: '. . . the "leaders" at the State and Central level seem to have devised a mutually self-serving protocol to keep their stranglehold on the organizational hierarchy at the expense of the party's democratic vitality'[3].

Rahul and his team seem to have been carried away with the exercise of organization building, its tools and technologies, rather than focus on the more practical and politically-relevant side of it. More internal democracy in the Congress is a pre-requisite for the entire Congress system becoming open. The internal elections idea in itself is sound. However, this needs to be done in conjunction with a devolution of powers from the 'high command'. New leadership has to be developed by the Congress in the states rather than relying on the old cliques of those who have become dependent on the 'high command' for survival. There is also need for a critical evaluation of the system employed by the Youth Congress before it is adapted for use in the Congress. What is clear is that the overt emphasis on corporate ideas and an NGO-centric conception of politics is not sufficient to bring about change in the Congress.

∼

The Youth Congress and NSUI internal democracy experiment was intended to produce youth leaders for the Congress and create a committed cadre-like support for the party. It was meant to help the Congress reach out to new young voters. However, at the moment it does not appear to be playing a decisive part in influencing election results in favour of the Congress. On the contrary, in states where the Congress organization is healthy and functions well, it is the Youth Congress which is able to capitalize on the Congress' strengths and put in a decent performance.

In Kerala, Uttarakhand and Punjab, the Youth Congress put in relatively decent performances. It managed a 50 per cent strike rate or thereabouts. In the 2012 Uttarakhand polls, the Congress with 32 seats out of 117 emerged as the single-largest party by a margin of one seat. In Punjab, it lost the elections (46 out of 117). The party had given tickets to five Youth Congress candidates in each state out of which two won the elections.

In the 2011 Kerala Assembly elections, the Congress-led United Democratic Front (UDF) alliance managed to win the elections by a slender majority. The UDF managed 72 seats in the 140-member house with a half-way mark of 71, while the CPM-led Left Democratic Front (LDF) won 68 seats. Eleven Youth Congress and NSUI candidates were given tickets out of which seven won in the elections. The Youth Congress also did well in Assam and West Bengal in the 2011 Assembly Polls where it won elections. In Assam it has been the dominant political player and in West Bengal it won elections in alliance with the Trinamool Congress which defeated the CPM-led Left Front which had ruled the state uninterrupted for thirty-four years.

In states such as UP, Tamil Nadu and Bihar where the Congress is not a principal political player, the infusion of new blood into the party organization through the Youth Congress and the NSUI is yet to kick-start the party's revival.

In UP the Congress' performance was a dismal 28 out of 403 seats in the 2012 Assembly polls. The party had given tickets to thirty-five Youth Congress candidates out of which just six won. The results once again showed that Rahul's initiative had been unsuccessful in producing new leaders who could connect with the electorate or create an organization that could double up as a cadre-base for the party. The UP performance, in which Rahul had invested personally, could, in turn, lead to a setback for the nascent Youth Congress experiment in the state. The rival Samajwadi Party's Akhilesh Yadav emerged as a youth icon in the polls. Earlier, in the 2011 Tamil Nadu Assembly polls, the Congress contested in 63 seats in alliance with the DMK. It could bag only five seats. All the ten Youth Congress nominees given tickets lost, including the state Youth Congress President M Yuvaraja. In the 2010 Bihar Assembly polls, the Congress was able to win a mere four seats out of 243. The Assembly elections were held close on the heels of the Bihar Youth Congress elections. When the tickets were finally given out, a surge of disappointment from Youth Congress ranks resulted in the youth organization playing a limited role in the electioneering process.

Politics for the Youth?

Rahul Gandhi made the connection between India's population profile as a young nation, and the fact that his own relative youth put him in a position to capitalize on this statistic. 'Yuva (youth) is a term which defines age, it also defines 70 per cent of our country. I am talking of the youth but I am also talking about the 70 per cent of the population today,'[4] he said at a press conference in Uttarakhand during the same tour. However, his politics as a leader of young Indians came to be centred on his work within the Congress organization.

He appeared to conflate the Congress' need to groom new leadership within its ranks with the needs of the youth. Even in India's most impoverished areas, the most important thing for the youth was never going to be about a way into politics. 'There are many issues facing the youth. Their biggest problem is that they don't have opportunities for economic betterment. Not being able to enter politics is not a big problem,' one Youth Congress leader said.

Rahul, however, clubbed education and jobs with political participation. Therefore, what was sold as Rahul's youth outreach mission could never go beyond a proposed large-scale overhaul of the Congress' youth and student wings. He continues to be projected by the Congress as its 'youth icon' but his work in the Youth Congress and the NSUI has not helped him build on that projection in a significant way. Rahul's efforts have at best lead to the setting up of a parallel Congress organization that he will himself lead someday.

For four years or so Rahul was fully immersed with the IYC and the NSUI. He refused to be drawn into a host of burning issues ranging from Kashmir to Telangana and even corruption for a very long time. His plea right through this period was that he was the AICC general secretary in charge of the IYC and the NSUI and his job was bringing young people into politics. Because Rahul has invested significant time and effort in the project, its shortcomings are reflected as the shortcomings of Rahul's politics.

PART FOUR

AN INCONSISTENT
AND OPPORTUNISTIC
BRAND OF POLITICS

13

BRAND-BUILDING AND THE 'TWO INDIAS' THEORY

Two days after Rahul Gandhi was inducted into the CWC, on 26 September 2007, a delegation of AICC general secretaries met Dr Manmohan Singh, and handed him a petition that requested him to immediately extend the government's flagship rural jobs scheme, the National Rural Employment Guarantee Act (NREGA), to the entire country. Rahul was the unofficial leader of this delegation, which included old hands such as Veerappa Moily, Margaret Alva and Janardan Dwivedi among others.

NREGA was already operational in 330 districts and had an in-built provision to roll it out across India in the future. The Congress wanted to convert it into an opportunity to get its first family to claim credit for popular measures. Through the petition it sought to boost the image of its freshly-anointed heir and associate him with the government's largest welfare scheme.

At that time, talk of mid-term elections was in the air. In the UPA-I coalition, Congress was headed for a showdown with its outside allies, the Left parties, over the Indo-US civilian nuclear cooperation agreement. Of course, Rahul could have done with an extra coat of 'pro-poor' varnish in those uncertain times. The delegation told the PM[1] that the move would be 'in the interest of the aam aadmi' and 'reinforce' the 'government's commitment to eradicating poverty'. Within two days, the government announced that NREGA would cover all 600 districts at an additional cost of Rs 8,000 crore, taking the annual allocation for the scheme to Rs 20,000 crore[2].

It was not just the Congress that worked hard to create Rahul Gandhi's political image between 2008 and 2011. Rahul too groomed himself for his future role as a key player in national politics, leading up to his becoming the top decision-maker in the Congress and maybe the prime minister when he felt the time was right.

This was part of a larger exercise, as he consciously aimed to create an image as a representative of the poor and marginalized.

The main plank of Brand Rahul was to view India as a country that comprised 'two Indias'; it was a simplistic division between a 'rich India' and a 'poor India'. To bolster his political theory, and back it with practical knowledge, he undertook several 'discover India' tours, and trudged through the poorest regions of the country. He spent nights in the homes of the poor and Dalits, and ate with them. Apart from NREGA, he wholeheartedly backed a Rs 60,000 crore farm loan waiver announced in the Union Budget of 2008-09. Like with the NREGA, the Congress projected this measure too as the UPA government's, and especially Sonia Gandhi's, gift to the farmers of the country. Rahul too was part of this projection. He backed various economic packages such as the one for the drought-hit Bundelkhand region straddling parts of Uttar Pradesh and Madhya Pradesh, and those for specific groups like weavers, found in significant numbers in Eastern UP.

He took up cudgels on behalf of Orissa's Dongaria Kondh tribe in the latter's fight to save the Niyamgiri hills from being mined by the global mining conglomerate, Vedanta. He undertook a padayatra to side with the farmers of Western UP who wanted better compensation for their land. He went to Mirchipur village in Haryana in April 2010, where members of the dominant Jat community allegedly set fire to eighteen Dalit homes. He went to Rajasthan's Bharatpur district in October 2011 where clashes between Gujjars and Meo Muslims and subsequent police firing resulted in the deaths of ten Muslims. He met rape victims in UP through 2011, ostensibly to highlight the precarious law and order situation in the state.

Even when he supported esoteric, global initiatives that seemed to have no connect with 'poor India', he couched them in the 'right' language. During the Indo-US nuclear deal debate in Parliament in July 2008, he said 'poverty was directly connected to energy security'[3]. He invoked the hardships of two women, Kalawati and Sasikala, whom he met on his earlier tour of Maharashtra's drought-prone Vidharbha region. For him, Kalawati, the widow of a farmer who had committed suicide, represented an ideal example of an individual who had diversified her income. A nation should do the same in the energy sector by seeking alternative sources, including nuclear. The nuclear deal, he maintained would benefit Sasikala, who did not have access to power.

Unfortunately, although there seemed to be a plan behind these endeavours, Rahul's politics came across as half-baked, inconsistent and opportunistic. It lacked a sustained engagement with the issues that he himself pursued from time to time. Somehow, his efforts acquired overtones of being opportunistic, or driven by the electoral needs of the Congress. His inability to deal with fast-unfolding and crucial political situations became apparent in the way he conducted himself during the thirteen-day Anna Hazare fast in August 2011. After days of conspicuous silence, Rahul made a brief appearance in Parliament, and proposed that the Lokpal institution should be given constitutional status. It had no bearing on the stand-off between Hazare and the government. Although he dubbed his proposal as a 'game-changer', it invited criticism and mockery from political opponents and critics.

According to Santosh Desai, CEO of Future Brands, an expert on branding and consumer insight, it would have been easier for Rahul to have become the Congress' 'educated face' as his father, Rajiv Gandhi had been. 'He could have chosen to speak for the new India, the international India, and the globally acceptable India. It was just a natural mantle waiting to be taken,' Desai said. However, Rahul, according to Desai, chose the 'much harder road' and decided to work at the district-level and with the internal party organization.

Possibly, after the Congress' 2004 electoral victory, which among other factors was credited to its *'Congress ka haath/aam aadmi ke saath'* (Congress' 'hand' is with the common man) slogan, Rahul believed the party had hit on the right formula. It matched his thinking too. Therefore, he set out to woo the old Congress constituencies of Dalits, tribals and the poor. Desai believes Rahul did grasp the 'deeper understanding of the idea of image' and that 'image is a consequence of action'. However, while Rahul did 'show signs of becoming something' and differentiating himself from other politicians, the image never 'crystallized'.

According to former editor of the *Times of India*, Dileep Padgaonkar, Rahul 'appeared to be a mix of the earnest jholawala, the social activist, or the NGO-type' while also having 'a certain degree of the element of the boy-scout in him.' Padgaonkar said Rahul was not an 'ideologue' and had 'endeavoured to be away from the categorization of right, left, right-of-centre and left-of-centre' which were the categorizations of Indian public discourse. 'There is a big risk he runs in political terms. How is he going to be perceived? This is a country which adores categories. As of now he is defying all categories, but has not yet emerged with a strong brand identity. This is something he has to make up his mind about,' he said.

He compared Rahul to other members of his family. 'His grandmother had cultivated that brand image to perfection. His father began to develop one but a series of things happened where he couldn't complete that exercise. His mother has a very strong brand image and one of the important reasons was the single gesture of renouncing the prime ministership which was offered to her on a platter.'

Rahul's 'Two Indias'

Over the past four years, the leitmotif of Rahul's speeches has been about 'two Indias'. He has relentlessly peddled the idea at election meetings, in Parliament, and at Congress conventions. At its basic level, there is an India of the rich (*amiron ka Hindustan*) and poor (*garibon ka Hindustan*). Congress was the only party that stood for 'poor India' or the 'aam aadmi'; all others represented the affluent India. That's why the BJP launched its 'India Shining' ad campaign before the 2004 general elections, the CPM stood for 'rich Bengal', and Nitish Kumar in Bihar ignored the poor and economically deprived in the state.

Although the idea of the 'two Indias' dates back to the 1960s, it grew rapidly due to the impact of economic liberalization post 1991. According to this view, the opening up of the economy had resulted in the emergence of two distinct classes – those who benefitted from reforms, and those who were left behind or further impoverished by them.

One of the first times that Rahul mentioned the idea was at the AICC session in November 2007[4] after he became the general secretary. Speaking in Hindi, he said, 'In our country on one side are those people who have had a chance to partake in the process of building India. On the other side are those who don't have an opportunity to partake in this growth . . . Some people believe that helping the poor to progress is a form of charity. This thinking is absolutely wrong. This view negates the fact that India's common people are its most valuable resource. In their hearts is that spark, that desire for change on whose strength India will be rebuilt. To convert that spark into fire, we will have to connect India's poor and marginalized people to India's and the world's economies. I believe this to be the biggest challenge facing our generation.'

Later, during the Budget discussion[5] in 2008-09, he added: '. . . there are two distinct voices among India's people today. The louder of these voices comes from an India that is empowered, an India that has proven to itself and to the world that it will shape the future. It is an India rich with opportunity and talent, straining to be unleashed. The other voice is yet to be empowered. It is not as loud, but reverberates across the country. It is the voice of disenfranchised people reminding us that they too have potential to fulfil . . . Some believe that the progress of these two Indias is not just separable but mutually exclusive. Some believe that India can shine only when we direct attention and resources to those Indians who already soar, while ignoring the aspirations of the disempowered . . . Our government believes that India's growth can and must be symbiotic . . . Our philosophy is not to choose which India to nurture, but to grow together.'

His most lucid presentation was in the keynote address[6] he delivered at the Bucerius Summer School in Hamburg in August 2009. He said he had experienced as much of a 'culture shock' when he travelled from New Delhi to rural Uttar Pradesh, as he had when he travelled from New Delhi to Hamburg for the lecture. Sixty years back, there was just one India which was poor but now the country stood at the 'crossroads' with 'two distinct Indias'. 'There is no simple way to categorize this divide. It is, for example, not a clear rural-urban divide. There are cities in India that are extremely disconnected and there are rural pockets that connect seamlessly to the world,' he said.

The 'connected India' was one which had roads, ports, airports, electricity and broadband Internet; boasted of 'a young and thriving middle class with global needs and practices' and produced 'goods and services valued in the world market'; it had access to education, healthcare and information and communicated fluently in English with the rest of the world. He said this India produced a large proportion of the country's wealth. 'It is growing rapidly and providing us with the financial resources to connect and transform the other India.' The other India according to him, did not 'produce the goods, deliver the services or supply the skills that the world uses' and was 'twice the size of its connected counterpart', but unlike it 'politically ... pack(ed) the punch of a super heavyweight'.

The academic Pratap Bhanu Mehta, in *Outlook*[7] magazine described 'the two Indias theme' as a 'self-fulfilling intellectual construct' in the context of Rahul's frequent invocation of it. According to him, 'the Congress's mistake is to project the idea that these so-called two Indias are not connected; that one is not creating the conditions for pulling the other up.'

This wasn't entirely true. Rahul grasped the fact that it wasn't easy to make clear distinctions about the 'two Indias'.

At the Burari plenary session of the Congress in December 2010, he defined what he meant by the 'aam aadmi'. 'The aam aadmi in India is that person who does not have a connection to the system,' he said. His examples not only included the tribal boy from Niyamgiri 'who is thrown off his land without justice', the Dalit boy in Jhansi 'who is forced to sit at the back of the class room', but also the young professional in Bengaluru 'who can't get her child into a good school', the university topper in Shillong who cannot get a job 'because he doesn't know the right people' and the businessman in Hyderabad 'who is pushed aside because he does not have connections'.

But as is the case with most political rhetoric, the nuances get lost. At the end of the day, the message that reached the sections of the two Indias was that Rahul could not think beyond his theory and NREGA.

14

INCONSISTENCIES AND
SYMBOLISM

Rahul Gandhi's 'discovery of India' tours (as the press cheekily labelled them) were sincere. In the first half of 2008, he travelled to Madhya Pradesh, Orissa, Karnataka, Chhattisgarh and Maharashtra. He wanted to see and understand people's problems at first-hand. This tied up with one of the core practices which characterized the 'Toyota Way', which was also at the core of Rahul's political strategy. As part of the problem-solving techniques employed by Totoya employees, from the juniormost to the seniormost, they are encouraged to get first-hand information about the issues they tackle.

Dr Jeffery K Liker in *The Toyota Way* held this principle, known in Japanese as *genchi genbutsu*, to be what distinguished Toyota from other management approaches. He says it means 'going to the place to see the actual situation for understanding'[1] and is not just restricted to the factory floor but is a philosophy that guides employees in all branches of the company from product development, sales, distribution, or public affairs. 'You cannot be sure you understand any part of the business problem unless you go and see for yourself first-hand. It is unacceptable to take anything for granted or to rely on the reports of others[2].'

However, unlike in the case of Toyota, Rahul's Indian excursions were seen as symbolic, rather than committed, and part of political one-upmanship. For example, take the case of the tactics to stay with poor families, especially the Dalits in UP, which became his political signature. His night halts enraged BSP's Mayawati, UP's Dalit chief minister at the time, who counts on a majority of the state's Dalits for unflinching support. Though Rahul denied that he specifically visited Dalits, Mayawati perceived a political challenge. At a public meeting in Azamgarh[3] on 7 April 2008, she said the Congress sent its 'yuvraj' or young prince, to live and eat with Dalits to garner their votes. She charged Rahul with using a 'special soap' and 'incense' to purify himself after staying with the Dalits.

When the former British foreign secretary and Labour MP David Miliband visited India in January 2009, Rahul took him to Amethi for an overnight stay at the home of a Dalit woman in Semra village, and to meet members of a women's self-help group. He wanted to show him a glimpse of 'rural India' rather than the India of the big cities. '. . . I thought it would be quite interesting for the foreign secretary to come to rural India and have a look at what people here are doing and the type of energy that is prevailing here and the type of energy India is going to use in the future,'[4] Rahul said. The Opposition said the Miliband episode proved that Rahul engaged in 'poverty tourism'.

A ride on Mumbai's suburban rail network in February 2010 was an attempt to score political brownie points over the Shiv Sena, which was vocal against the growing population of North Indian migrants in Mumbai. Rahul decried the

Sena's stance; the Sena warned that if Rahul visited the city, he would be black-flagged. But being some sort of a political guerilla fighter[5], Rahul outwitted them when he travelled on the Mumbai 'local', the lifeline of the city's working population, from Andheri in Western Mumbai to Dadar in the central part of the city and then to Ghatkopar in the central suburbs, a distance of less than 25 kms that he covered in under an hour. In the process, he avoided the road routes where the Sena planned to show black flags to him. Though his Mumbai train ride was a success from an image-building point of view, he could not capitalize on the political mileage he gained. It was a one-off. He could not repeat the chutzpah he displayed to trump Shiv Sena in its backyard. He tried a similar strategy in Western UP's Bhatta and Parsaul villages which he entered by stealth to side with farmers protesting against the Mayawati government's land acquisition practices. However, in that instance he could not pull it off. The benefits from that trip were lost because he over-played his hand. In his eagerness to harness local disaffection, he made over-the-top allegations implying the state government's hand in mass murders in the two villages which could not be substantiated.

To return to Rahul's train rides, it was not just in Mumbai that Rahul took the local transport. He made several trips on Delhi's Metro rail network. He even undertook a 36-hour train journey from Gorakhpur to Mumbai on the Gorakhpur-Lokmanya Tilak Superfast Express to understand the problems of migrants from Eastern UP and Bihar who travelled to Mumbai in search of livelihoods.

The symbolic nature of his visits and travels came to the fore, when the media reported that many of those he spent a night with in UP or Maharashtra continued to live in dilapidated homes, and their financial conditions remained wretched. 'Going and staying in somebody's house is a very powerful symbol to use in politics. The question that needs to be asked is whether Rahul followed through after his visit,' a Congress functionary said, pointing out that a problem with Rahul's politics was its lack of 'deliverables'.

~

Niyamgiri should have been a feather in Rahul's political hat. His intervention in this politico-socio-economic minefield sparked off a huge debate on the rights of local communities, especially the tribals. It led to a refusal of environment clearance for a huge mining-cum-aluminium project mooted by an Indian MNC, Vedanta Group. It triggered sweeping changes in the new mining bill, which is before the Parliament, to protect local communities. It resulted in a heated discussion on whether the state should give up economic development at the expense of social costs and implications.

However, this was not to be. At the end of day, Rahul's politics in this case was seen as inconsistent, incomplete and incoherent. It was seen as an amateur act.

When Rahul began his 'discovery of India' tour in March 2008, the first state on his itinerary was Orissa. On 7 March 2008 the very first day of his tour, he went to Ijurpa, a small tribal village in Lanjigarh on the foothills of the Niyamgiri hills in the backward Kalahandi district.

He met the members of the Dongaria Kondh tribals, who welcomed him to the beat of drums, garlands and even by the traditional washing of his feet[6]. The tribals told him of their opposition to the 1.7 billion-dollar alumina refinery being set up by the UK-based entrepreneur Anil Aggarwal's Vedanta group[7]. The Orissa government and Vedanta had signed an agreement in October 2004 to set up the refinery complex, which included the supply of bauxite from the proposed mine in Niyamgiri. According to Vedanta[8], the Orissa government had to supply 150 million tonnes of bauxite and had identified the Niyamgiri mines as the initial source for 78 million tonnes.

The Kondh tribals, Dongari and Kutia, consider the hill to be sacred and believe it to be the abode of their god-king 'Niyam Raja'. They feared a loss of habitat and ecological destruction of the Niyamgiri hills, a rich bio-diversity zone known for rare flora and fauna including twenty types of orchids and the golden gecko lizard. The hills provided the Kondhs with a livelihood. Protests against the refinery and the proposed mine had been on since 2005.

Speaking at a 'Save the forest rally' in Bhawanipatana, the district headquarter of Kalahandi, the same day in March 2008, Rahul said: *'Kalahandi ka, aur adivasiyon ka Delhi mein ek sipahi hai. Uska naam Rahul Gandhi hai'*[9] (Kalahandi and its tribals have a soldier in Delhi. His name is Rahul Gandhi). At a press conference in Bhubaneshwar three days later, Rahul was asked whether or not mining should be allowed in the Niyamgiri hills. 'It's a broader question than the Niyamgiri hills. The question is what happens to the resources that the state has? What happens to the people who live on the land on which these resources are? I am not against industrialization per se. What I am for is fairness . . . My personal view is that doing mining there will destroy the environment. It will destroy the water supply of thousands of people, it will destroy the culture of thousands of people. And I am against it personally.'[10]

Two years after Rahul had spoken out against mining in the Niyamgiri hills, on 24 August 2010, the Ministry of Environment and Forests refused to grant clearances for the Odisha Mining Corporation Ltd and Vedanta subsidiary, Sterlite Industries (India) Ltd's, proposed bauxite mine in Niyamgiri. It was Rahul's first political victory. He had played a direct role in influencing the Niyamgiri decision.

Rahul Gandhi went back to Lanjigarh on 26 August 2010 to address a Congress-organized tribal rally. He congratulated the tribals on their victory against the MNC conglomerate. '. . . I told you . . . your voice . . . is being crushed . . . I will be the soldier for that voice . . . I have come to tell you that your voice reached Delhi and it is you who have saved your own land. I was standing by your side. I helped in whatever way I could. However, this victory is yours. It is the victory of the Adivasis,' he said.

What went unnoticed was that Rahul's win had come against all adversities. In August 2008, the Supreme Court gave its go-ahead to the proposal. Then it was believed that it was only a matter of time before the mining project came up in Niyamgiri. It was just before the apex court ruling that Rahul became a part of the story. In 2009, once UPA II came to power, the environment ministry was headed by Jairam Ramesh, one of the few Congressmen who had access to Rahul. In end-June 2010, he appointed a committee headed by N C Saxena, a retired IAS officer who was also a member of Sonia Gandhi's NAC, to decide whether Vedanta should be allowed to mine bauxite in Niyamgiri. It was mandated with investigating the 'specific impact on the livelihood, culture and material welfare' of the local tribal groups in Orissa affected by the project[11], or all the points that Rahul had raised during his 2008 trip.

In August 2010, the committee recommended that mining should not be allowed in Niyamgiri. 'Allowing mining in the proposed mining lease area by depriving two Primitive Tribal Groups of their rights over the proposed mining site in order to benefit a private company would shake the faith of tribal people in the laws of the land. Since the company in question has repeatedly violated the law, allowing it further access to the proposed mining lease area at the cost of the rights of the Kutia and Dongaria Kondh, will have serious consequences for the security and well-being of the entire country,'[12] it concluded. Days after the report, Ramesh rejected forest clearances to the mining proposal[13].

Rahul's 'sipahi' act was lauded by his mother Sonia Gandhi. In her customary 'letter to Congresspersons' in the September 2010 issue of the party mouthpiece *Congress Sandesh*, she said: 'The Congress's commitment to the welfare of the underprivileged and weaker sections was reinforced after the decision to protect the Niyamgiri region from mining by party general secretary Rahul Gandhi, who assured the tribal people that their fundamental interests would not be sacrificed.'[14]

But it ended as a limited victory for Rahul. For people questioned whether Niyamgiri was only a one-off case, and did not reflect a firm ideological view and sustained engagement with tribal issues. More importantly, it was perceived to be an inconsistent position on the part of the future PM.

Before his 2008 tour, Rahul had never been to Lanjigarh or spoken up in favour of the anti-Vedanta protesters, whose agitation began in 2005. Moreover, he did not visit the area between March 2008, when he first went there, and August 2010, when he visited it after the government's refusal to grant environment clearance. He did not visit the area subsequently, even though protests continued as the matter is still tied up in the courts. But to give credit to Rahul, there have been two attempts to clear Vedanta's project since August 2010 by the Union Ministry of Environment and Forests (MoEF), but he has indirectly stepped in both times to scuttle it.

What is critical is that during the same period, there were similar protests against the South Korean steelmaker Posco's steel plant in Orissa. There were also furious agitations against land acquisition for the Indonesia-based Salim Group's chemical hub and Tata's proposed car factory in West Bengal's

Nandigram and Singur respectively. However, Rahul did not engage in public with these issues. In July 2011, Rahul did say that if non-agricultural land was available for Posco's 12-million tpa (tonnes per annum) steel plant, it would be a 'better solution' to the log-jam. He felt the need to ensure proper compensation and rehabilitation for those affected by the project. However, anti-Posco activist Prafulla Samantara said that 'Rahul Gandhi has not taken an interest in the Posco issue. The prime minister's office is directly monitoring the developments in the Posco case.'

15

POLITICAL OPPORTUNISM AND INACTION

It was another case of shoot-and-scoot politics that has become Rahul Gandhi's hallmark. In the pre-dawn hours of 11 May 2011, he rode pillion on a bike and sneaked into the villages of Bhatta and Parsaul in Western UP, where the state government had imposed Section 144 of the Criminal Procedure Code (CrPC), prohibiting the assembly of more than five people.

The restriction was lifted a few hours before Rahul's entry. But the situation continued to be tense after clashes between the state police and the villagers in the area a few days back. Rahul's daredevil entry into the two villages was broadcast by several TV channels through the day. The scenes showed Rahul as the anti-establishment, angry young man, who was ready for a political showdown. He was arrested late night along with other Congress leaders like Digvijay Singh, Rita Bahuguna Joshi and Raj Babbar. Rahul was immediately released on bail, but was escorted out of UP to the Delhi border, located 60 kilometres away.

For many political pundits, this seemed like a perfect way to launch the campaign for the UP Assembly elections, slated to be held in early 2012. An emotional connect here with the voters, and upstaging the state government would ensure that Congress won more seats than before. The political prey lay before him, but Rahul could not attack directly as his strategy was opportunistic, rather than realistic.

The issue in Bhatta-Parsaul was linked to demands for higher compensation for land acquisition from the farmers. The row had seen sporadic eruption of violent protests since 2008, when the state government acquired land for the 165-km-long Yamuna Expressway project, which aimed to connect Greater Noida with Agra, and develop residential and commercial properties along the six-lane highway. *Down to Earth[1]* magazine reported that the local body wanted to develop 44,000 ha (hectares) of land, of which only 9.3 per cent was for the expressway. While 4,100 ha was given to the Jaypee Group, the builder, for the expressway, 2,500 ha was handed over as five 'land parcels' for residential and commercial purposes.

Farmers held demonstrations against the low compensation rates. They resented the fact that sellers situated closer to Delhi got higher rates. More importantly, there was a wide discrepancy between the rates at which the state government acquired the land and the ones that it charged from Jaypee and other real estate developers. There was up to a ten-fold difference or more in the two rates and the farmers I met during a trip to Western UP in July 2011 alleged that officials had taken a substantial cut from the land sales.

As a result, violence broke out between the protestors and state police. In Aligarh's Tappal block, in August 2010, it left five people dead, including one provincial arms constabulary personnel. Rahul made an unannounced visit to Tappal in pouring rain to back the agitating farmers. He visited some of the families who had lost their kin in the fighting. Since then, he disappeared from the scene until he reappeared, almost magically, in Bhatta-Parsaul on 11 May 2011.

The two villages in UP's Gautam Budh Nagar district were the epicentre of the farmers' protests. A few months ago, when Manveer Tewatia, a farmers' leader from the adjacent Bulandshahar district, came to lead the agitation, trouble brewed between the farmers and police. On 7 May, the two clashed after the farmers held two employees of the state transport corporation captive. Four people, including two policemen, died in the violence; the district magistrate Deepak Agarwal was shot in the leg. Tewatia went absconding and the UP police announced a cash reward of Rs 50,000 for information leading to his arrest. The state clamped down Section 144; the roads leading into the two villages were sealed. There was an air of fear in Parsaul when I visited the village on 11 May 2011. Large crowds gathered outside the house where Rahul rested in the afternoon. A sizeable Youth Congress contingent from Delhi managed the crowds.

Locals said that all the men had gone away from the village fearing more reprisals from the police. They claimed the police misbehaved with the women who had been left alone after the men left. The villagers seemed grateful that the incidents in Bhatta and Parsaul had become public due to Rahul's visit. Rahul held an indefinite dharna; the Congress demanded a judicial probe into the incidents of firing on 7 May. It wanted the villagers who had been arrested to be released.

This was viewed as Rahul's turning point in politics. His team was convinced that Bhatta-Parsaul would develop into a Singur-like agitation against the UP Chief Minister Mayawati. The facts were before them; two days after Rahul's visit to the area, election results were announced in West Bengal. Trinamool Congress' Mamata Banerjee, currently the chief minister of West Bengal, who had spearheaded the Singur agitation, decisively defeated the Left Front, which had been in power for more than three decades. Rahul's team set up a website named after the twin villages to garner support for the 'movement'.

To keep the issue simmering, Rahul met Manmohan Singh with a delegation of farmers from Bhatta-Parsaul on 16 May 2011. 'People are being murdered ... there is a large ... seventy-foot ashes there with dead bodies inside (sic). Everybody in the village knows ... Women have been raped, people have been thrashed, houses have been destroyed,'[2] Rahul told the media later. His statements sparked a huge controversy as they suggested that the state's machinery had committed mass murders and rapes in Bhatta-Parsaul.

Unfortunately for Rahul, the charges could not be proved. Media teams from Delhi found no evidence of either mass murders or rapes. Subsequently, the UP government said the preliminary forensic tests of ash samples collected from the villages showed no evidence of any human remains. It revealed only the presence of 'molten synthetic material' and 'cowdung ash'[3]. The question of whether the state police had raped women in Bhatta-Parsaul became entangled in a number of contradictory accounts. The matter is still under investigation and is being looked into by the state's crime and criminal investigation branch on the directions of the Allahabad High Court.

The Congress was forced to come out in Rahul's defence. Party spokesperson Janardan Dwivedi said Rahul had not mentioned the number seventy-four or talked of seventy-four bodies (as was reported in some places) in the ash heap in Bhatta-Parsaul; his words had been distorted by the media. But the BSP, Mayawati's party, and BJP came out strongly against Rahul. BSP said that he had made 'baseless allegations' and advised him to show restraint; BJP spokesperson Nirmala Sitaraman counselled Rahul against 'exaggeration'.

The impression that gathered ground was that Rahul was politically naïve; his insinuations about large-scale killings and rapes appeared to vindicate the Opposition leaders' public references to Rahul's greenhorn status. BJP's Rajnath Singh once described him as a 'bachcha' or child and, in private, many Congress leaders agreed with such an assessment.

To be fair to Rahul, Bhatta-Parsaul forced the Centre to do something about land acquisition. The UPA government made attempts to change the colonial Land Acquisition Act in India dating back to 1894. The 1894 Act gives the government inordinate powers to acquire land for 'public purposes'. Over the years, this has not only come to imply land meant for public infrastructure projects but also for private industry and real estate developers. If the Centre introduced a new law, it would standardize and set the benchmark for an equitable process to acquire land, pay compensation, and rehabilitate the affected.

The earlier attempts to amend the old Act had failed until then due to the lack of political consensus. In 2007, UPA-I introduced two separate Bills to tackle problems associated with land acquisition – The Land Acquisition (Amendment) Bill and The Resettlement and Rehabilitation Bill. The Bills were passed by the Lok Sabha in 2009, but lapsed as the term of the Lok Sabha ended. During UPA II's tenure, the Trinamool Congress opposed the two Bills.

However, immediately after Bhatta-Parsaul, Union Home Minister P Chidambaram announced that the government planned to introduce an amended Land Acquisition Bill in the next session of Parliament, which was a couple of months away. Within a few weeks, the Sonia Gandhi-backed NAC submitted its recommendations for a consolidated Bill that combined the earlier Bills.

Shortly after that Jairam Ramesh was moved from the environment to the rural development ministry. This time, his job was to introduce the new Bill in Parliament at the earliest. By the end of July 2011, the ministry released the draft of an integrated Land Acquisition, Rehabilitation and Resettlement Bill, 2011 (LARR). Over a month later, the Cabinet passed it with a few amendments and introduced it in the Lok Sabha on 7 September 2011.

'Without Rahul Gandhi's intervention and involvement at every step, the Bill would not have been prepared and introduced in fifty-five days,'[4] Ramesh said. He admitted that the 'political context' in which the Bill had been introduced was Rahul Gandhi's July padayatra in Western UP when he toured the districts which had witnessed land acquisition agitations. Rahul made 'key suggestions' for the proposed legislation. The Bill was sent to the Parliamentary Standing Committee on Rural Development headed by BJP's Sumitra Mahajan. The committee failed to finalize its report by the 2011 Winter Session of Parliament. As a result the Bill could not be passed before the UP elections in February-March 2012 which is what the Congress and Rahul had wanted.

The Standing Committee submitted its report to Parliament during the Budget Session of Parliament in May 2012. It recommended important changes in the government's Bill to effect a further tightening of land acquisition norms, especially with regard to the definition of 'public purpose'. It spoke of completely doing away with the State's role in acquiring land for private enterprises, public-private-partnership (PPP) projects, and even public enterprises. But Ramesh indicated the government might find it hard to accept the panel's proposals on PPP projects. 'The government must have a role in land acquisition . . . We must recognize that we are not at a stage of development where the government's role can be eliminated.'[5] He indicated that the government would introduce a revised Bill in the Monsoon Session of Parliament after further political consultations.

However, Rahul himself did not speak on the subject after the UP polls in March until the end of the Budget Session of Parliament in May 2012. This reinforced the impression that Rahul's intervention in Bhatta-Parsaul, and the land acquisition issue, was driven by political opportunism. He knew what Mamata had achieved electorally in West Bengal, as she rode a wave on land acquisition. He thought he could do the same in the forthcoming UP Assembly elections. Which is why he chose UP as his political playground, and not other states, and it was timed to reap political benefits. Rahul's role in Niyamgiri too can be partly seen as an opportunistic tactic to script a political comeback in a state where the Congress had been out of power since 2000. It provided an opportunity for him to challenge Naveen Patnaik, BJD's leader and three-time chief minister whose popularity is attributed to his 'pro-development' credentials. That the Orissa government through its MoU with Vedanta was an involved party helped the bid to challenge the BJD. Rahul's effort did help the Congress' revival in Kalahandi. Bhakta Charan Das, who brought Rahul to Lanjigarh in 2008, became the MP from the seat in the 2009 general elections. The Congress was also able to get four MLAs elected from the region. Beyond this, the gambit was unlikely to pay off. 'It will not be an easy task for Rahul to win the confidence of tribals just by enacting plays,' said writer, activist and journalist Sudhir Pattnaik. The Congress was trounced by the BJD in the panchayat union polls in early 2012.

～

The further weakening of Brand Rahul was due to inaction on several issues of national importance, chief among them being corruption. By the middle of 2011, UPA II was on the back-foot over corruption charges in connection with the 2G spectrum scam, which according to one estimate of the Comptroller and Auditor General (CAG)could have cost the exchequer as much as 1,76,000 crore, the Commonwealth Games scam, and the Adarsh housing society scam among others.

The anti-corruption sentiment against the Congress-led Central government was further catalysed by the Anna Hazare movement. The 74-year-old social worker and activist from Maharashtra became the face of an agitation to evolve a comprehensive anti-corruption legislation in India. On 5 April 2011, he began the first of his two fasts-unto-death for the setting up of an independent anti-corruption watchdog, the Lokpal, and the passage of the Jan Lokpal Bill by Parliament. A self-proclaimed Gandhian, Hazare had led anti-corruption crusades in Maharashtra.

The UPA government was caught unawares by the response evoked in cities and small towns, and the round-the-clock coverage by TV channels. It agreed to set up a committee to draft a new Lokpal Bill which would have members from the government and 'Team Anna', as the group of activists around Hazare came to be known. The group included the RTI activist and Magsaysay award-winner Arvind Kejriwal, former IPS officer Kiran Bedi, and Supreme Court advocate Prashant Bhushan. Hazare broke his five-day fast on 9 April 2011 after a gazette notification about the joint drafting panel. He set a deadline of 15 August 2011 for the Jan Lokpal Bill to be passed.

However, the joint drafting panel failed to reconcile the differences between the separate Lokpal Bill drafts. There was a difference of opinion among civil society groups themselves over the Lokpal Bill. Activist Aruna Roy, a member of the National Campaign for People's Right to Information, a group that framed another version of the Lokpal Bill, felt the Jan Lokpal Bill was 'impractical and complicated'[6]. She felt giving widespread powers to an unelected body was a 'threat to democracy'[7]. The government introduced its own Lokpal Bill in Parliament in the Monsoon Session of Parliament on 4 August 2011. The Bill was rejected by Team Anna, which announced Hazare would undertake his next fast from 16 August 2011 for a strong anti-corruption law.

As things turned out, Sonia Gandhi went abroad for surgery for an undisclosed medical condition at the beginning of August. She was likely to be away for two to three weeks, the Congress said. Rahul accompanied her but was expected to be back soon. Sonia had included him in a four-member committee tasked to look after the Congress' day-to-day affairs in her absence that also had senior Congress leaders A K Antony, Ahmed Patel and Janardan Dwivedi in it. His presence in the committee conveyed the message that Sonia had put him in charge during her absence.

Rahul returned to India from the US on 14 August, where Sonia Gandhi had reportedly gone for her surgery. On 15 August, after the Independence Day flag-hoisting ceremony at AICC headquarters, 24 Akbar Road, Manmohan Singh and Rahul held a meeting to discuss the Anna situation. The meeting was attended by other senior Congress leaders including Pranab Mukherjee and Ambika Soni.

On the morning of 16 August, the Delhi police took Hazare into preventive custody as he was about to set out for the fast venue, Delhi's Jayaprakash Narayan Park. He was sent to seven days of judicial custody. The police arrested his teammates soon after Hazare's detention. The arrests sparked outrage. Parliament was adjourned over the incident and Opposition parties demanded a statement by the prime minister on the 'undemocratic' action[8]. It galvanized support for Hazare from urban Indians. Delhi's Chattarsal Stadium turned into a temporary jail as people willingly courted arrest. Candlelight marches were held in many cities. UPA-II had miscalculated the impact of Hazare's arrest. On the sixteenth evening, Manmohan Singh and Rahul met; soon after, Hazare was released. TV channels reported that this was done at Rahul's behest. Hazare refused to leave Tihar Jail. He would not agree to the Delhi police's restrictions on the number of days he could fast. He started his fast inside Tihar. Outside, his supporters gathered in the hundreds if not more.

Over the next two days, as the Delhi police and Team Anna bargained over the fast conditions, Rahul gave the impression of being unconcerned about the developments. Since his mother was away, and deemed Rahul as her representative during her absence, Rahul should have taken charge. Instead, on 18 August, he turned up in Maharashtra's Maval district to visit the families of three farmers who had died after being fired upon by the state police. On 19 August, Hazare's fast shifted to Delhi's Ramlila Maidan. Support for the agitation grew as the government appeared clueless. On 20 August, Manmohan Singh said there was a 'lot of scope for give-and-take' on the draft Bill[9]. However, attempts at informal mediation proved futile. By 22 August, it was apparent that the Congress would have to find a way out. All eyes were on Rahul to see how he would respond in his mother's absence. It was the first test of his leadership as far as handling a big crisis went. Rahul remained silent.

Over the next two days, Pranab Mukherjee, Salman Khurshid, and MP Sandeep Dikshit negotiated with Team Anna. The talks broke down. On 25 August, the prime minister made an appeal in Parliament. 'I urge all Members of the House (Lok Sabha) to join me in making an appeal to Shri Anna Hazare that he has made his point. It has been registered with us. I respect his idealism. I respect him as an individual. He has become the embodiment of our people's disgust and concern about tackling corruption. I applaud him, I salute him. His life is much too precious and therefore, I would urge Shri Anna Hazare to end his fast.'[10]

The PM proposed a formula to break the log-jam so that the Parliament could debate all versions of the Lokpal Bill, including Hazare's. The proceedings of the Parliament's debate, which would reflect a sense of the House[11], could be sent to the Standing Committee on law and justice, which would examine the government's Bill. The PM sent Union minister Vilasrao Deshmukh as his emissary to Hazare. Tensions seemed to de-escalate.

Rahul had still not spoken publicly. His views on the Lokpal Bill(s) were unclear. Only on 26 August did he intervene in Parliament during the Zero Hour. 'An effective Lokpal law is only one element in the legal framework to combat corruption. The Lokpal institution alone cannot be a substitute for a comprehensive anti-corruption code. A set of effective laws is required. Laws that address the following critical issues are necessary to stand alongside the Lokpal initiative: (1) government funding of elections and political parties, (2) transparency in public procurement, (3) proper regulation of sectors that fuel corruption like land and mining, (4) grievance redress mechanisms in public service delivery of old age pensions and ration cards; and (5) continued tax reforms to end tax evasion,' he said.

He proposed that the Lokpal be given constitutional status. 'Madam Speaker, why not elevate the debate and fortify the Lokpal by making it a Constitutional body accountable to

Parliament like the Election Commission of India? I feel the time has come for us to seriously consider this idea,' he said. Later, he described this idea as a 'game-changer'. In Parliament, he made a veiled attack against Hazare. 'Individual dictates, no matter how well intentioned, must not weaken the democratic process ... A tactical incursion, divorced from the machinery of an elected government that seeks to undo the checks and balances created to protect the supremacy of Parliament sets a dangerous precedent for a democracy.'

Until this time, Rahul stayed away from the debate on corruption. He spoke in generic terms about the necessity to bring about 'systemic changes' by reforming the political system itself. At the Congress' 83rd plenary session on 19 December 2010 held in Burari, on the outskirts of Delhi, he said: 'Corruption is the symptom of closed and opaque economic and political structures.' He also referred to a five-point action plan to fight corruption that his mother, Congress President Sonia Gandhi presented at the same conclave and advocated the strictest punishment for those found guilty.

Just over a month later, he said: '. . . Corruption is a serious issue in our politics. And it is not only in one place. It is everywhere in our politics. We have to look at this issue systemically, not in individual cases ... The single biggest reason why it is taking place ... is that the doors of the political system are closed. And your average person who wants to do good . . . who would never allow something like that to happen is not allowed into the political system. And what the youth of this country need to do is they need to start stepping forward and changing the way this political system is structured . . . The answer lies in opening the door of politics to the clean, young person.'[12]

Rahul's 'game changer' of an idea in August 2011 played little part in solving the confrontation between the government and Team Anna. On 27 August, both Houses of Parliament passed a resolution which backed the three issues Hazare had insisted to be included in the Lokpal Bill. A triumphant Hazare called off his thirteen-day fast the next day.

Rahul did not come out smelling of roses in the Anna episode. His inexperience and inability to deal with fast-unfolding political situations became apparent. The general perception was that Sonia Gandhi would have handled the situation differently had she been in India. It appeared as though without the benefit of her advice, he could not come up with a concrete roadmap to resolve the stand-off or defuse the crisis. He seemed disinterested and unable to connect with the rising sentiments against corruption among the middle class. He made a brief, blink-and-you-will-miss-it intervention in Parliament that had no bearing on the debate.

In the months after Anna's autumn fast, the message went out that there were huge question marks over Rahul's brand of politics. Rahul has so far been unable to engage with the many big-ticket issues that confront India. A senior Opposition leader and prominent minister in the previous NDA government compared Rahul Gandhi's role in the Congress to that of an item girl in Bollywood cinema. 'Rahul Gandhi is the Congress party's Mallika Sherawat. He comes, he does his item number and he disappears. He has nothing to do with the script (of the movie),' the leader said.

If Rahul takes credit for NREGA, the loan waiver and the other social security measures, he has to take flak for corruption, policy paralysis and inflation. But like his mother, Rahul has stayed away from taking responsibility for the problems that have gripped the UPA II. Santosh Desai, who believes Rahul started out on the right note says 'there is an uncertainty and a larger lack of clarity' about him. He pointed out that successful brands rely on giving a clear message to their target constituency, but there was an 'overall lack of communication' with Rahul.

Dileep Padgaonkar said it was not sufficient for Rahul to be 'good natured, well-mannered, well-intentioned' as all these qualities were 'taken for granted'. He indicated that Rahul had so far failed to emerge as a well-defined brand. 'At some point, the leadership of the country will demand there is a certain brand image.'

16

THE 'REAL' RAHUL: ON THE ROAD WITH RAHUL DURING HIS WESTERN UP PADAYATRA

Between 5 and 8 July 2011, almost two months after his pillion-ride to Bhatta-Parsaul, Rahul Gandhi undertook a 75 km padayatra from the two villages through over twenty more on the way. He travelled through the three districts of Gautam Budh Nagar, Aligarh and Mathura, which had witnessed the most number of land acquisition protests. Rahul found people wanted to share their grievances and vent anger against the Mayawati government's land acquisition methods.

They expected Rahul to redress their problems. He was the scion of the Nehru-Gandhi family and one of the most influential figures in the ruling establishment in Delhi. Many elderly people at the chaupal sabhas or village square meetings addressed him as pradhan mantriji or prime minister. This drew amused smiles from those present as well as from Rahul himself. The one refrain Rahul heard was that the Centre should immediately pass a new land acquisition Bill in Parliament.

On the first day of his padayatra, Rahul went to Rampur

Baangar village where a local politician, Billu Neta, told Rahul: 'You walk ahead and we will walk behind you.' Another villager used an earthy metaphor: 'Like the hungry look at the roti, people are looking at you. You have to find the solution.' At the Khankhera village on the third-day of the journey, a middle-aged man asked him angrily: 'What can you do for us? Please tell us when you talk what we should expect from you.'

Rahul listened intently to many people. However, this was not always the case. I noticed that he would lapse into inattentive spells while the sabhas were on. As villagers spoke, Rahul would fidget with his BlackBerry or play with something in his hand like a leaf or a piece of thread. He would become conscious of his fidgeting, throw it away and recline into a purposeful listening position.

He would sit on a charpai with village elders and small children. At Syarol village on the second day of his journey he played with two young girls sitting near his feet in the crowd. He took their photos with his phone camera and asked them to smile. When he listened seriously, he would usually sit with his head slightly cocked to one side and his hands would cover his mouth or a part of his face.

His speeches had an unvarying template during the padayatra. They were dull, lacked emotional content, and were unable to tap into the resentment that people felt. He spoke of how the rich were given market rates for their land but the poor were not even told that their land was being taken away. He said their land was being taken for as little as Rs 700–800 per square metre and was being sold for thousands of rupees. He reminded them of how he had gone to Tappal and Bhatta-Parsaul where 'atrocities' were committed against farmers. He promised a 'good Bill' in Parliament to replace the old Land Acquisition Act; at one place he admitted that coalition compulsions could lead to a delay in the passage of the Bill.

He invoked the Haryana government's land acquisition policy to draw a comparison between the BSP and the Congress. He spoke of how farmers in the neighbouring Congress-ruled state were happy to part with their land. He pointed out that there was a process of consultation before land was acquired in Haryana. What he did not point out was that Haryana's methods are far from model. The courts have criticized the policies of the state government, and quashed land acquisition in several instances.

Towards the end of the padayatra, Rahul's attack on Mayawati became direct. He said the problem was not the old land acquisition Bill, which had worked well in Haryana, but the UP government's insincere 'intentions'. He said the Supreme Court had quashed land acquisition in villages of Greater Noida. He added the government acquired large tracts of land to favour a real estate group. The reference to the Jaypee Group was unmistakable though he did not name the company directly. 'India needs development. (What is happening in UP) is not development but loot. All of this being done for one person,' he said.

'They are running the government for big builders,' he told villagers at Khankhera village. At the same meeting, Mandsaur MP Meenakshi Natarajan, a member of his core team, spoke about how land had been taken away from people for the expressway first, but subsequently acquired forcibly to build shopping malls and golf courses. IYC president Rajeev Satav, also an important member of Rahul's team, spoke of the atmosphere of fear in UP. Rahul took his cue from Natarajan. He said it was 'absolutely wrong' that land was being acquired to give it to private parties for malls and golf courses.

One has to say that Rahul seemed a better speaker when he engaged in direct dialogues with his audience at the chaupal sabhas. He presented his point of view with greater emphasis.

The connection with the audience came alive during some of these discussions. The padayatra was originally aimed to send a message to the farmers that the Congress cared for them; it was, therefore, named the 'Kisan Sandesh Yatra' (message to the farmers).

However, it boiled down to project Rahul as the face of the Congress in the 2012 Assembly elections. The four-day journey was like a well-choreographed event for a high-profile product launch. The use of media was integral to the exercise. Teams of TV and print journalists followed Rahul through the fertile rural swathe. If he climbed up the elevated expressway still under construction, the TV crews went after him. If he took a diversion, the cameras followed him.

But it was not just the media that created the impression that the trip was about Rahul. The bulk of the padayatris were those who came from outside the area. Locals joined the procession only when he entered a new village. The team which accompanied him had Youth Congress workers from Delhi, UP, Rajasthan, Maharashtra and Tamil Nadu and other states. Each group had a duty assigned to it: logistics, food, publicity, organization of sabhas, and creating cordons to keep out the press and onlookers.

There were members of Rahul Gandhi's extended team in the troupe. There was the mandatory presence of Kanishka Singh, who wore a navy blue baseball cap and grew a beard during the journey. In charge of logistics and media management was Baiju, a former SPG member who has transitioned into Rahul's team. He spent the trip in jeans and a half-kurta. Pankaj Shankar was there with a camera slung around his neck. On the second or the third day Sachin Rao joined in with the quintessential cotton jhola that is identified with social activists. He stopped along the way to click photographs of some local boys who greeted the padayatra with the national flag.

Meenakshi Natarajan and Rajeev Satav joined the trip midway as did Haryana Chief Minister Bhupinder Hooda's son, Deepender Hooda. A floating population of those who came for a day or so included the former IYC president of Goa, Girish Chodankar, Ashok Tanwar, Vijay Mahajan, Krishna Byre Gowda and Varad Pande, a graduate of the Harvard Kennedy School of Government who is attached to Jairam Ramesh's rural development ministry as an officer on special duty.

The homes, where Rahul and his core team stayed, were not chosen randomly. A group of Youth Congress boys on motorcycles would go ahead of the procession to shortlist a few houses in the villages. The SPG would select one of the houses that had been shortlisted based on security considerations. This meant that on all the three nights Rahul slept in fairly well-off households. However, the facilities at these homes were not luxurious by any standards.

In Rampur Baangar where Rahul spent the first night, he reportedly slept on a bare charpai with just a pillow under his head. He is reported to have eaten the food served in these homes. But I saw soft drink bottles with the SPG men, who stood guard outside; their MUVs appeared to have more supplies. I asked a Youth Congress leader why Rahul's team carried soft drinks when the idea was to understand the conditions in which people lived. He said it would have been pretentious of Rahul to behave as though he did not have soft drinks.

'In Rahul's team there are people who drink cola daily and when they go to the villages they carry them. After a day out in the rural countryside, people feel like a Pepsi at the end of the day,' the leader said. He added Rahul has stopped at local village shops, bought soft drinks and snacks where they were available. Rahul was not fussy about food and ate whatever was available. 'If you give him a choice between a pizza and masala dosa, he prefers the latter. That too, he likes the paper masala dosa but he will eat it without the potato curry,' the leader remarked.

The trip was physically demanding as it entailed a walk of 15-20 km a day in hot and humid conditions. However, Rahul didn't appear tired. The sleeves of his white kurta were pushed back and bunched up on his forearm. On the second day he had red spots on his left forearm probably due to the heat or insect bite. Rahul copied his father's sartorial preference for white khadi kurta-pyjama and sports shoes. While Rajiv donned Italian-made Lotto sneakers, Rahul wore the Japanese sportswear brand, Acics (the company is the official kit supplier for the Australian cricket team). It was evident he exercised a lot. He told a TV reporter who asked him how he managed to stay fit that he ran a few kilometres daily.

A gym-going Rahul appears to set himself – and his team-members – physically demanding targets like he did during the padayatra, and also during the 2012 UP elections when he travelled an approximate 9000 kms during the three months of canvassing, according to figures from his office. This is possibly inspired by his interest in outdoor and adventure sports. He is into cycling, mountaineering and scuba-diving. He has also learnt to box, he is a motorsports buff and plays squash.

At the end of the four-day trip, Rahul addressed a 'kisan mahapanchayat' or a big farmers meet in Aligarh city's Exhibition Grounds. He responded to BSP's and BJP's characterization of his padayatra as 'nautanki' or drama. 'Many people are saying this is a nautanki ... I think a politician should talk to the people and move among the people ... If your government comes to you and listens to you there would be no need for bullets or to wield the baton,' he said in Hindi.

17

AT RAHUL'S JAN SABHA: A
MEETING WITH RAHUL GANDHI

'What can I do for you?' Rahul Gandhi asked me, as he leaned back against a railing in a concrete enclave in one of the lawns inside 10 Janpath, his mother's residence. It was a bright October morning, barely four months after the Congress had returned to power at the Centre in May 2009. The white-kurta-pyjama-clad Rahul was polite but couldn't hide his impatience to wind up his meetings with the thirty odd people, including me, invited to one of his Jan Sabhas.

I did not know how to answer the question he asked me. In a fit of anger, frustration and desperation, I had shot off a letter to Rahul less than a week ago about Delhi's child beggars. News reports said the Delhi administration was thinking of shifting them out of the city, and out of the view of foreign visitors, who would descend on Delhi during the forthcoming Commonwealth Games, to be held in October 2010.

A few days after I read the news item, I saw young girls begging at a prominent traffic junction, as I had seen them several times earlier. This time, I was more appalled. Perhaps naively and putting my cynicism aside for a moment, I wrote to Rahul about the problem. Since I covered Rahul for my newspaper, and wrote about him on a regular basis, I felt in a moment of helplessness after having watched young girls begging barefoot on burning asphalt roads that here was a person who was in a position to bring about change. Lingering at the back of my mind was the thought that since he had projected himself as a young and idealistic politician, and had toured some of India's poorest parts, he might be willing to help find more permanent ways to rehabilitate child beggars ahead of the Commonwealth Games.

I was surprised, mildly shocked, and excited when I received a response from his office within two days; I was invited to discuss the matter with Rahul the same week. To be frank, I hadn't mentioned I was a journalist. The prompt response from his office suggested that Rahul was open to meeting private citizens who felt strongly about the plight of urban poor, especially destitute children who can be found begging in cities all over India.

On a Friday morning a few days later, I was in the motley bunch that waited outside 10 Janpath for Rahul. It included older politicians, earnest-looking students, an African contingent and young Congress workers. Each person had been screened by Rahul's office, and given a personal invitation. A stern-looking bespectacled man, who carried a piece of paper with our names on it, kept the gathering at bay outside the house. Only when he called out our names were we allowed to go past the first security barrier into the address that has become the nerve centre of political power. There were several more rounds of security checks before coming within close range of the Nehru-Gandhi scion.

In the lawn, there were rows of chairs upholstered in white cloth. Noisy pedestal fans whirred away in another half of the little enclave. The resident peacocks that I had heard of seemed away that day. Only the gardeners and sweepers went about their morning chores and provided some distraction for us. As the news of Rahul's arrival circulated amongst us, there was a buzz. When he arrived, it was without much fanfare.

He looked cheerful; he smiled at us but was immediately business-like. Without formalities, he dived into the meetings. First in line were a group of men, whom I guessed by their attire, to be corporate executives. He disposed them quickly, within a few minutes. Then it was the turn of four Sikhs, who wore jeans and flashy half-sleeve shirts with sneakers. Rahul spent more time with them, and I thought they must be Congress workers from Punjab. They were directed by Rahul to his chief aide Kanishka Singh, who heard them out in a cool and unruffled manner.

It was now the turn of a backpack-carrying student from Kerala who beamed when Rahul keenly pored over her file, which contained clippings and documents. She must have been an NSUI member whom Rahul had spotted on one of his tours, a whiz kid who had won several awards, certificates and had been written about in the media.

I was among the last to meet Rahul. Taken aback by his direct question, and unable to come up with an immediate answer, I mumbled something about the need to help child beggars, who might be moved out of sight during the Commonwealth games. I spoke to him about coming up with a lasting solution.

'Don't you think this is a symptom of a larger problem?' he asked.

I was flummoxed and stared back at him.

'Child beggars in cities such as Delhi are a result of migration from rural areas,' he said.

I agreed but still urged him that something had to be done immediately for these kids. He warmed up to the subject, and asked me what he should focus on. Should he tackle every small manifestation of poverty? Or should he focus on the root causes?

'Earlier, I would go wherever I spotted a problem. A DTC (Delhi Transport Corporation) bus would run over somebody and I would go there.' But now, he needed to 'focus' since he had limited energy. He asked Kanishka to put me in touch with Meenakshi Natarajan, the AICC secretary, who worked with him, to see how the issue could be taken forward. I got in touch with Meenakshi who in turn directed me to someone else.

As I was about to leave, I told him I was a journalist. He was amused and asked about my 'background'. I immediately took the opportunity and enquired if I could ask him a few questions. I had to try since he hardly spoke to the media. He was quick to say 'no' but added that may be some other day I could interview him.

The meeting left me with the impression that Rahul had the right intentions. But I was also somewhat disappointed that nothing much had come out of the meeting with Rahul and his colleagues. Nonetheless, it made me look at his work more intently. That is how I got interested in Rahul's initial years in politics. However, the more I studied his politics, the more I felt his actions lacked the prized 'focus' he was so keen to acquire. It was as though he didn't understand how to route his ideas and plans through political actions and initiatives. Even the things he did right, like meeting an unknown middle-class young woman from Delhi who had wanted to talk over the urban poverty issue with him, did not get reflected in his politics.

PART FIVE

UP 2012

18

THE HUMILIATION

The 2012 Uttar Pradesh Assembly elections were meant to be Rahul Gandhi's political Kurukshetra. In Rahul's mind, it was a fight between Right (Congress) and Wrong (BSP, SP, and BJP). It was a fight to conquer Congress' legitimate territory, which it had lost during the late 1980s. But more importantly, Rahul had a point to prove in UP. He was working in the state since the 2007 Assembly poll debacle. If he could deliver UP to the Congress, he would have fulfilled an important part of his duty as the Nehru-Gandhi heir. This was his do-or-die battle. It was mentored by Sonia Gandhi who, like Lord Krishna, provided the moral and philosophical strength to the party's campaign. The twenty-first century democratic war was fought by the modern-day Arjuna, or Rahul, whose eyes could not look at anything beyond a victory in the state. But, it threatened to become Rahul's Waterloo.

This is why, a day after the UP election results came out on 6 March 2012, Sonia came out to support her son. 'In UP our (party) organization is weak. This is the main problem. After that, the people of UP were very angry with the BSP and the alternative in front of them was the SP,'[1] she said. Rahul had stepped up to 'accept responsibility' on the day the results were announced. Like his mother, he too blamed the defeat on organizational weakness. Sonia also suggested that the Congress' problem was not a lack of leadership, but that it had 'too many leaders'[2].

However, try as they might, it was not easy to justify Congress' performance in the UP elections. The party finished fourth with 28 seats[3]. Though the Congress' vote share went up to 11.63 per cent, a gain of 3 per cent from 2007, it improved its seats tally by just six. Even its realistic assessment was a lot more than that. Its seasoned political leaders gave the party a minimum of 50-60 seats, along with its alliance partner the Rashtriya Lok Dal (RLD); on its own, it hoped to at least touch 50, and more than double its tally of 22 in the 2007 polls. The result was a big embarrassment for Rahul. He had staked his personal reputation on the Congress' performance in the elections. He addressed 211 rallies, undertook 'roadshows' in eighteen constituencies and spent forty-eight days between 14 November 2011, when he kicked off his campaign from Jawaharlal Nehru's constituency, Phulpur, and 29 February 2012. A senior Congress functionary associated with UP said that Rahul monitored 'every small detail' of the electioneering process.

Yet, the strategy fell apart. It left the Congress as decimated as it was in the state for over two decades. Critics questioned Rahul's ability to win elections, and Congress leaders were uncertain about the party's future under his leadership, which is imminent. Rahul admitted himself to the media after the UP results that he was 'standing at the front'[4], leading the campaign.

This is because of two factors. The first was the pressure

on Rahul to finally deliver results for the Congress. He had failed to win a single state in the past seven years with the exception of the party's performance in UP in the 2009 general elections, when it won an unexpected 21 seats and its vote share went up to 18.25 per cent. In the run-up to the UP 2012 elections, he had no excuses; he was connected with the state since 2007 and micro-managed the strategy in 2012.

The second was Sonia's uncertain health. After Sonia's August 2011 surgery for an undisclosed medical condition, when she was out of political action for more than a month, there was speculation about Rahul's impending takeover as the party president and even as the prime minister, before the 2014 general elections. The Congress looked out for that event to springboard him to the top. If he managed to pull off UP for the Congress, anointing him as the party president would could be a cakewalk.

Therefore, UP was the test case. This was apparent in the manner in which Rahul ran the campaign, unlike what he had done in the past. One, he showed a willingness to set aside old ideas like fight elections alone, and adopted a more pragmatic line to forge electoral alliances. Before the 2012 UP elections, the Congress inked a pre-poll pact with Western-UP centric Ajit Singh-led RLD; while the Congress contested 355 seats, RLD got to fight 46 seats[5].

As a politician, Rahul worked on his speeches. In the past, he had shied away from this despite criticism about his below-par public speaking skills. An IYC leader, whom I asked about his resolute refusal to hone his speeches, said that Rahul 'was happy being a man of action rather than a man of words'. Words became more important in the 2012 polls.

The 'angry young man' image was improved. In terms of looks, it included a stubble or a beard. The bearded look was meant to showcase a rustic personality, but it drew flak as a means to woo Muslim voters. The words acquired an edge. His attack on other parties in the state, the SP and the BSP was pointed. A constant refrain was that in the past twenty-two years (since the Congress was out of power) the state had seen no development.

For instance, in Rampur during one of the last days of the UP campaign Rahul criticized other parties for making all manner of promises during election time. He said SP's Mulayam Singh had promised free electricity, but not one power plant had been set up in UP in the last twenty-two years. 'Where will the electricity come from, will it drop from the skies?' he asked using the Hindi phrase 'aasman se tapkegi kya'.

The actions became aggressive. During a rally in Lucknow on15 February 2012, he took on SP's Mulayam Singh Yadav in a bid to prove that all that he had done was to make promises but never delivered on them. He read out from a piece of paper. '. . . I will give you electricity, I will give you water, I will give you employment. If I cannot give you employment, I will give you an unemployment dole . . . The same list comes out of the pocket (of Mulayam Singh) and is used for twenty-two years . . . A list of promises.'[6]

He dramatically tore the paper and flung the pieces away. 'Do you understand what I am saying. This state will not be run by these lists, by promises. (This state) runs due to your blood and sweat. These people (the non-Congress parties) don't respect you. These people think we will make money in government through corruption and get away. What will happen to you? What will happen to the thousands of youth who are wandering here and there . . . You have heard promises for twenty-two years.'[7] He appeared overcome by rage.

At the same time, he used humour and sarcasm to good effect. He peppered his speeches with 'bhaiyya' and used colloquial Hindi phrases. He came up with catchy phrases, such as Mayawati's 'jaadoo ka haathi' (the magic elephant; elephant being Mayawati's BSP electoral symbol)) which gobbled up huge amounts of money instead of leaves and grass. It drew applauses from the audience each time he repeated it.

On the SP's 'umeed ki cycle' (cycle of hope; cycle being its symbol) campaign, Rahul asked where was the 'umeed' for the people of the state. He said the voters had 'trusted the cycle three times' but the SP had 'punctured' their future.

Rahul said in his speeches that he mixed with the people, which was his style. He spent nights at poor homes, ate with them, and drank the 'dirty water' from their wells. He said Mayawati and Mulayam Singh did not know the problems of the poor. He was 'angry' with the condition of UP, especially when he saw that young people were forced to migrate to Maharashtra, Delhi and other states to seek work.

The Centre backed Rahul's efforts. The UPA made its announcement sanctioning a Rs 6,234 crore economic package for weavers across India on 19 November 2011. It was timed to woo the Muslim weavers in Eastern UP. This was after Rahul toured the weavers' belt and wrote to Union Commerce Minister Anand Sharma the same month.

Then came the controversial 4.5 per cent sub-quota for 'minorities' within the 27 per cent Central reservation for OBCs in jobs and education. This was announced on 22 December 2012, two days before the Election Commission (EC) notified the poll dates, when the Model Code of Conduct would have come into force. The move aimed to retain the support of Muslim voters, who constitute about 18 per cent of the voting population.

However, during the campaign, Union Law Minister Salman Khurshid said that if Congress was voted to power, it would impose a 9 per cent sub-quota for backward Muslims in state jobs[8]. His statement was tantamount to a policy statement and meant a doubling of the 4.5 per cent quota. It got Khurshid into trouble with EC, which censured him for violating the Model Code of Conduct by making a 'new promise'[9] to a 'distinct targeted group of the electorate among the minorities'[10].

In UP 2012, the Congress openly pandered to communal sentiments. Khurshid said Sonia had 'wept' when he showed her the pictures of the Batla House encounter in Delhi's Jamia Nagar in September 2008 in which two suspected Indian Mujahedeen terrorists and a police inspector died. His statement was made at a rally in Azamgarh, where the two alleged terrorists hailed from. Digvijay Singh, who was in charge of the UP campaign, described the Batla House encounter as 'fake' and stood by his earlier call for a judicial probe into the shoot-out. This was in early January 2012 in Azamgarh, when Rahul faced protests during his election tour of the area.

The government refused to promise Salman Rushdie, the author of *The Satanic Verses,* adequate security to attend the annual literary festival in Jaipur. Rushdie, whose work is considered blasphemous by Muslims across the world and whose book was banned in India, faced the ire of the Islamic seminary Darul Uloom Deoband, which asked for the cancellation of his Indian visa.

Though Rushdie did not require a visa as he was a Person of Indian Origin (PIO), the Congress scared him away from the literary event. Speaking at a conclave in New Delhi after the UP elections, where the Congress fared miserably, Rushdie described the incident as '. . . predictable Deobandi bigotry pandered to by, as it turns out, pretty useless electoral calculations by the Congress Party'[11]. He went further: 'Didn't even work, Rahul. Didn't even work. Years and years of kneeling down in front of every mullah you could find, and it did not even work.'[12]

These tactical moves to woo Muslims were a part of a larger electoral arithmetic. In Rahul's view, Muslims formed a part of the voters' constituency that he hoped would vote for Congress. It included the most backward classes (MBCs) and the Ati-Dalits, or the poorest among the OBCs and Dalits. Rahul thought he could build on the support his party got in the 2009 national elections from the Muslims, and the Kurmis, an OBC sub-caste whose leader Beni Prasad Verma joined the Congress from the SP.

In 2012, Verma was projected as the leader of MBCs. Party strategists[13] said they had identified 100 seats, where the combination of Muslims and Kurmis would prove decisive. The party gave 110 tickets, or just less than a third of its election nominations, to MBCs. The Ati-Dalit calculation was to split Mayawati's Dalit vote into the Jatav (the caste Mayawati belongs to) and non-Jatav blocks.

'Through his stays at Dalit homes, Rahul targeted the non-Jatavs,' Ram Kumar, a Lucknow-based Dalit activist said. The Congress gave nominations to Ati-Dalit candidates.

The party's 'vision document' titled 'Nav Uttar Pradesh 2020' – attributed to Rahul – and its manifesto made promises, especially on the education and employment fronts, for the two groups. The manifesto specifically spoke of introducing an MBC sub-quota within the OBC reservations.

While Rahul was the Congress' star campaigner, Priyanka monitored the progress in the Assembly seats that fell under the Amethi and Rae Bareli Lok Sabha seats. Priyanka, who had campaigned in the area since 1999, addressed several rallies in the ten Assembly segments. Along with Rahul, she undertook a roadshow in the neighbouring Sultanpur constituency, and signalled her willingness to go to other parts of UP if her brother wanted her to. Her husband Robert Vadra joined the campaign, which led Mayawati to tell *Al Jazeera*: 'For the Gandhi family, the UP elections have always been a big picnic.'[14]

Everything was in vain. In UP 2012, SP made a stunning comeback with 224 seats, exceeding Mayawati's performance in 2007 (206 seats). SP's spectacular victory, like Mayawati's earlier, was possible due to the support of its core base, Muslims and Yadavs, and a wider social coalition that included Brahmins, MBCs, and even non-Jatav Dalits in some pockets. SP won 58 out of 85 seats reserved for Scheduled Castes[15].

Almost all the constituents, on whom Rahul had pinned his hopes, voted for the SP. In the Amethi-Rae Bareli-Sultanpur belt, the Congress won just two out of the 15 Assembly seats. Its candidate lost even in Jewar, the constituency in Western UP under which the villages of Bhatta and Parsaul fall. Rahul had undertaken a dharna against the Mayawati government's land acquisition policies there in May 2011 and later started his Western UP padayatra from the twin villages. Jewar, a BSP stronghold, was retained by Mayawati's party by a margin of 9,500 votes though the Congress' Dhirendra Singh was the runner-up.

In the days and weeks following the rout, Congress leaders big and small took part in an exercise to absolve Rahul of the responsibility for the defeat. Immediately after the results came out on 6 March 2012, Digvijay Singh, the AICC in charge of UP said[16] the elections were not Rahul's 'litmus test'. He summed it up as 'the failure ... of the organization, state leadership, and mine personally'. Uttar Pradesh Congress Committee (UPCC) chief Rita Bahuguna Joshi tendered her resignation a few days after the results came out and was also eager to take the blame for the defeat. During a post-mortem of the debacle Rahul held about a month after the results,

Congress leaders from the state cited a number of reasons for the party's loss. Chief among them were organizational weakness, faulty distribution of election nominations, lack of coordination between the state leadership and Central leaders, controversial statements made by Union ministers such as Salman Khurshid, Sriprakash Jaiswal, and party leaders such as Digvijay Singh. Among other things, Jaiswal and Singh spoke of the possibility of President's Rule in the state if the Congress did not win a majority. Nobody directly mentioned Rahul's role as campaign in charge, the one thread that linked all these disparate reasons for failure.

Why Did Rahul's Election Pitch Fail?

The writing was on the wall before the first vote was cast in UP. Without a core vote base, a political organization that worked on the ground, and strong local leaders, the Congress' chances to win 100-plus seats that a few over-enthusiastic Congressmen bragged about, was out of the question. Even the modest tally of 50-60 seats eluded it because it depended on a flawed, immediate strategy, which was hatched months before the elections on the basis of the results in the 2009 Lok Sabha polls.

Let us begin with the new socio-political alliance the Congress planned with the Muslims, MBCs and Ati-Dalits. Included among them were a section of upper-caste Brahmins (10-11 per cent of the state population), who were its traditional supporters. All of them voted for the party in 2009, and the UP math was based on it. But Rahul forgot that there were differences between 2009 and 2012.

He thought the 2009 verdict signalled the return of the Muslims to the Congress fold, after they had deserted the party post the Babri Masjid demolition in 1992. However, the

Muslims voted for Congress in 2009 for varying reasons. Congress spokesperson and UP leader Rashid Alvi identified three reasons: SP's tie-up with the former BJP leader Kalyan Singh, who was chief minister of UP when the Babri Masjid was demolished; Mulayam Singh's strained relationship with his top Muslim leader, Azam Khan; and the fears that the BSP might join a Central coalition headed by BJP's prime ministerial candidate L K Advani.

In 2012, none of the above factors were valid. Instead, the Congress' attempt to give sops to Muslims, like the 4.5 per cent minority sub-quota, backfired; the Muslims felt it was too little, too late. 'It left the backward Muslims nowhere, as they felt that they had to compete with other minorities such as the Christians, Sikhs, Parsis and Jains for the reservations,' Alvi said.

Others felt the announcement came too close to the polls. 'The announcement of the 4.5 per cent reservations for backward minorities should have come earlier. We could not explain the policy properly. More MBCs could have come to the Congress (if it wasn't for the confusion over the policy),' Uttar Pradesh Congress Committee President Rita Bahuguna Joshi said. In the end, the Muslims stood solidly behind SP which, according to Joshi, emerged as the 'biggest supporter of their interests at the regional level'. The MBCs voted for the SP.

The 'Beni factor' that Rahul believed would influence the Kurmi belt didn't work for other reasons in 2012. There was internal dissent against Verma, who was given a free hand during the ticket-distribution process. He got his own candidates in about 25-30 out of the 55 seats in Central Uttar Pradesh and parts of the Terai or North-east region that went to polls in the first phase of campaigning, according to media reports. Many of the nominees were outsiders. 'These candidates were not from the Congress system. They could not win the support of Congress workers,' said Joshi.

The problem with the Ati-Dalit voters was that they were never a homogenous or a consolidated group of voters as they comprised sixty-five[17] sub-castes. While in Bihar, they are known as Mahadalits and are politically mobilized, it is not so in UP. 'It is only an attempt at the moment,' Dalit activist Ram Kumar said. It is an idea before its time in UP. So, the Ati-Dalits (as also some sections of Brahmins) voted SP in 2012, partially due to the anti-incumbency factor or dissatisfaction against BSP.

Another issue with Rahul's social rejigging was that it seemed more like an election-eve stunt. The building of such social coalitions requires long-term and sustained engagement. This was especially the case with Jats, whom the Congress failed to woo through the poll-eve alliance with the RLD in Western UP, and other OBCs such as Kurmis, who are not traditional Congress voters. But unmindful of the effort required for building a political constituency, all the Congress did was to try and get Muslims on their side through quotas announced at the last minute, pull Kurmis by bestowing Verma with a Cabinet post five months before the polls, and wean away Ati-Dalits through Rahul's visits to their homes. All these bore the stamp of tokenism. 'We thought the Muslims have come back to us in 2009, but we didn't do anything for them,' Alvi said.

In fact, Rahul spent the bulk of the mid-2009 to early 2011 period on IYC- and NSUI-related issues. He neglected UP and never capitalized on the 2009 gains. In 2012, the Congress won four out of 19 seats in Bundelkhand, only because Rahul visited the region in this interim period[18]. A former legislator from UP said the Congress had a distinct advantage for about a year after the Lok Sabha polls and emerged as a main challenger to the BSP. A year before the UP campaign kicked off, the leader said: 'There is a political vacuum in UP. It just requires Rahul to concentrate full-time on the state.'

But he did not, and the opportunity vanished into thin air. Observers felt he should have prepared for UP earlier. This lack of focus can be traced back to Rahul's confusion about whether he is in politics to win elections and occupy positions of power, or to 'improve the political system'[19], which he reiterated after the 2012 defeat. Unfortunately, Rahul has done neither.

More importantly, UP is a political theatre, where the two regional parties, SP and BSP, tussle with each other. In an era where voters aim to form stable governments – this has been the trend in verdicts in a majority of the states across India as well as the Centre in recent years – they choose between the principal players, rather than those unlikely to form a government. In UP, both Congress and BJP fall in the latter category as they are no longer seen as alternatives.

Some Congress leaders said the only way their party could become a catch-all formation in the state once again – which was what the 2012 strategy envisaged – was by rebuilding its core vote bases among dominant groups like Dalits and Muslims. 'Both Muslims and Dalits don't have a representative within the Congress,' a leader who is part of Rahul's extended team said.

Connected to this is Rahul's failure to fix the Congress' organizational problems in the state. Rahul cited the party's organizational weakness as one of the primary reasons for its failure, but Rahul who had taken it upon himself to revive the party in UP, was partly responsible for the poor condition of the organization.

Congressmen pointed out that one of the chief reasons for the Congress' organizational weakness is the lack of leadership at different levels of the party structure and among specific communities. Rahul had been speaking of the imperative to build leaders since 2006 when he first addressed a Congress conclave in Hyderabad. However, despite working in UP for at least five years, Rahul was not anywhere close to achieving this when the 2012 polls arrived. Rahul chiefly attempted organization building in the state by trying to revitalize the Youth Congress. The UP 2012 polls proved that the IYC experiment to produce new leaders as well as to strengthen the organization on the ground came a cropper.

Another reason cited by the Congress for the party's loss was the fact that it did not project a chief ministerial 'face'. 'People did not vote for us because we did not have a face in the state. We need to project one person for the next five years,' UPCC chief Rita Bahuguna Joshi said. This was the same strategy the Congress had adopted in the 2007 elections when its principal plank in the state was the projection of Rahul Gandhi. Despite that attempt having failed, the Congress, under Rahul, did the same thing in 2012. It was conclusive proof that just the Nehru-Gandhi name alone was not enough to facilitate a Congress revival in the state. 'When a national leader puts all his eggs in the basket of a state election, it will either make him or break him. Rahul should have hedged his bets,' said Ajay Upadhyay, the editor of the Hindi daily *Amar Ujala*.

So, even factors that should have worked in his favour hurt him. His decision to play traditional politics, which he was opposed to, in UP was one example. The perception, as brands expert Santosh Desai put it, was that 'when you lose belief, you start using ideas you have denied. The moment you do that you become a thick-skinned politician, who is ready for give-and-take.' He added from being an 'unbending, presumptive ruler' Rahul began to act like a 'politician'.

Rahul's act of tearing the list of Mulayam Singh's promises went against his earlier image, and as that of a member of the Nehru-Gandhi clan. Upadhyay described it as 'one of Rahul's biggest blunders'. He said that 'what Rahul did was not proper and dignified. People expect this from a Raj Narain or a Lalu Yadav, not from the scion of the Nehru family.'

This was an election where the Congress sought young voters. However, Rahul's overt appeal to caste sentiments and the Congress' communal campaign, which reflected on Rahul, showed him up as the face of the old school of politics that did not sync with the new India. SP chief Mulayam Singh's son, Akhilesh, who is three years junior to Rahul and was competing for young voters, presented a more forward-looking image. In fact, Mulayam's Australia-returned engineer son was responsible for giving the SP an image-makeover. The SP had come to be associated primarily with caste politics, criminal elements in the party, and anti-modern ideas such as opposition to computers and English. Akhilesh, whom even Congress leaders admitted emerged as SP's 'new face', stood for change. This was because of several factors. First, Akhilesh was instrumental in denying an election nomination to the Western UP 'don' and alleged criminal D P Yadav. This sent out a strong signal that the party wanted to correct its earlier image of having allowed criminal elements a free-run between 2002 and 2007 when it was in power. Thus, Akhilesh indirectly admitted that SP needed to change the perception that it had presided over 'goondaraj'. Second, the party's ticket distribution bore his stamp. The party tried to strike a balance between the old and the new, with a number of young people getting tickets but also keeping local factors and Mulayam's old associations in mind during the ticket distribution process. He also undertook a mass-contact programme by travelling across the state in a refurbished mini-van or a rath covering

9000 kms and 250 constituencies[20]. Akhilesh's 'Kranti Rath Yatra' began in September 2011 and he was way ahead of all his opponents including Rahul who began their campaigns only later. Akhilesh covered some stretches of the journey, between Noida and Agra for instance, through a cycle yatra. The yatras made it possible for him to touch each part of the state and become accessible to party workers and candidates. He promised to withdraw the alleged 'false' cases framed by BSP against SP cadres. In his speeches, Akhilesh kept the focus on 'development', promising electricity, water, power, and fertilizers to farmers and later talked of the party's promise of waiving agricultural loans of up to Rs 50,000. He also spoke of an unemployment dole of Rs 1,000 per month for those above thirty-five years of age, also promised in the SP manifesto, and highlighted SP's commitment to education, especially free education for girls. He attacked Mayawati over corruption and for having spent crores on memorials to Dalit icons and for having put up statues of herself. His clincher proved to be the promise of free laptop computers and tablets to students which connected with the youth.

Congress leaders spoke of how the SP's manifesto was one of the important reasons for its inability to capitalize on the voter disenchantment against Mayawati. Many disparaged it as a list of 'freebies' but admitted that it worked. 'There was an overall appreciation by people about the dynamic leadership of Rahul Gandhi. But the youth were swayed by the promise of Rs 1,000 per month (of umemployment dole), the SP also promised to waive off farmers' loans, provide free irrigation, and laptop computers. This led the youth who was totally with Rahul Gandhi and the Congress to move away (to the SP),' Congress leader P L Punia said. What differentiated Akhilesh from Rahul was the way he was perceived. Akhilesh was no less a yuvraj than Rahul, but he was seen as an accessible young leader who belonged to the state and its soil. Rahul was the remote crown prince of the Congress who lived in Delhi and came to UP to do his politics. The memories of this grand debacle will not be erased in a hurry. If Congress had done well, some sections of the party would have projected him as an interim PM, and may be pushed him into the seat in 2013. However, it still does not discount the possibility of Rahul being projected as the party's prime ministerial candidate in 2014.

But whenever he becomes the PM, can Rahul grapple with the tough economic and political issues the country will confront?

EPILOGUE

PRIME MINISTER RAHUL GANDHI: WHAT THIS WOULD MEAN FOR INDIA

Despite the Congress' lackadaisical electoral performance in UP 2012, the Rahul Gandhi era is almost inevitable. Many experts contend that Sonia Gandhi's son will be a prime ministerial candidate in 2014. During the UP election campaign, Beni Prasad Verma said Prime Minister Manmohan Singh would be eighty-two in 2014 and his age would make it hard for him to take work pressures. 'Under these circumstances, Rahulji will be made the prime minister,'[1] he told the crowd in Jaunpur. Through 2011, senior Congressmen such as Pranab Mukherjee and Digvijay Singh kept such a prospect alive when they declared Rahul as fit and ready to be PM. Even Manmohan Singh agreed that 'younger people'[2] should take over.

Post-UP, Rahul, who was earlier reluctant to expand his role beyond the IYC and NSUI, has signalled he is ready for a bigger profile. In an April 2012 trip to Maharashtra, Rahul not only met elected leaders of the IYC and the NSUI but also held discussions with block and district committee presidents of the state's Congress Committee. He did the same in Chhattisgarh, which he visited a month later, meeting leaders of the state Congress Committee, MPs and MLAs, and Karnataka which he visited in June. He also took a keener interest in Andhra Pradesh, another big Congress-ruled state where the party is gripped with leadership troubles in the aftermath of its tallest leader Y S Rajasekhara Reddy's death, the emergence of YSR's son Y S Jaganmohan Reddy as a challenger to the Congress (his breakaway YSR Congress swept the crucial Assembly by-elections held in June 2012) and the crisis triggered by the agitation for a separate Telangana state. And the chances of him becoming the next PM are fair. The disarray in the BJP, which is faced with the conundrum of whom to project as prime minister, gives hope to many in the Congress of a win in 2014. However, the Congress' numbers itself may be diminished due to several factors including the coalescing of pan-India anti-Congress forces. On the flip side, one has to see whether the Congress' chances in 2014 will be diminished by allegations of corruption and non-governance.

Still, it may be germane to figure out what a potential Rahul prime ministership holds for India. To begin with, despite his seemingly-imminent rise as PM, Rahul seems unsure, as of now, on the role that he wishes to play in politics. Rahul's brief speech after the UP results came out on 6 March 2012 hinted at this uncertainty: 'I view my work as trying to work for the people. I view my work as trying to improve the political system. That will continue. Certainly, I expect to have victories along the way and I expect to have defeats. This is one of the defeats and I take it in my stride. I think it will be a very good lesson for me, because it will make me think things through in a detailed way which I like to do.'[3]

The statement indicated that Rahul doesn't know if he should continue as the selfless political activist who wants to ring in fundamental changes in the system. Or should he be a little less ambitious, and geared towards keeping the Congress a robust and electable political outfit. In the past, his major thrust on developing inner party democracy – strengthening the IYC and NSUI – hasn't yielded results. The new Youth Congress has come to be dominated by children of established party leaders. And when it comes to electoral politics, Rahul has been unable to cultivate a constituency of voters or display the tactical nous to forge profitable alliances. His experiment to accumulate non-core and peripheral castes and classes into a single and sizeable vote bank failed in UP 2012.

'He wants to become a radical but cannot. He must strike a balance,' senior journalist Ajay Upadhyay said. This confusion about why he is in politics has meant he has neither engaged sufficiently with politico-economic issues nor has he become a part of the political processes within the Congress as its future leader. The confusion is magnified by other factors. Rahul and his mother remain inaccessible. Within his own party, he is perceived to be aloof. Senior Congress functionaries and ministers have trouble getting past the apparatus Rahul has put in place. He gives the impression of appearing and disappearing from the political scene at will. He disappeared from the political scene for more than a week immediately after the UP debacle, missing the opening of the Budget Session of Parliament.

Couple this with the fact that in this era of coalition politics, Rahul has not nurtured relationships with too many alliance partners. One of Sonia Gandhi's strengths as Congress president has been her ability to reach out to prospective and existing alliance partners at key junctures. Rahul has not shown a flair for this kind of political tight-rope walking. While it is true that he has not had reason to play this role yet, he has not even shown a willingness to engage with political allies whether it is the DMK, the NCP or the Trinamool

Congress. The only UPA allies that Rahul seems to share a rapport with is National Conference's Omar Abdullah, who like him is the scion of a well-entrenched political dynasty, and RLD's Ajit Singh, which was more of an expediency to somehow do well in UP.

Rahul's quest for building up the Congress in states where it has been weakened has seen him adopting indifferent or even haughty public postures towards the leaders of regional parties, who also happen to be allies of the Congress at the Centre. In the case of Tamil Nadu's M Karunanidhi, his refusal to call on the octogenarian DMK leader on his trips to Tamil Nadu was perceived as a snub by the regional party. Rahul as prime minister would have to strike a far more conciliatory posture towards regional players. A failure on this front would mean all kinds of alliance trouble, especially in a situation where the Congress' strength in Parliament is weakened in 2014.

Rahul's approach to change, through his backing for measures such as the Unique Identification Authority of India (UIDAI) scheme reveals an unwillingness to engage with the existing system. It is an attempt to superimpose new systems over existing structures. This approach is bound to meet the fate of his experiments in the IYC and the NSUI, where the existing system finds a way to infiltrate the new one and scuttle change. Similarly, the UIDAI, which envisages a unique identification number – or an Aadhaar number – for each Indian after collection of biometric information, is a technocratic quest to identify the poor and target benefits to them. This initiative too is unlikely to bypass the inefficiencies of the delivery mechanism in the current system.

Also in the name of better targeting of the poor for state-sponsored schemes, the UID programme pays little attention to privacy issues. Critics argue that once implemented, the

UID will help government gain access to private information such as medical records of citizens. The Parliamentary Standing Committee on Finance examining the UIDAI Bill was scathing in its rejection of the scheme finding it 'riddled with serious lacunae'[4] and disapproving of the hasty manner in which the scheme was approved without a comprehensive feasibility study.

The reliance on technocrats and subject experts on the one hand and the lack of political managers in his own team on the other hand could mean Rahul going the same way as his father did years back. Rajiv Gandhi's dramatic fall from the heights he scaled after his win in 1984, when the Congress won a near three-fourth majority in the Lok Sabha, was primarily due to political mismanagement. Rajiv had sidelined senior members of his mother's inner coterie such as R K Dhawan who were adept at political management, and got in technocrats like Sam Pitroda who, he thought, would ring in radical changes. Rahul as prime minister is likely to do the same. Members of Rahul's core team at the moment such as Kanishka Singh are process-driven corporate managers rather than canny political operatives. Then the churning within the Congress which will see Rahul's new Congress and the old Congress leaders go head-to-head could have its own fallout on politics.

It is in such a political environment that Rahul would have to deal with the economy. India's fabled growth story is suddenly a subject of black humour at investor conclaves, after a slowdown in 2011-12 threatens to turn everything upside down. Even ministers of the government, who at the annual World Economic Forum at Davos lost no opportunity to remind everyone that India was the world's second fastest growing economy, after China, seem to have forgotten that phrase. The storm clouds of economic uncertainty threaten to wash away everything, thanks to the decision-making paralysis of UPA II, global crises, especially in Eurozone, corruption charges, and an inability to improve the investment sentiment among domestic and foreign investors.

The international rating agency Standard and Poor's (S&P) reduced the outlook on India's credit rating to 'negative' in April 2012. It spoke of a one-in-three chance of an actual downgrade within the next 12-24 months 'if the external position continues to deteriorate, growth prospects diminish, or progress on fiscal reforms remains slow in a weakened political setting'[5]. Moody's Analytics said the Indian government was the 'single biggest drag'[6] on business activity in a report published at the same time.

In June 2012, S&P brought out another report that warned India could become the first among the BRIC (Brazil, Russia, India, China) nations to lose its investment grade credit rating. It threatened to downgrade India's credit rating to 'speculative'[7] or junk status from the current lowest investment grade rating it enjoys. 'Slowing GDP growth and political roadblocks to economic policy making could put India at the risk of losing its investment grade rating,'[8] the report said. It additionally blamed the governing arrangement at the Centre with a division of powers between a 'powerful' Congress chief Sonia Gandhi and an 'unelected' Prime Minister Manmohan Singh for 'weaken(ing) the framework for making policy'[9]. It pointed out that '. . . paramount political power rests with the leader of the Congress, Sonia Gandhi, who holds no Cabinet position, while the government is led by an unelected Prime Minister Manmohan Singh, who lacks a political base of his own.'[10]

Until a couple of years ago, buoyed by high GDP growth rates, there was some semblance of a balance between the welfare state policies of Sonia Gandhi, like the rural employment guarantee scheme and the latest food security

Bill, and economic reforms that Manmohan Singh pursued. It was a mix of inclusive growth and economic growth. But that has changed now. The Sonia-led NAC has pushed India in the direction of becoming a cumbersome welfare state and Singh's image as the poster-boy of reform lies in tatters. Opposition to reform measures from within the Congress and coalition partners has played an equal part in undoing the optimism about the economy.

From what we know about Rahul's economic mindset, he may possess the bandwidth to deal with both the left and right spectrums of economic policies. He has backed big ticket social sector schemes such as the proposed National Food Security Bill (conservatively estimated to cost the government Rs 50,000 crore a year). He has also advocated measures such as FDI in organized retail. Rahul's economic position can be pinned down to looking at growth as a means to fund large social sector schemes aimed at the poor and, at the same time, enabling the poor to participate in the growth story.

He can be identified within the large-left of centre space in India. It can be argued that Rahul's positions are close to Sonia's though he does not exactly mirror her position either. On many issues, he would be closer to Manmohan Singh. Therefore, while a member of Sonia's NAC described him as a 'growthwallah' (or a reformist), at the same time, a microfinance champion and Rahul advisor spoke of an 'ideological shift' between the Sonia and the Rahul generations. The fact is that Rahul is not opposed to development, but wants the poor to get their due, like the right price for their land.

The problem with Rahul, though, is that there has been no conviction or consistency in his economic views. While he has opposed Vedanta's Niyamgiri mining proposal, he has not done the same with Posco or other similar projects. His initiatives to influence the land acquisition Bill was somewhat guided by political expediency, or the forthcoming elections in UP. If investors look for predictability from a new government headed by Rahul, they might be hard-pressed to find it.

For other huge questions, there are few pointers to the direction Rahul will take. His refusal to reveal his mind on pressing domestic and foreign policy issues is worrying. For instance, when he was asked at the height of the Kashmir stone-throwing protests in 2010 for his prescription, he evaded a direct response. Asked if he would personally intervene, he responded that his focus was on bringing young people into politics and that 'solving Kashmir is not a part-time problem . . . It is a full-time problem'[11].

It would require a reorientation of Rahul's attitude to politics and a willingness on his part to learn the tricks of political management if Rahul expects to manage the complex tasks he faces as a potential prime minister. That process has begun. The government's plummeting credibility and the uncertainty surrounding his mother's health might have forced Rahul's hand. After casting his vote in the Presidential election that concluded in July 2012, Rahul Gandhi for the first time told the media that he is ready for a bigger role in the party and the government. Newspapers reported that when Rahul was asked whether he would play a more active role in the Congress, he told *NDTV*: 'That decision has been taken. It has been under discussion of the party leadership.' Queried whether he would take up a bigger role in the party or the government, he replied, 'both options are open'. He added the decision on the timing of the move was left to his 'two bosses' – Congress President Sonia Gandhi and Prime Minister Manmohan Singh. Rahul's announcement came amidst a steadily growing clamour from within the Congress for his greater involvement in the party. In the months before the next general elections, Rahul's performance in his chosen role will be watched closely. It will have a strong bearing on his party's electoral fortunes. He has put himself through a self-styled apprenticeship in the first eight years of his career, but his real apprenticeship has only just begun.

NOTES

PART ONE: THE FORMATIVE YEARS

1. YESTERDAY ONCE MORE

1. Bose, Raktima, 'Rahul Gandhi charms the crowd in Purulia', *The Hindu*, Online edition, 25 April, 2009. http://www.hindu.com/2009/04/25/stories/2009042550511400.htm

2. 'Mrs Gandhi braves stone-pelting demonstrations', *The Hindu*, Madras, 20 June 1970.

3. 'Brickbats hurled at P.M., crowd lathi charged', *The Hindustan Times*, New Delhi, 20 June 1970.

4. 'Mrs Gandhi braves stone-pelting demonstrations', *The Hindu*, Madras, 20 June 1970.

5. 'P.M. tackles hostile mob ignoring all security measures', *The Tribune*, Chandigarh, 20 June 1970 quoting PTI and UNI reports.

6. Merchant, Minhaz, *Rajiv Gandhi – End of a Dream,* Viking, Penguin India, 1991, p. 41.

7. From Rajiv Gandhi's profile on the Prime Minister of India's website, www.pmindia.nic.in

8. Kidwai, Rasheed, *Sonia – A Biography*, Viking, Penguin India, 2009, pp. 1, 2.

9. Merchant, Minhaz, *Rajiv Gandhi – End of a Dream*, Viking, Penguin India, 1991, p. 109.

10. Ibid. p. 62.

11. Ibid.
12. Gandhi, Sonia, *Rajiv*, Viking, Penguin India, 1992, p. 71.
13. Merchant, Minhaz, *Rajiv Gandhi – End of a Dream*, Viking, Penguin India, 1991. p. 360.
14. Rasheed, Kidwai, 'Priyanka's Tiger Mom Days', *The Telegraph*, Calcutta, 3 August 2011.
15. Gandhi, Sonia, *Rajiv*, Viking, Penguin India, 1992, p. 68.
16. Jayakar, Pupul, *Indira Gandh – A Biography*, Viking, Penguin India, 1992, pp. 144, 146.
17. Sam Pitroda interviewed by Aziz Haniffa. 'He has a vision of India like his dad', 22 May 2009, *election.rediff.com*
18. Merchant, Minhaz, *Rajiv Gandhi – End of a Dream*, Viking, Penguin India, 1991.
19. Nugent, Nicholas, *Rajiv Gandhi – Son of a Dynasty*, BBC Books, London ,1990, p. 43.
20. Gandhi, Sonia, *Rajiv*, Viking, Penguin India, 1992, p. 6.
21. Ibid.
22. Ibid.
23. Ibid.
24. Ibid. p. 8.
25. Malhotra, Inder, *Indira Gandhi: A Personal and Political Biography*, Hodder and Stoughton, Great Britain. p. 183.
26. Jayakar, Pupul, *Indira Gandhi: A Biography*, Viking, Penguin India, 1992. p. 7.
27. Ibid.
28. Malhotra, Inder, *Indira Gandhi: A Personal and Political Biography*, Hodder and Stoughton, Great Britain, 1989, p. 183.
29. Ibid.
30. Priyanka Gandhi interviewed by Barkha Dutt, *NDTV*, 25 April 2009. Transcript downloaded from www.pressbrief.in
31. Ibid.
32. Ibid.
33. Bhagat, Usha, *Indiraji: Through My Eyes*, Viking, Penguin India, 2005.
34. Ibid.
35. Ibid.

36. Bhagat, Usha, *Indiraji: Through My Eyes*, Viking, Penguin India, 2005, p. 252.

37. Ibid.

38. Alexander, P.C., *My Years with Indira Gandhi*, Vision Books, 1991, New Delhi, p. 69.

39. Rai, Raghu, *A Day in the Life of Indira Gandhi*, Nachiketa Publications, New Delhi, 1974. Text edited by Jug Suraiya.

40. Jayakar, Pupul, *Indira Gandhi: A Biography*, Viking, Penguin India, 1992, p. 417.

41. Ibid.

42. Rajiv Gandhi interviewed by Dilip Bobb, *Best of India Today: 1975-1990,* August 1980.

43. Jayakar, Pupul, *Indira Gandhi: A Biography*, Viking, Penguin India, 1992, p. 417.

44. Ibid.

45. Ibid.

46. Ibid. p. 415.

47. Ibid. p. 416.

48. Priyanka Gandhi interviewed by Barkha Dutt, *NDTV*, 25 April 2009. Transcript downloaded from www.pressbrief.in

49. Ibid.

50. Ibid.

51. Ibid.

52. Ibid.

53. *Star News,* 12 Novermber 2010. Report from: http://www.youtube.com/watch?v=en4gDD0wCKs 'Rahul pahunche bhanjon ke school'

54. Ibid.

55. Ibid.

56. Masood, Basharaat, 'In Valley, Rahul waits for questions – and gets some answers too', *The Indian Express*, Online edition, 27 September 2011.

57. Gandhi, Sonia, *Rajiv,* Viking, Penguin India, 1992, p. 8.

58. Ibid.

59. Alexander, P.C., *My Years with Indira Gandhi*, Vision Books, New Delhi, 1991, p. 154.

60. Gandhi, Sonia, *Rajiv,* Viking, Penguin India, 1992, p. 9.
61. Ibid.
62. Ibid.
63. Ibid.
64. Gandhi, Sonia, *Rajiv,* Viking, Penguin India, 1992, p. 10.
65. Ibid, p. 13.
66. Uploaded by pressbrief.in on http://www.youtube.com/watch?v=nTYXc26Kb.
67. Rajiv Gandhi interviewed by Dilip Bobb, *Best of India Today: 1975-1990,* August 1980.
68. Interview to author.
69. www.pressbrief.in, 'Rahul Gandhi remembers Rajiv Gandhi', from: www.youtube.com
70. 'Admission of PM's son invalid: BJP', Times of India News Service, New Delhi. From *The Times of India,* Bombay, Saturday, 8 July 1989 edition.
71. Shukla, Rajiv, 'Marks and the man: Did Rahul Gandhu get into St Stephen's because of his marksmanship? The BJP doesn't think so', *Sunday,* 16-22 July 1989.
72. 'Admission of PM's son invalid: BJP', Times of India News Service, New Delhi. From *The Times of India,* Bombay, Saturday, 8 July 1989 edition.
73. Shukla, Rajiv, 'Marks and the man: Did Rahul Gandhu get into St Stephen's because of his marksmanship? The BJP doesn't think so', *Sunday,* 16-22 July 1989.
74. Gandhi, Sonia, *Rajiv,* Viking, Penguin India, 1992.
75. Merchant, Minhaz, *Rajiv Gandhi – End of a Dream,* Viking, Penguin India, 1991, p. 305
76. Ibid. p. 308.
77. Ibid.
78. Ibid. p. 309.
79. Ibid.
80. 'The last journey', Bandyopadhyay, Saumya, on board the special train, *Sunday,* 9-15 June 1991.
81. 'My hands are tied, admits Rahul Gandhi', Reuters, 06 August 2004, from: www.expressindia.com

82. Ibid.
83. Simi Garewal's *India's Rajiv.* ('Rajiv's India', Part IV, from www.youttube.com. Uploaded by www.pressbrief.in)
84. Priyanka Gandhi interviewed by Barkha Dutt, *NDTV,* 25 April 2009. Transcript downloaded from www.pressbrief.in
85. Merchant, Minhaz, *Rajiv Gandhi – End of a Dream,* Viking, Penguin India, 1991.
86. Rajiv Gandhi interviewed by Rajiv Shukla, 'The everyday Rajiv', *Sunday,* 4-10 September, 1988.
87. Priyanka Gandhi interviewed by Barkha Dutt, *NDTV,* 25 April 2009. Transcript downloaded from www.pressbrief.in
88. Sonia Gandhi interviewed by Vir Sanghvi, 'Do you really want to be PM?', *The Hindustan Times,* 18 April 2004, from: www.aicc.org.in

2. EDUCATION AND WORK

1. www.youtube.com, 'Congress leader Rahul Gandhi on Education', uploaded by www.pressbrief.in
2. Gandhi, Sonia, *Rajiv,* Viking, Penguin India, 1992, New Delhi.
3. Rajiv Gandhi interviewed by Rajiv Shukla, 'The everyday Rajiv', *Sunday,* 4-10 September, 1988.
4. Rajiv Gandhi felt Rahul was 'a much more outgoing, sporting type of a person and much more sensitive perhaps' as compared to Priyanka who he described as 'much tougher . . . a lot like my mother (Indira Gandhi), strong willed'. The comments figure in Simi Garewal's 1991 documentary on Rajiv Gandhi, 'India's Rajiv'. ('Rajiv's India, Part IV' From www.youttube.com Uploaded by pressbrief.in)
5. Rajiv Gandhi interviewed by Rajiv Shukla, 'The everyday Rajiv', *Sunday,* 4-10 September, 1988.
6. These comments don't figure in the write-up that appeared in the *Varsity* issue of 12 February 2010 but are in Ashleigh Lamming's typed-up notes of the actual interview that she kindly shared with the author.

7. 'Back to School', *Sunday*, 13-19 October 1991 reported in a short piece in its Spotlight section that Priyanka Gandhi had made a 'return to school' after her father's death.

8. Election Commission of India, affidavits of candidates in general elections 2004, from: www.eci.nic.in

9. 'Charisma is not enough', *Newsweek*, 24 December 2006, from: www.dailybeast.com

10. Ibid.

11. 'Newsweek apologizes to Rahul Gandhi', *The Indian Express*, 17 January 2007, from: www.indianexpress.com

12. 'The truth about Rahul's M Phil', *The New Indian Express*, 7 April 2009, from: Google webcache of story.

13. 'Rahul was awarded M Phil degree in 1995: Cambridge', www.indianexpress.com, 29 April 2009.

14. Official website of The City of Winer Park, from: www.cityofwinterpark.org

15. U.S. News & World Report, from:http://colleges.usnews.rankingsandreviews.com/best-colleges/rollins-college-1515

16. Merrow Golden and Ashleigh Lamming, 'Eastern Promise', *Varsity*, 12 February 2010, from: http://www.varsity.co.uk/paper-edition (PDF version).

17. These responses don't figure in the write up that appeared in the *Varsity* issue of 12 February 2010 but are in Ashleigh Lamming's typed-up notes of the actual interview that she shared with the author.

18. *New Palgrave Dictionary of Economics* second edition, 2008.

19. 'Economics A-Z terms', *The Economist*, from: www.economist.com

20. This comment does not figure in the write-up that appeared in the *Varsity* issue of 12 February 2010 but is in Ashleigh Lamming's typed-up notes of the actual interview that she shared with the author.

21. Ibid.

22. Merrow Golden and Ashleigh Lamming, 'Eastern Promise', *Varsity*, 12 February 2010, from: http://www.varsity.co.uk/paper-edition (PDF version).

23. This comment is a lengthier version of a quote that appears in the write-up in the *Varsity* issue of 12 February 2010. It is part of the notes shared by Ashleigh Lamming with the author.

24. In Ashleigh Lamming's typed-up notes of the actual interview with Rahul Gandhi for *Varsity*, 12 February 2010, that she shared with the author.

25. Ibid.

26. From email conversation with Ashleigh Lamming.

27. These comments don't figure in the write-up that appeared in the *Varsity* issue of 12 February 2010 but are in Ashleigh Lamming's typed-up notes of the actual interview that she shared with the author.

28. 'I prefer to fight today's battles', *Outlook*, 17 August 2009. Amartya Sen interviewed by Vinod Mehta and Anjali Puri, from: www.outlookindia.com

29. 'Putting growth in its place', *Outlook*, 14 November 2011. Dreze, Jean, and Amartya Sen, from: www.outlookindia.com

30. Gopinath, Vrinda, 'My girlfriend is Spanish: Rahul Gandhi', 24 April 2004, *www.expressindia.com*

31. Ibid.

32. *Press Trust of India*, 29 July 2004, from www.indianexpress.com

33. Tewari, B.C., *The Times of India*, Bombay, 21 August 1995.

34. 'Sonia hits out at govt. for delay in Rajiv probe', *The Times of India*, Bombay, 25 August 1995.

35. Agarwal, Amit, 'Only mild ragging for Rahul', *The Times of India*, Bombay, 19 July 1989.

36. Porter, Michael E., *Competitive Strategy: Techniques for analyzing industries and competitors*, originally published: Free Press, New York, 1980.

37. Rahul Gandhi interviewed by George Iype, 'I will create a new brand of politics', 23 April 2004, *www.rediff.com*

38. 'Rahul Gandhi's Mumbai millions', *Mid Day*, 27 May 2004, from: www.mid-day.com

39. Jha, Nilanjana Bhaduri, 'Rahul Gandhi: Gen Y to the rescue', m.timesofindia.com, 23 March 2004.

40. Vivek, T R, 'Rahul on the lookout for a CEO', *Business Standard*, 24 June 2004, from www.business-standard.com

41. Gopinath, Vrinda, 'My girlfriend is Spanish: Rahul Gandhi', 24 April 2008, *www.expressindia.com*

42. Rahul Gandhi interviewed by Sagarika Ghose, 24 April 2004. 'Flashback: Won't indulge in tit-for-tat politics, says Rahul', *ibnlive.in.com*

43. Gandhi, Rahul, speech at 82nd Congress Plenary Session, Hyderabad (22 and 23 January 2006).

PART TWO: ENTER RAHUL

3. FAMILY AS POLITICS

1. Akbar, M.J., *Nehru, the Making of India*, Viking in association with Rupa and Co, London, 1988, p. 132.

2. Gopinath, Vrinda, 'My girlfriend is Spanish: Rahul Gandhi', *The Indian Express*, 28 April, 2004, from: www.expressindia.com

3. Sonia Gandhi interviewed by Vir Sanghvi, *Hindustan Times*, 17 April 2004, from www.aicc.org.in

4. Priyanka Gandhi interviewed by Barkha Dutt, *NDTV*, 25 April 2009. Transcript downloaded from www.pressbrief.in

5. Ibid.

6. Mike Wooldridge, 'Priyanka: Daughter of the dynasty', 1 October 1999, *news.bbc.co.uk*

7. Amartya Sen interviewed by Vinod Mehta and Anjali Puri. 'I prefer to fight today's battles', *Outlook*, 17 August 2009, from: www.outlookindia.com.

8. Rahul Gandhi interviewed by Sharat Pradhan, 'Inexperience is my biggest handicap', 15 June 2004, *www.rediff.com*

9. Gopinath, Vrinda, 'Private prince', *The Indian Express*, 28 March 2004.

10. *www.youtube.com* (uploaded by pressbrief.in) 21 January 2004. Date corroborated by PTI story filed on the same press interaction published in *The Telegraph*, Calcutta, India, 21 January 2004, 'Siblings keep suspense alive'.

11. Sonia Gandhi interviewed by Vir Sanghvi, *Hindustan Times*, 18 April 2004, from www.aicc.org.in

12. Ibid.
13. www.pressbrief.in, 'Rahul Gandhi remembers Rajiv Gandhi', from: www.youtube.com
14. Nelson, Dean, 'The next Gandhi: I'll make India better off than Britain', *The Sunday Times*, London, 30 April 2006, from www.thesundaytimes.co.uk
15. Singh D K, 'Rahul: If I'd not come from Gandhi family, I wouldn't be here', *The Indian Express*, 21 October 2008, from: www.indianexpress.com

4. THE CONGRESS THAT RAHUL INHERITED

1. Sridharan, E, 'The fragmentation of the Indian party system' in *Parties and Party Politics in India*, ed., Hasan, Zoya, Oxford University Press, New Delhi, 2002, p. 477.
2. Ibid.
3. Malhotra, Inder, *Indira Gandhi*, National Book Trust, India, New Delhi, 2006, p. 33.
4. Ibid, p. 49.
5. Ibid.
6. Sridharan, E, 'The fragmentation of the Indian party system' in *Parties and Party Politics in India*, ed., Hasan, Zoya, Oxford University Press, New Delhi, 2002, p. 481.
7. Thakur, Janardan, *All the Prime Minister's Men*, Vikas Publishing House Pvt Ltd., 1977, p. 23.
8. Ananth, Krishna V, *India Since Independence: Making sense of Indian Politics*, Pearson, 2011, p. 97.
9. Thakur, Janardan, *All the Prime Minister's Men*, Vikas Publishing House Pvt Ltd. 1977, p. 84.
10. Mehta, Vinod, *The Sanjay Story: From Anand Bhavan to Amethi*, Jaico Publishing House, Bombay, 1978, p. 96.
11. Ibid, p. 87.
12. Ibid., p. 112.
13. Ananth, Krishna V, *India Since Independence: Making sense of Indian Politics*, Pearson, 2011, p. 171.
14. Ibid.

15. Dayal, John and Ajoy Bose, *For Reasons of State: Delhi under Emergency*, Ess Ess Publications, Delhi, 1977, p. 143.

16. Mehta, Vinod, *The Sanjay Story: From Anand Bhavan to Amethi*, Jaico Publishing House, Bombay, 1978, p. 85.

17. As quoted ibid, p. 85.

18. Mehta, Vinod, *The Sanjay Story: From Anand Bhavan to Amethi*, Jaico Publishing House, Bombay, 1978, p. 90.

19. Sengupta, Bhabani, *Rajiv Gandhi: A Political Study*, Centre for Policy Research, Konark Publishers Pvt Ltd., New Delhi, 1989, p. 80.

20. Merchant, Minhaz, *Rajiv Gandhi, The End of a Dream*, Viking, 1991, p. 101.

21. Ibid.

22. Rajiv Gandhi's speech delivered to the Congress centenary session at Mumbai in 1985. From http://www.congresssandesh.com/rajivgandhi/rajivgandhi.html

23. Sengupta, Bhabani, *Rajiv Gandhi: A Political Study*, Centre for Policy Research, Konark Publishers Pvt Ltd., New Delhi, 1989, p. 80.

24. Ibid.

25. Ananth, Krishna V, *India Since Independence: Making sense of Indian Politics*, Pearson, 2011, p. 313.

26. Sridharan, E, 'The fragmentation of the Indian party system' in *Parties and Party Politics in India*, ed., Hasan, Zoya, Oxford University Press, New Delhi, 2002, p. 485.

27. Ibid.

28. Ibid.

29. Sridharan, E., 'Electoral Coalitions in 2004 General Elections', *Economic and Political Weekly*, 18 December 2004.

30. The Pachmarhi Declaration, 6 September 1998, from: www.congressandesh.com

5. THE 'PROFESSIONAL' POLITICIAN

1. Rahul Gandhi interviewed by Vijay Simha, *Tehelka,* 24 September 2006, from: www.tehelka.com

2. *The Times* of London, 2 March 1982. Quoted in Sengupta, Bhabani, *Rajiv Gandhi: A Political Study*, Konark Publishers, New Delhi, 1989.

3. Rahul Gandhi interviewed by Vijay Simha, *Tehelka,* 24 September 2006, from: www.tehelka.com

4. Rahul Gandhi interviewed by Sharat Pradhan. 'Inexperience is my biggest handicap', 25 June 2004, www.rediff.com

5. Rahul Gandhi interviewed by Vijay Simha, *Tehelka,* 24 September 2006, From:www.tehelka.com

6. Ibid.

7. Ibid.

8. Ibid.

9. Ibid.

10. Ibid.

11. From www.loksabha.nic, Rahul Gandhi's member's page.

12. Ibid.

13. Rahul Gandhi interviewed by Vijay Simha, *Tehelka,* 24 September 2006, from: www.tehelka.com

14. Ibid.

15. Rahul Gandhi's closing keynote speech at Bucerius Summer School, 2009, http://www.bucerius-summer-school.de

16. Datta-Ray, Sunanda K, *Looking East to Look West – Lee Kuan Yew's Mission India*, Viking by Penguin India in association with The Insitutute of South East Asian Studies, 2009, p. 313.

17. Ibid.

18. Ibid.

19. Manoj, C L, *The Economic Times,* 1 September 2005, from: www.economictimes.indiatimes.com 'Rahul gets report on Bharat Nirman'; *DNA*, 1 September 2005. Seetha. From: www.dnaindia.com 'Rahul, now at planning commission meet'

20. Video from http://pressbrief.blogspot.com/2011/08/rahul-gandhis-first-press-conference.html

21. 'Regrets if there are any errors in Rahul interview: Tehelka', *PTI*, 17 September 2005, from: www.outlookindia.com .

22. Ibid.

23. Ibid.

24. Ibid.

6. A TEAM TAKES SHAPE

1. As stated in an email from Phyllis Stevenson, media relations coordinator, at The Wharton School.
2. http://www.lazard.com/careers/FA-NA-mba.aspx?Level=3
3. Singh, Kanishka, 'Why Sonia is like John Kerry', *Outlook*, 12 April 2004, from: www.outlookindia.com
4. Hebbar, Nistula, 'Rahul Gandhi – Who are his pals?', *Business Standard*, 26 November 2005, from www.business-standard.com
5. Mishra, Manjari, 'Like Rajiv, Rahul too has his team in place', *The Times of India*, 28 April 2006, from www.timesofindia.indiatimes.com; 'Candidate Sonia', *The Indian Express*, 7 May 2006, from: www.indianexpress.com .
6. Jeelani, Mehboob, 'Reform School', *The Caravan*, 1 August 2011, from http://caravanmagazine.in/Story.aspx?StoryID=1017&Page=1
7. Rao, Sachin, 'Reflections on the MAP and working with Dr. Prahalad C K', *Journal of Management Inquiry*, July 2005, vol. 14. no. 2 pp. 178-80, from http://jmi.sagepub.com/content/14/2/178.extract
8. Singh, Kanishka, 'Growing Young', *Indian Express*, 9 June 2004, from: http://www.indianexpress.com/oldStory/48567/
9. Singh, Kanishka, 'Dreaming of India in 2010', *Seminar*, December 2005. From: http://www.india-seminar.com/2005/556/556%20kanishka%20singh.htm
10. *Indian Express*, Kanishka Singh, 'Growing Young', June 9, 2004. From: http://www.indianexpress.com/oldStory/48567/
11. Singh, Kanishka, 'Communication', *Seminar*, February 2004, from: http://www.india-seminar.com/semframe.html
12. 'Jitendra Singh, the Rahul man and Ist time MP who makes it big', *Deccan Herald*, 22 July 2011, *PTI*, from: www.deccanherald.com

7. RAE BARELI BY-ELECTION, 2006

1. 'Delegates dazzled by plenary arrangements', *The Hindu*, 22 January 2006, from web edition. http://www.hindu.com/2006/01/22/stories/2006012211130100.htm

2. The following set of events regarding slogan-shouting at the plenary have been reconstructed from press reports in *India Today* (Menon, Amarnath K, 'Idle Worship', 6 February 2006, from: http://archives.digitaltoday.in/indiatoday/20060206/nation2.html), Prasad, K V, 'Congress seeks to return to power on its own', *The Hindu*, 23 January 2006, from: http://www.hindu.com/2006/01/23/stories/2006012309780100.htm), rediff.com (http://www.rediff.com/news/2006/jan/22cong3.htm), Roy, Bhaskar, 'Delegates can't wait for sonrise', *Times of India*, 23 January 2006, from: http://articles.timesofindia.indiatimes.com/2006-01-23/india/27792944_1_delegates-rahul-gandhi-amethi-mp) –

3. Estimates across newspapers and magazines varied between 10,000 to 15,000 people.

4. 'Sonia heads council to implement CMP', *The Hindu*, 5 June 2004, from: http://hindu.com/2004/06/05/stories/2004060512021300.htm

5. Sahgal, Priya, 'The hot seat', 17 April 2006, www.indiatoday.intoday.in,

6. 'To stop office-of-profit axe, UPA gets ordinance', *The Indian Express*, 22 March 2006, from: http://www.indianexpress.com/news/to-stop-officeofprofit-axe-upa-gets-ordin/922/

7. 'BJP opposes any ordinance of office of profit', *PTI*, 22 March 2006, from: http://articles.timesofindia.indiatimes.com/2006-03-22/india/27794985_1_ordinance-opposition-bjp-profit

8. Ibid.

9. Raghuvanshi, Umesh, 'Rahul to launch Sonia blitzkrieg', *The Hindustan Times*, 24 April 2006, from: www.hindustantimes.com The story says this particular poster had the pictures of Feroze Gandhi, the first to represent the seat, Indira Gandhi, Rajiv and Sonia Gandhi.

10. Mishra, Manjiri, 'The Sonia-Rahul show', *The Times of India*, 17 April 2006, from: www.timesofindia.indiatimes.com

11. 'Candidate Sonia', *The Indian Express,* 7 May 2006, from: http://www.indianexpress.com/news/candidate-sonia/3912/

12. Ibid.

13. Ibid.

14. 'Rahul: Sonia committed to Rae Bareli's progress', *The Times of India*, 27 April 2006, from: http://articles.timesofindia.indiatimes.com/2006-04-27/lucknow/27829084_1_rae-bareli-rahul-gandhi-star-constituency

15. This was verified by listening to Rahul Gandhi's speeches and interactions with mediapersons trailing him available on YouTube. Radhika Ramaseshan mentions this in *The Telegraph*, Calcutta. 8 May 2006 ('Rae Bareli and Priyanka give their verdict on eve of poll'.)

16. 'Rahul connects with voters in Rae Bareli', *PTI*, 1 May 2006, from: http://www.hindu.com/2006/05/01/stories/2006050116961100.htm

8. THE BIG BATTLE – UTTAR PRADESH ASSEMBLY ELECTIONS, 2007

1. Video from www.youtube.com dated 16 May 2007, New Delhi, as corroborated from www.rediff.com

2. Ananth, V Krishna, postulates in 'Rahul Gandhi Illusion', *Economic and Political Weekly*, 1 October 2005, that while it could be argued that the first time Dalits left the Congress fold was with Jagjivan Ram's exit from the party before the 1977 election to form the Congress for Democracy with H N Bahuguna. Ram was never able to 'consolidate his own political base . . . because he lacked a vision or a strategy to reflect the aspirations of the Dalits in the evolving political scenario.' He says therefore, Indira Gandhi was able to 'retrieve the situation' with her visit to Belchi in Bihar where Dalits had been massacred.

3. Lok Dal (Ajit) was led by Charan Singh's son Ajit Singh and Lok Dal (Bahuguna) had leaders such as Devi Lal, Mulayam Singh Yadav and Lalu Prasad. Krishna Ananth says in 'Rahul Gandhi Illusion' that Janta Dal was formed with the merger of Lok Dal (A) and Lok Dal (B) along with the rank and file and most of the important leaders of the Janata Party except Subramanian Swamy.

4. Ananth, V Krishna, 'Rahul Gandhi Illusion', *Economic and Political Weekly*, 1 October 2005, from beta.epw.in.

5. Ibid.

6. *Economic and Political Weekly,* 2 September 2006, from beta.epw.in

7. Zerinini-Brotel, Jasmine, 'The BJP in Uttar Pradesh: From Hindutva to Consensual Politics?' in *The BJP and the Compulsions of Politics in India,* eds., Thomas Blom Hansen, Christopher Jaffrelot, Oxford University Press, 1998.

8. *Economic and Political Weekly,* 2 September 2006, from beta.epw.in 'Congress Illusion'.

9. Stone, Brewer S, *Asian Survey*, vol. 28, no. 10 (Oct., 1988). pp. 1018-30.

10. James, Manor, 'Anomie in Indian Politics', *Economic and Political Weekly*, vol. XVIII, no. 19, 1 May 1983.

11. Ibid.

12. Stone, Brewer S (1988) cites two important studies done by Paul Brass, *Factional Politics in an Indian State: The Congress Party in Uttar Pradesh* (Berkeley: University of California Press, 1965) and BD Graham, *The Succession of Factional Systems in the Uttar Pradesh Congress Party, 1937-66* in Mark J. Swartz, ed. *Local Level Politics* (Chicago: Aldine Publishing Company, 1968) to argue that factions in UP politics used to be 'inclusive of diverse caste and religious groups' to compete for the 'leadership of the state'.

13. Ananth, V Krishna, in the 'Rahul Gandhi Illusion', *Economic and Political Weekly,* 1 October 2005, says the intermediate caste groups gathered round the socialists in the 1950s.

14. Manor, James, 'Party Decay and Political Crisis in India,' *Washington Quarterly,* Summer 1981, p. 28. In Brewer S Stone (1988).

15. Ibid.

16. Pai, Sudha, 'The Congress Party and Six National Elections: 1964-1984', *A Centenary History of the Indian National Congress*, Academic Foundation, New Delhi, 2001, p. 78.

17. Ibid.

18. Ibid.

19. Rahul Gandhi, speech at 82nd Congress plenary session at Hyderabad, from www.aicc.org.in

20. Rahul Gandhi's election tour interview. 'Rahul Gandhi talks to the media during election campaign Part 8' at www.youtube.com

21. Khan, Atiq, 'Congress busy preparing strategy for U.P. elections', *The Hindu*, 11 February 2007, from web edition.

22. Ibid.

23. 'Sonia, Rahul show all the way, locals missing', *The Economic Times*, 5 April 2007, from epaper.timesofindia.com http://epaper.timesofindia.com/Default/Scripting/ ArticleWin.asp?From=Archive&Source=Page&Skin= pastissues2&BaseHref=ETD/2007/04/05&PageLabel= 2&EntityId=Ar00203&ViewMode=HTML

24. From pressbrief.com, rediff.com and other newspapers/websites.

25. George, Varghese K and Priya Sahgal, 'Double Jeopardy – Mayawati's Triumph – A lesson for the Congress and the BJP', *India Today*, 21 May 2007, from www.indiatoday.intoday.in

26. Ramachandran, Aarthi, *The Economic Times*, 11 April 2007.

27. Ibid.

28. 'Rahul Gandhi talks about UP' video from www.youtube.com

29. Ibid.

30. 'Rahul Gandhi talks about UP', video clipping from www.youtube.com of Rahul Gandhi's 2007 UP election tour uploaded by www.pressbrief.com

31. 'Rahul Gandhi promises development in UP' video from www.youtube.com

32. 'Rahul Gandhi promises to bring change in UP' video from www.youtube.com

33. 'Rahul Gandhi warns against divisive forces', video from www.youtube.com

34. 'Rahul Gandhi on political scenario in UP', video from www.youtube.com

35. Chatterjee, Manini, Varghese K George, 'If a Gandhi was active, Babri wouldn't have fallen: Rahul', *The Indian Express*, 19 March 2007, from www.indianexpress.com

36. 'Friends, foes slam Rahul's remark', *PTI*, 20 March 2007, from www.expressindia.com .

37. 'They have fooled you, says Rahul Gandhi', 14 April 2007, Bareilly, Rahul Gandhi's speech as reported by www.pressbrief.in

38. Press statement of Prakash Jawadekar, 16 April 2007, from www.bjp.org.in

39. WikiLeaks Cable: 07NEWDELHI1915 From www.wikileaks.org

40. Merchant, Minhaz, *Rajiv Gandhi – End of a Dream*, Viking, Penguin India, 1991. p. 109.

41. Ibid.

PART THREE: IYC AND NSUI REVAMP

9. A 'NEW BRAND' OF POLITICS

1. 'Rahul's appointment hailed', *Tribune*, 25 September 2007, www.tribuneindia.com .

2. Rahul Gandhi interviewed by Vijay Simha, *Tehelka*, 24 September 2005, www.tehelka.com

3. 'Inexperience is my biggest handicap', Rahul Gandhi interviewed by Sharat Pradhan, 15 June 2004, *www.rediff.com*

4. Rahul Gandhi interviewed by George Iype, 'I will create a new brand of politics', 23 April 2004, *www.rediff.com*

5. Rahul Gandhi interviewed by Vijay Simha, *Tehelka*, 24 August 2005, from: www.tehelka.com

6. Rajiv Gandhi, speech delivered to the Congress centenary session at Mumbai in 1985. From http://www.congresssandesh.com/rajivgandhi/rajivgandhi.html

7. Rahul Gandhi's speech at Congress' 82nd plenary session in Hyderabad, 22 and 23 January 2006. Downloaded from: www.aicc.org.in

8. 'Time for house-cleaning in the Congress', *The Hindu*, 4 April 2012, www.thehindu.com

9. Rahul Gandhi's speech at the AICC session on 17 November 2007, from www.youtube.com
10. Ibid.

10. A STRATEGY CONSULTANT GOES TO WORK

1. www.ilid.org
2. Liker, Jeffrey, K. *The Toyota Way*, Tata McGraw-Hill, 2004, New Delhi, p. 37.
3. Ibid.
4. Liker, Jeffrey, K. *The Toyota Way*, Tata McGraw-Hill, 2004, New Delhi, p. 40.
5. Media release from Rahul Gandhi's office on the Thiruvananthapuram press conference, 7 October 2009.

11. 'TRANSFORMATION'

1. Misra, Udit, 'Rahul Gandhi: His tryst with destiny', *Forbes India*, issue of 9 September 2011, from www.forbesindia.com
2. Singh, D K, 'Rahul: If I'd not come from Gandhi family, I wouldn't be here', *The Indian Express*, 21 October 2008.
3. 'Congress leader Rahul Gandhi's press conference at Bhopal (MP) part 1', 6 October 2010, www.youtube.com
4. 'Rahul Gandhi on Youth Congress & NSUI elections', www.youtube.com. Uploaded by www.pressbrief.in
5. Ibid.
6. 'Congress leader Rahul Gandhi's press conference in Amritsar, Part II, www.youtube.com. Uploaded by www.pressbrief.in
7. Video clip of Rahul Gandhi's press conference in Bhopal. 6 October 2010, www.pressbrief.in
8. *Buniyaad* (Youth Congress national convention November 2011) organizational resolution. From www.iyc.in The description of the seven core pillars are also from the same document.
9. 'Rahul Gandhi's press conference in Amritsar, Part 1', www.youtube.com. Uploaded by www.pressbrief.in 18 November 2008.

10. Ibid.
11. Liker, Jeffrey, K. *The Toyota Way*, Tata McGraw-Hill, 2004, New Delhi, p. 38.
12. The following statistics regarding membership of the Youth Congress as well as the numbers of elected office-bearers is from the IYC newsletter of November 2011.
13. http://www.unilever.com/images/es_Project_Shakti_tcm13-13297.pdf
14. http://www.hul.co.in/sustainability/casestudies/enhancing-livelihoods/Shakti.aspx
15. IYC Training Manual. From http://pehchaan.iyc.in/pls/apex/f?p=400:46:4372604878858562
16. 'Rahul Gandhi's interaction with young professionals Part II'. Programme date: 24 February 2009, www.youtube.com
17. Rahul Gandhi's speech at the AICC session on 17 November 2007, from www.youtube.com
18. 'Rahul Gandhi's interaction with young professionals Part II'. Programme date: 24 February 2009, www.youtube.com

12. WITHER 'TRANSFORMATION'?

1. 'With many Youth Congress ticket hopefuls joining the fray, party to pick those winnable', *The Indian Express*, 27 December 2011, www.indianexpress.com
2. Sharma, Ashwani, 'Cancel Virbhadra son election, agency tells Youth Cong', *The Indian Express*, 21 January 2012, www.indianexpress.com
3. 'Time for house-cleaning in the Congress', *The Hindu*, 4 April 2012, www.thehindu.com
4. 'Rahul Gandhi on Youth Congress & NSUI elections', www.youtube.com. Uploaded by www.pressbrief.in

PART FOUR: AN INCONSISTENT AND OPPORTUNISTIC BRAND OF POLITICS

13. BRAND BUILDING AND THE 'TWO INDIAS' THEORY

1. Statement issued by Prime Minister's Office on 26 September 2007. Press Information Bureau, Government of India. www.pib.nic.in

2. Rural development minister Raghuvansh Prasad was quoted as saying the scheme would cost the government Rs 20,000 crore annually in several newspapers including *The Hindu* and *Business Standard*. The figures for increased allocations were also mentioned in the two papers on 29 September 2007.

3. Rahul Gandhi's speech during the debate on the Motion of Confidence in the Lok Sabha, 22 July 2008. Downloaded from aicc.org.in

4. Rahul Gandhi's speech at AICC meeting on 17 November 2011. Transcript downloaded from www.aicc.org.in

5. Rahul Gandhi's speech made during the discussion on the general budget 2008-09. Trancript downloaded from www.aicc.org.in

6. Rahul Gandhi's closing keynote address at Bucerius Summer School, 28 August 2009. Downloaded from: www.bucerius-summer-school.de

7. Mehta, Pratap Bhanu, 'Beyond Club and Cabal', *Outlook*, 2 January 2012, fromwww.outlookindia.com

14. INCONSISTENCIES AND SYMBOLISM

1. Liker, Jeffrey, K. *The Toyota Way*, Tata McGraw-Hill, 2004, New Delhi, p. 224.

2. Ibid, p. 223.

3. 'Rahul Gandhi takes bath after visiting Dalits', *PTI*, 7 April 2008, at www.indiatoday.intoday.in .

4. 'Congress leader Rahul Gandhi and David Miliband in Amethi (part 03), www.youtube.com. Uploaded by pressbrief.in

5. Journalist Vijay Simha in 'Congress begins to think of plan B' (www.tehelka.com, May 23, 2011) speaks about how Rahul is much more at home with youngsters, whether politicians or students he meets at campuses, than with older politicians. He says with the latter he is constantly forced to 'out-think' them. He cites the Mumbai train ride and Rahul's early morning motorcycle ride into Bhatta-Parsaul in Western UP as examples of this behaviour.

6. Das, Subrat, '"Soldier" on save forest mission – 23 years on, *Mahapuru* wields Gandhi wand', *The Telegraph*, 8 March 2008, www.telegraphindia.com .

7. Ibid.

8. Bisoi, Dilip, 'Vedanta looks at Orissa govt for alternative bauxite source', *The Financial Express*, 26 August 2010, www.financialexpress.com .

9. Das, Prafulla, 'Rahul starts discovering India', *The Hindu*, 8 March 2008, www.thehindu.com

10. 'Congress leader Rahul Gandhi speaks to the press in Orissa (Part IV)', www.youtube.com. Uploaded by pressbrief.in

11. 'New panel on Vedanta may force more delay', *Mint*, 30 June 2010. Reuters. www.livemint.com

12. Report of the Four Member Committee for investigation into the proposal submitted by the Orissa Mining Company for Bauxite Mining in Orissa, 16 August 2010 www.moef.nic.in

13. Ghosh, Padmaparna, 'Vedanta's Orissa project nixed', *Mint*, 24 August 2010, www.livemint.com

14. Jha, Sanjay K, 'Sonia salutes *sipahi* & strategy', *The Telegraph*, 16 September 2010, www.telegraphindia.com

15. POLITICAL OPPORTUNISM AND INACTION

1. Sood, Jyotika and Moyna, 'Road to Disaster', *Down to Earth*, 15 June 2011, www.downtoearth.org.in

2. 'Rahul takes farmers' fight to PM'. Uploaded by NDTV, www.youtube.com

3. 'Bhatta-Parsaul: No bodies only burnt plastic, cow dung says lab', *The Indian Express*, 20 May 2011, www.indianexpress.com

4. 'Rahul behind speedy introduction of Land Bill: Ramesh', *PTI*, 7 September 2011, from www.outlookindia.com .

5. 'Government to continue provision for acquiring land acquisition for PPP projects', 19 May 2012, www.economictimes.indiatimes.com

6. 'Aruna Roy: Jan Lokpal Bill impractical, undemocratic', *IANS*, 21 August 2011, from www.economictimes.indiatimes.com

7. Ibid.

8. Parsai, Gargi, 'Government arrests Anna, then blinks', *The Hindu*, 17 August 2011, www.thehindu.com

9. Reddy, B Muralidhar, 'Manmohan: scope for give-and-take on Lokpal Bill', *The Hindu*, 21 August 2011, www.thehindu.com

10. 'PM's speech in the Lok Sabha debate on corruption', 25 August 2011, from www.pmindia.nic.in

11. 'Anna's proposals on Jan Lokpal to be discussed in Parliament', *The Hindu*, 26 August 2011, www.thehindu.com .

12. 'Rahul Gandhi addresses the media in Aurangabad (Maharashtra) Part II, www.youtube.com, 29 January 2011, uploaded by pressbrief.in

PART FIVE: UP 2012

18. THE HUMILIATION

1. 'Sonia Gandhi talks to the media after the Assembly poll results 7 March 2012'. Video at www.pressbrief.in

2. Ibid.

3. The numbers and statistics about the UP 2012 election results are from 'Sixteenth Assembly elections in Uttar Pradesh', *Economic & Political Weekly*, 7 April 2012, Vol. XLVII, No. 14. In Special statistics: 2012 state elections'

4. 'Rahul Gandhi interacts with media', Rahul Gandhi's interaction with the press on 6 March 2012. Video at www.pressbrief.in

5. 'Sixteenth Assembly elections in Uttar Pradesh', *Economic & Political Weekly*. 7 April 2012. Vol. XLVII No. 14. In Special statistics: 2012 state elections'

6. Rahul Gandhi's speech in Lucknow, Bakshi ka Talab, on 15 February 2012. At www.pressbrief.in

7. Ibid.

8. 'Another Cong quota googly in UP', *The Times of India*, 10 January 2012, from: epaper.timesofindia.com

9. Election Commission of India's order regarding violation of model code of conduct by Salman Khurshid, 9 February 2012 www.eci.nic.in

10. Ibid.

11. 'Salman Rushdie blames Congress for Jaipur fiasco', published by ibnlive.com 17 March 2012, www.youtube.com

12. Ibid.

13. Benedict, Kay, 'Congress eyes Muslim-Kurmi alliance for Uttar Pradesh', 4 January 2012, www.indiatoday.intoday.in

14. 'UP polls a big picnic for Gandhi family: Mayawati', *The Times of India*, 21 February 2012, www.articles.timesofindia.indiatimes.com

15. The numbers and statistics about the UP 2012 election results are from 'Sixteenth Assembly elections in Uttar Pradesh', *Economic & Political Weekly*, 7 April 2012, vol. XLVII, no. 14. In Special statistics: 2012 state elections'.

16. 'UP polls no litmus test for Rahul: Digvijay Singh', *NDTV*, 6 March 2012.

17. Verma, A K, 'Subalterns in Uttar Pradesh: A new trajectory', *Economic & Political Weekly*, 7 November 2010, vol. XLV, no. 48.

18. 'Sixteenth Assembly elections in Uttar Pradesh', *Economic & Political Weekly*, 7 April 2012, vol. XLVII, no. 14. In Special statistics: 2012 state elections'.

19. 'I take responsibility, says Rahul Gandhi about UP results', published by *NDTV* on 6 March 2012, www.youtube.com

20. Chaudhary, Shoma, 'Two men and a vote', 3 March 2012, www.tehelka.com

EPILOGUE

1. 'Rahul Gandhi could be PM in 2014: Beni Prasad', *PTI*, 10 February 2012, www.articles.timesofindia.indiatimes.com
2. 'PM Manmohan Singh says open to Rahul Gandhi succeeding him', *PTI*, 29 June 2011, from www.articles.economictimes.indiatimes.com
3. 'Rahul Gandhi interacts with media'. Rahul Gandhi's interaction with the press on 6 March 2012. Video at www.pressbrief.in
4. Report of the Parliamentary Standing Committee on Finance presented to Lok Sabha on 13 December 2011. From www.loksabha.nic.in
5. Dasgupta, Neha and Tony Munroe, 'S&P cuts India outlook; investment rating in peril', 25 April 2012, www.in.reuters.com
6. 'Moody's: Indian government single biggest factor weighing on outlook', *PTI*, 26 April 2012, from www.articles.economictimes.indiatimes.com
7. 'S&P: India risks losing investment grade rating', *The Hindu*, 12 June 2012.
8. Ibid.
9. Ibid.
10. Ibid.
11. Rahul Gandhi press conference in Kolkata part 1, 16 September 2010, www.youtube.com. Uploaded by pressbrief.in

INDEX